SOCIAL MEDIA ABYSS

SOCIAL MEDIA ABYSS

Critical Internet Cultures and the Force of Negation

Geert Lovink

polity

First published in 2016 by Polity Press

Polity Press
65 Bridge Street
Cambridge CB2 1UR, UK

Polity Press
350 Main Street
Malden, MA 02148, USA

ISBN-13: 978-1-5095-0775-7
ISBN-13: 978-1-5095-0776-4 (pb)

A catalogue record for this book is available from the British Library.

Library of Congress Cataloging-in-Publication Data

Names: Lovink, Geert, author.
Title: Social media abyss : critical internet cultures and the force of negation / Geert Lovink.
Description: Malden, MA : Polity, 2016. | Includes bibliographical references.
Identifiers: LCCN 2015041526 (print) | LCCN 2016001138 (ebook) | ISBN 9781509507757 (hardback) | ISBN 9781509507764 (paperback) | ISBN 9781509507788 (Mobi) | ISBN 9781509507795 (Epub)
Subjects: LCSH: Social media. | Online social networks–Sociological aspects. | Popular culture. | BISAC: SOCIAL SCIENCE / Popular Culture.
Classification: LCC HM742 .L698 2016 (print) | LCC HM742 (ebook) | DDC 302.23/1–dc23
LC record available at http://lccn.loc.gov/2015041526

Typeset in 10.5 on 12 pt Sabon
by Toppan Best-set Premedia Limited
Printed and bound in Great Britain by CPI Group (UK) Ltd, Croydon

For further information on Polity, visit our website:
politybooks.com

CONTENTS

ACKNOWLEDGEMENTS

Social Media Abyss is book 5 in the series on critical internet culture that I began working on fifteen years ago. After *Networks Without a Cause* (April 2011), this is my second title with Polity Press, thanks to John Thompson, his team and their readers. I would like to thank Sabine Niederer, head of the Create-IT Knowledge Centre, and Geleyn Meyer, Dean of the Media & Creative Industries faculty at the Amsterdam University of Applied Sciences (HvA) where our Institute of Network Cultures (INC) is based, who have both been very supportive. In 2013, Geleyn Meyer gave me the opportunity to convert my three-days-a-week position into a full-time one. This change meant my departure from Mediastudies, University of Amsterdam (UvA), where I'd been involved in developing the one-year New Media master's degree since 2006.

The recent period at HvA has been marked by uncertain funding and a centralization of applied research towards the 'creative industries'. Despite the cultural-budget cuts in the Netherlands and increased pressure to work within the commercial sector, the INC has been able to run a number of research networks, publication series and conferences on topics such as 'Unlike Us: Alternatives in Social Media' (2011–13), 'MyCreativity Sweatshop: an Update on the Critique of the Creative Industries' (2014), the 'Hybrid Publishing Toolkit: Research into Digital Publishing Formats' (2013–14), 'Society of the Query: the Politics and Aesthetics of Search Engines' (2013), 'MoneyLab: an Ongoing Collective Investigation into Internet Revenue Models' (2014–15) and 'The Art of Criticism: a Dutch/ Flemish Initiative on the Future of Art Criticism' (2014–16). Early in 2015, a part of the INC was split off as The Publishing Lab, led by Margreet Riphagen.

ACKNOWLEDGEMENTS

I have developed many ideas in the two-day masterclasses that I lead around the world. I am particularly thankful to Larissa Hjorth and Heather Horst at RMIT's Digital Ethnography Research Centre in Melbourne for inviting me in 2013 and 2014, to Henk Slager from the MA of the Hogeschool voor de Kunsten (HKU) in Utrecht for our long-term collaboration, Florian Schneider at the Art Academy Trondheim, Wolfgang Schirmacher for the annual three-day sessions at the European Graduate School in Saas-Fee (where I've supervised my first four Ph.D. students), Christiane Paul at the New School who facilitated three classes from 2010 to 2012, Leah Lievrouw at UCLA, Michael Century at Renselaer, Ingrid Hoofd while at the National University of Singapore, and Mariela Yeregui for organizing my visit to Buenos Aires.

There have always been collaborations, and it is a great passion of mine to write with others, to push the discursive boundaries in order to break out of one's own invisible premises. In the case of this book there are three co-authorships that need to be mentioned. First of all, that of the Sydney media theorist Ned Rossiter, my friend and commentator on my work, with whom I have developed the organized networks concept (a project which will be the subject of a separate publication soon). Second, INC's ambassador and news connoisseur Patrice Riemens, with whom I co-authored the chapter on Bitcoin. And finally, Nathaniel Tkacz (Warwick University) with whom I initiated both the Critical Point of View network in 2009 and MoneyLab in 2012/13, and co-authored the chapter on the MoneyLab agenda.

Peter Lunenfeld in LA encouraged me to dive into contemporary American literature. I would like to thank him for his hospitality and friendship, thriving over long distances for almost two decades. The Jonathan Franzen essay is dedicated to him.

Writing the Uganda chapter would not have been possible without the generous support of Ali Balunywa, a former master's student at UvA, who organized my visit to Uganda in December 2012.

I would also like to thank Joost Smiers, Sebastian Olma, Mieke Gerritzen, Daniel de Zeeuw (re: lulz) and Michael Dieter for their encouraging Amsterdam dialogues; Margreet Riphagen, Miriam Rasch and Patricia de Vries at the INC for all their work; Henry Warwick for the collaboration on our offline library project; Saskia Sassen for her extraordinary support; and Bernard Stiegler and Franco Berardi for their friendship.

During the writing period, *Frankfurter Allgemeine Zeitung* publisher Frank Schirrmacher died of heart failure in Frankfurt. In his case, the ambulance crew didn't get to him soon enough. Frank was exactly my age (b. 1959). Over the past years Frank encouraged me, via his favourite medium Twitter, to search for wider publics for my work, despite the considerable political differences between us. As Frank was, I am motivated by direct exchanges with American colleagues to create European alternatives. Despite recent despair and setbacks, this book was written in his spirit, in order to build an independent public European dialogue and infrastructure.

Some of the chapters were edited early on by Morgan Currie in LA. An amazing copy-editing job was done out of Berlin by Rachel O'Reilly, assisted by my long-term German translator and friend Andreas Kallfelz, who this time came on board early to identify the missing bits in the English original manuscript. *Social Media Abyss* is dedicated to the love of my life, Linda Wallace, and our DJ son Kazimir, going strong together, beyond the most extraordinary survival. A family hug.

Amsterdam, September 2015

INTRODUCTION: PREPARING FOR UNCOMMON DEPARTURES

Sloganism: 'The Beginning is Near.' (Anonymous) – 'The internet feels like a trashy magazine I automatically pick up in my dentist's waiting room. It's irresistible, yet pointless.' (Johanna DeBiase – Pump-and-Dump) – 'Journalists should not be expected to make a lasting difference.' (John Young) – 'But it says so on Facebook!' – 'Your worst enemy is not the person in opposition to you. It is the person occupying the spot you would be fighting from and doing nothing.' (Georgie BC) – 'Artists survive by doing something else.' (X) – 'If you want to find a needle in a haystack, you first must have a haystack.' (Dianne Feinstein) – All that is air solidifies into fossilized institutions – 'Wear your best LinkedIn face.' (Silvio Lorusso) – 'Most of the inspirational quotes attributed to me on the internet are shit I'd never say.' (Albert Einstein – He only read low-impact journals.) – 'No such thing as a free lunch. No such thing as a free search engine. No such thing as a free webmail. No such thing as a free cloud storage.' (Mikko Hypponen) – Cyberspace: Our Home of the Useless Truth – 'Everyone has a plan until they get punched in the mouth.' (Mike Tyson) – 'This conversation is missing your voice.' (Vimeo) – 'Fund Yourself' (Get Real) – 'The Internet of Thugs' (Christian McCrea) – Operational theory for the catastrophic everyday – 'Accelerate your Exit: The Politics of (System) Migration.' (e-book title)

Social Media Abyss describes the drying up of a horizon, from the unbounded space of what was the internet into a handful of social media apps. In this global slump, IT giants such as Google and Facebook have lost their innocence. Existing governance models no longer have the necessary consensus to function. After Snowden, Silicon Valley reveals itself as deeply compromised, entangled in facilitating state surveillance and reselling the private data of its customers. For the first time, the Valley is confronted with waves of activism, from Wikileaks, Anonymous and Snowden to protests around Google busses, Uber and Airbnb. The tide has broken, and while negations of this net culture are on the rise, controversies turn over into open conflict. Many have now understood the 'sharing economy' meme as a scam. The self-evident Californian Ideology no longer works. Two decades after the publication of the essay with the same name,[1] the hegemony of the once powerful libertarians is finally being contested – but what can replace it?

In studying this question, I kicked off with social media architectures and internet revenue models to arrive at the organizational stakes: how can protest movements, from Occupy to Bangkok, prolong their presence and interconnections? Will eruptions transform into political parties or will the decentralized anarchist approach prevail? It sounds like post-1848 all over again. Are we waiting for our version of the Paris commune? But the present stagnation, interrupted by waves of dissent, indicates that we're in a post-revolutionary period, with the *ancien régime* having lost its legitimacy, hanging onto power, while counter-forces still search for modes of organization.

In the aftermath of the Snowden revelations, internet users find themselves in a situation of tension that the pragmatic engineering class, who've handled internet governance so far, always tried to avoid. Everyone is exposed but supposedly no one should worry. The past years have been a period of social media consolidation with the overall trends moving from PC to smart phone, and from established to emerging markets.[2] The pathos of this campaign phase would be that 'The Internet is Broken', but the registration of our defeat is better captured in the maxim 'We Have Lost the War', because it's unclear who will fix it and how it could be rebuilt.[3] The genuine techno-optimism amongst the white male geeks that a free and open internet, tied together by rebel code, would always persevere, has been replaced by the digital version of state monopoly capitalism, as Lenin once defined it. The innocent age of a laissez-faire consensus is well and truly behind us. Will capitalism's infrastructure ever be considered important enough not to be left to a bunch of buccaneers?

Let's Talk About Platform-Capitalism

If the 1980s gave birth to media theory, and the 1990s were the decade of networks, we are now living under the spell of the platform. As the word indicates, the tendency is to move upwards – to

2

centralize, integrate and synthesize. While network ideology boasted its decentralized nature, platform culture stands proud to announce that the Family of Man has finally found its common home.[4] In his 2010 paper, Tarleton Gillespie summed up neatly the various reasons why the platform concept emerged in the aftermath of the dotcom crash. According to Gillespie, the word 'platform' was strategically chosen to present the contradictory activities of online services as a neutral ground for DIY users and major media producers, while enabling the collision of privacy and surveillance efforts, community and advertising investments.[5] 'Platform' also hints at the integration of and by different players, through a variety of applications, into a higher synthesis.

Imagine disliking everything. Positive reformers will do whatever they can to stop us exploring the subterranean forces of negative empowerment. The power of critique is quickly dismissed as 'extreme' (if not terrorist). The fear of the crowd that abruptly unfollows itself brings back ancient traumas of the violent populist mob – and this fear at the level of (self)governance is no different in the age of platform capitalism. Where will the amorphous collective energies flow after we have overheated the internet? Why is it so hard to imagine a world in which all platforms or 'intermediaries', such as Google, Facebook and Amazon, have been dismantled – not just the old ones, but also, and in particular, the latest and the coolest?

Along with many others, I'm calling for a critical theory of intermediaries that is technical, cultural and economic in nature.[6] In his *Digital Tailspin* essay, Berlin net critic Michael Seemann calls for 'platform neutrality', while keeping in mind the pitfalls that come with the term 'neutrality'.[7] He also argues in favour of 'filter sovereignty' as a new form of information ethics. On the positive side, Seeman acknowledges 'the most important feature of these platforms is the unlimited, manifold network effects they can have'. In the social media debate, we urgently need to go beyond the culture of complaint that inherently comes with the bourgeois emphasis on the loss of privacy. Getting a better understanding of the political economy of private data is one thing – however, it could very well be that this does not automatically translate into a political programme. For Seemann, 'loss of control' is an important reframed starting point, for coming up with new strategies:[8] 'The most effective way of ridding ourselves of platform dependency is by building decentralised platforms.' For a while, WhatsApp was such an alternative, becoming a retreat from Facebook – until Facebook purchased it.

3

In the past few years, a small number of attempts have been made to kick-off 'platform studies' as a separate discipline, so far without much success.[9] We will have to wait a while for a comprehensive theory of 'platform capitalism'. Is *Platform Society*, two decades after Manuel Castells' classic trilogy *Network Society*, able to reach the same public as Thomas Piketty or Naomi Klein? Whereas the internet is now fully integrated with society, this cannot be said of academic efforts in this field. In part, there are institutional reasons for this. Internet studies is still situated in-between all secure departmental chairs, as it was neither allowed to become a fully fledged discipline of its own nor eagerly taken up by others. Nevertheless, the speed of the field's development, twenty-five years on, is still breath-taking, making it hard for struggling academics to stay ahead of the game. The role that's left to them is to measure the effects of the IT roll-out in a fast-expanding range of sectors.

In this monopoly stage, markets are fake and merely a belief system for dazed and confused outsiders. With Wall Street, Silicon Valley and Washington DC converging instead of competing (as the official version still proclaims), power itself is becoming a black box, with the algorithm as its perfect allegory. And algorithms have consequences, as Zeynep Tufekci has so clearly described. Her analysis of the 2014 protests in Ferguson makes very clear the powerfully contingent relationship of Facebook's algorithmic filtering to political cause-and-effects, the impossibility of net neutrality rules in times of crisis, and the weird, incomprehensible logic to what is – and what's not – 'trending' on Twitter.[10]

The digitization and networking of all fields of life has not yet slowed down; there are still plenty of 'innocent' under-mediated contexts out there. But most worrying is the obscuring of the technology itself, which Frank Pasquale so accurately describes in his study *The Black Box Society*. The aim of more applied net criticism, as practised at the Institute of Network Cultures in Amsterdam, has been to focus on particular online services such as search, social media, Wikipedia and online video, amongst other topics. But what have we gained from such case studies? Are we merely rearranging the deck chairs on the *Titanic*? What's the status of speculative critical theory in the light of the growing divide between the social sciences and humanities? Can we be confident that the development of new and alternative tools is the most effective way to undermine the current platforms?

That our 'thermidor' moment in internet development has arrived is clear also in 'clickbait' technology. Clickbaiting is when a publisher posts links with headlines that encourage people to click to see more, without offering much information about what will be viewed.[11] This is tabloid press 2.0, *Gleichschaltung* on a global scale.[12] What clickbaits do is to raise curiosity for an amorphous genre. The presented items are not quite news but present themselves as such, in being scattered formally and technically between news websites and social media. 'Clickbait' technology is reaching its moment of being ousted, as it is now widely understood by online audiences to be a sinister technique to raise online advertising revenue; media companies will soon have to look for other means to attract audiences. There is also a Facebook version of clickbaiting. Facebook was observed to start penalizing the type of page 'that excessively posts repeated content and encourages *like-baiting*. Like-baiting is when a post asks News Feed readers directly to like, comment or share a post.'[13] Global current affairs news has meanwhile become fully interactive. Take the Taboola software, which helps news site administrators fine-tune their content. The Taboola founder explains: 'For everyone who hates one piece of content, many others love it, and click on it. So we register it as a popular story, and leave it up, so more people can see it. If no-one clicked on it, or tweeted about it, then we would remove it.'[14]

Recently, we've seen a cultural shift away from the active, self-conscious user towards the subject as docile, ignorant servant. In a variation on what Corey Robin writes about conservatives, we could say that we feel sorry for internet users here, and identify them as victims. In the public imagination, the user has flipped sides and has morphed from an empowered citizen to a hopeless loser. Now the genre of our engagement is a tragic one, but we're not sure of which plot, which repetitions or histories (see Franzen) even apply. Users are simultaneously aggrieved, convinced of the righteousness of their cause, and of the unlikeliness of their heroic triumph. Whether we are rich or poor or somewhere in-between, this user is one of us.[15] But why should humility come from what is incontrovertible about the present defeat? Piety is not compatible with dignity. How can the user become a master of his or her fate again in this 'administrated world', to use the term from Adorno and Horkheimer's universe? This might only be possible if the surveillance infrastructure is dismantled. Much like the nuclear threat during the Cold War, the knowledge of how to employ cameras, bots, sensors and software that, for instance, came to light in the Snowden files, is clearly revealed. Only when the technology is decommissioned and neutralized will collective fear dissipate. A first step here is to 'make things visible', as Poitras, Greenwald, Appelbaum, Assange and so many others are doing. This is the 'Berlin' strategy[16] presently in operation: creating a critical mass of civil techno intelligence non-profit orgs to relentlessly annoy the bourgeois mind with a never-ending stream of revelations.[17]

Silicon Realpolitik

'War is life, peace is death' is one of the Orwellian slogans in Dave Eggers' Silicon Valley parable *The Circle*. How do these motifs play out in this era of monopolistic consolidation? In this digital age of Total Integration, there are no old industrial giants anymore that need to be overthrown. Today's barons live in Mountain View – and they shy away from war and imperial occupation. Instead of our image of Bay Area industries as the fortuitous tech-evolution of Whole Earthers that has trans-morphed, been co-opted and corrupted, I would propose another reading of Silicon Valley as the degeneration of libertarian conservatism, in the opposite direction to its realization. My guide here, so powerful to read in the internet context, is Corey Robin's *The Reactionary Mind*. Robin's lead forces us to shift our mindset and no longer see the Silicon Valley as fallen hippies betraying progressive goals but to read their cruel yet innocent minds as reactionary, aiming to further strengthen the power of the conservative 1 per cent. The real hippies retired long ago. Their legacy was easy to delete.[18] This perspective gives us the liberty to instead reread the dotcom age as a 'weakened moral fiber', dominated by a 'lost martial spirit'. The problem with bourgeois society as Robin describes it is its lack of imagination: 'Peace is pleasurable, and pleasure is about momentary satisfaction.' Peace 'erases the memory of bracing conflict, robust disagreement, the luxury of defining ourselves by virtue of whom we were up against'.[19] Once Silicon Valley lost its innocence, it took a bit of time to realize that it was now gearing up for war and conflict.

In contrast to most DC think tanks, Silicon Valley calculates with, and not against, the Apocalypse. Its ever-implicit slogan is: 'Bring it on'. Writing about the neo-cons, Robin notes that 'unlike their endgame, if they have one, there is an apocalyptic confrontation between good and evil, civilization and barbarism – categories of pagan conflict diametrically opposed to the world-without-borders vision of America's free-trading, globalising elite'.[20] This openness of conflict is absent from the Valley. Google's over-identification with, and then later abandonment of, its old slogan 'Don't be Evil' says it all. Against this initial do-good mentality, we need to be able to occupy the mindset of venture capitalist guru Peter Thiel, who is willing to think with Evil, and one of the few to talk openly about the autistic tendencies of the tech elite. In his book, *From Zero to One*, Thiel formulates four rules for start-ups: '1. It is better to risk boldness than triviality. 2. A bad plan is better than no plan. 3. Competitive markets destroy profits. 4. Sales matters just as much as the product.' To get there, companies must remain 'lean', which is code for 'unplanned': 'You should not know what your business will do; planning is arrogant and inflexible. Instead you should try out. Iterate and treat entrepreneurship as agnostic experimentation.'[21] All this applies to the logic of the war economy, run by a cold cynicism that looks down on the naïve idealism of free market advocates.

Peter Thiel publicly admonishes Hobbesian status-quo thinking. Frank Pasquale, meanwhile, comes to similar conclusions but voices a new social realism. With competition muted and cooperation accelerating, 'most start-ups today aim to be bought by a company like Google or Facebook, not to replace them. Rather than merely hoping for competition that may never come, we need to assure that the natural monopolization now at play in fields like search and social networking doesn't come at too high a cost to the rest of the economy.'[22] In the blurb for Julian Assange's *When Google Met Wikileaks*, we can find the following contrast between the hacker-whistleblower Assange and the Google executive Eric Schmidt: 'For Assange, the liberating power of the internet is based on its freedom and statelessness. For Schmidt, emancipation is at one with US foreign policy objectives and is driven by connecting non-Western countries to Western companies and markets.'[23]

A Quick Update on Attention

Let us now focus on what has been going on in internet theory over the past few years. Leaving aside the usual techno-optimists and Silicon Valley marketing gurus, there are two trajectories that need discussion. The American approach, coming from Nicholas Carr, Andrew Keen and Jaron Lanier, who are primarily business writers, not academics – with the exception of Sherry Turkle – critiques social media for its superficiality: the fast, short exchanges within people's 'echo chambers' (that can even affect the brain, as Carr tried to prove) are causing loneliness and a loss of focus. More recently,

Petra Löffler from Weimar has given these concerns a Euro-historical twist in her study on the role of distraction in the works of Walter Benjamin and Siegfried Krakauer.[24] The case study in this book on the Europhilic 'net resentment' of the American writer Jonathan Franzen can be situated between these positions. Net criticism cannot pretend that it sits outside of these very real concerns around info overload, multi-tasking and loss of concentration, and related work, as dealt with by scholars such as Trebor Scholz and Melissa Gregg. However, it is also good to sometimes forget such anxieties and turn our attention to the material roots that underlie pressurized social media timelines.

In contrast to the moralistic turn in US mainstream outlets, Europeans such as Bernard Stiegler, Ippolita, Mark Fisher, Tiziana Terranova and Franco Berardi (and I include myself here) stress the wider economic and cultural context of (the crisis in) digital capitalism which is producing its own 'pharmacological' effects (directly linking to self-adjustment through medicines).[25] According to these authors, an embodied approach is necessary in order to overcome simple resignations into 'offline romanticism' – a position taken all too easily when we feel that our bodies no longer cope and routine takes over. The politics of the internet, including its interface aesthetics, should go beyond the Sloterdijkian mental training proposal, 'mastering' away the temptations of technology via life-changing individuated routines. Prescriptions of therapeutics must always combine with a political economic position on the financialization of the economy, the effects of 24/7 availability and invisible infrastructures, and the role of climate change, while we are working through the digital.

Irrespective of our feelings and resentments about a technology that overwhelms us with too much data, what are we going to do when, as David Weinberger says, it is all 'too big to know', and the eye candy of info visualization does not give us easy answers either?[26] Whether we are North America industry sensitives or up with the Euro-theory, the current downturn in critical theory production around distraction and disciplining of the workforce only means that this is here to stay. Nevertheless, moral memes might occasionally step in – for example, to make staring at smart phones in public uncool overnight.

One author who so far has been able to productively overcome the information overload thesis would be Evgeny Morozov. In his 2013 study *To Save Everything, Click Here*, he presented a general theory that leaves behind surface-level media and representation analysis. Central to this critical project is the IT marketing tactic he calls 'solutionism'. Cost cutting and disruption have become goals and industries in themselves that can – and will – be applied to all fields of life. After his first book on US foreign policy and the 'internet freedom' programme of former Secretary of State Hillary Clinton, Morozov expanded his analysis to healthcare (the quantified self), logistics, fashion, education, mobility and the control of public spaces. He warns us that technology cannot solve social problems: we must do that ourselves. Remaining sceptical about human nature, his message is that programmers should take the complexity of human customs and traditions into account and hold back from making bold claims.[27]

Early in 2015, Morozov made an interesting change of tack. In an extensive personal interview with *New Left Review*, the ownership of IT infrastructure becomes the key issue: 'Socialise the Data Centres!' – 'I am questioning who should run and own both the infrastructure and the data running through it, since I no longer believe that we can accept that all these services ought to be delivered by the market and regulated only after the fact.'[28] He dismisses Europe's attempts to regulate Google.[29] A European search algorithm won't do the job: 'Google will remain dominant as long as its challengers do not have the same underlying user data it controls. For Europe to remain relevant, it would have to confront the fact that data, and the infrastructure (sensors, mobile phones, and so on), which produce them, are going to be the key to most domains of economic activity.' The reason Europe can't do much against its dependency on American companies is because such measures 'would go clean against what the neoliberal Europe of today stands for'. Morozov proposes that one company should never own citizen's data: 'Citizens can own their own data and not sell it, to enable a more communal planning of their lives.'

The Internet as Techno-Social Unconscious

Having turned into a general infrastructure for everything, the internet is now entering its maturity phase. 'Reification' is not our social media problem. Nor does 'rationalization' capture the challenging behind-scenes processes of our time. In *The Uprising*, Franco Berardi states that 'in the digital age power is all about making things easy'.[30] Leaving behind the modern age of mass education and class compromise, operating as that did under the umbrella of the welfare state and the Cold War, datafication and financialization are taking command as two sides of the neoliberal society of control. There must be a 'Universal Reason of the Digital' but what does it consist of? Without a plan or decision in sight, the digital presents itself as the comfortable yet unquestioned new norm. There is nothing anymore to verify, nothing to see (but cute cats). New-school clueless users, busy with their everyday lives, have installed the apps, signed-in, created an account and agreed on the terms and conditions, to enter the world of smoothness. Welcome to the regime of liminal comforts, the unbearable lightness of swiping, clicking and liking.[31]

Here lies the thesis of this book: tomorrow's challenge will not be the internet's omnipresence but its very invisibility. That's why Big Brother is the wrong framing. Social media are anything but monstrous machines. The sweet 'eye' of the screen is a spectacle that easily distracts us. Mind control is more subtle, and does not congeal in exemplary images and objects. Social media gather influence in the background. We need the input here of a new generation of techno-psycho-analysts to radically update the disappeared 'mass psychology' discipline, from Freud and Canetti onwards, to explain these new states of collective unconscious. These insights, in turn, should be paired with an equally new batch of sociologists who can think through the abstraction of work (due to digitization and automation). How can sociology be lured away from Big Data and, once again, contribute to critical theory? Is a new *Methodenstreit* necessary or can the regressive obsession with quantitative analysis be countered in a different way? Needless to say, our expressionist science has to get over its own defensive, depressive state. One way of doing this would be a radical reassessment of 'French theory' and the mechanical way theory has been utilized in the recent past.[32] It is all very well to dream of swarms and proclaim the networked multitude (and warn of its dark side), but it is equally important to design new forms of sociality that harness these energies, for instance in 'collective awareness platforms' that emphasize long-term collaborations over spontaneous one-off gatherings.[33] The power of concepts that are implemented and start to live a life of their own is still imminent, and there are plenty of examples of this, also, in this book.

Where do you find comrades to work with, to live with, to love and care for? How can we envision new organizational forms that are both horizontal and vertical, with an external arm and a rich internal structure? Are we ready for political dating sites and hyper-local social signaling? What's a 'like' with technical consequences? How can we move on from the simple 'clicktivism' level of Avaaz to scalable local organizations that can respond to sudden events while

10

having a long-term agenda? What could peer-to-peer solidarity look like?[34] This is why the Anonymous episode of 2009–12, so accurately documented by Gabriella Coleman,[35] remains so deeply subversive and inspiring, despite all the tragic mistakes and betrayals, leading to the lengthy prison sentences of Barrett Brown and others.[36] 'What is to be done?' is a question of not merely how to address world leaders during their summits, but also how to design digital sensibility, so as to forge direct and ongoing involvements with as yet unknown others.

Furthermore, as Michael Seemann writes: 'Decentralised approaches will only work if you keep the data open. Only open data can be centrally queryable and avoid misappropriation at the same time.'[37] Is the 'federated web' a viable alternative to the centralization strategy of the status quo? What does it mean when we federate? Obviously federation is an ancient political concept, meaning voluntary association into a larger state unit. In the internet context, federation goes beyond direct, peer-to-peer connections and addresses protocol issues and governance. But can we also speak of a federation of abilities? When we mash data from various sources and bring them together in our browser, we oppose the logic of the centralized data silos. Would this be an effective answer to the uncontested rise of data centres? It's easy to dismiss this approach as a techno-fix. *Engineering Our Way Out of Fascism*, as Smari McCarthy proposed, should be taken seriously as a strategic contribution.[38] Fascism is defined here as 'the perfect union of state and business'. Today's questions of political organization are technological in nature. Those who argue alongside Machiavelli, Hobbes, Hegel or Schmitt repeat the problems of the ruling elites and implicitly desire to overrule social movements and their dynamics with a higher body (the Party) that will coordinate and control political dissent.

Technology is always political; there can be a consensus about this, yet it is hard to consider that politics is technical in nature. We're attracted to the purity of the separated realm of intrigue where interests clash and the power game is being played out, rather than confronting ourselves with the 'Albert Speer' legacy: we, the programmers, are hacktivists and geeks; the technocrat is always the other.

We need a shift from the attention economy to a web of intentions. The strategy should be to crystallize the social through 'networks with consequences'. The current social media architectures merely capture value (from a business perspective). They monitor events and commodify news (without producing it) for audiences whose

11

preferences can be sold to the highest bidder. Abstraction is our black hole. The proposed solution here is focused user groups (also called organized networks) that can operate outside of the 'like' economy and its weak links. Mutual aid outside the recommendation industry. Sharing outside of Airbnb and Uber. A cooperative renaissance on the internet is possible.[39] We should not give up on the multitude of attempts to design general software and related machine languages, as these are our only viable strategy against the monopolistic inter-mediates. We will have to define a seductive mix between federalism and 're-decentralization'. Celebrate the aesthetics of collective mean-ingfulness and develop the tools that encode the principles that we value in society. This will only become possible when we say farewell to the free and built-in counter-monetization procedures on all levels, so that the gift will, once again, become a precious gesture, not a slippery, hidden default. In order to get there, we need to recapture the network as a distinct form, different from the working group, the party and the old hierarchies inside companies, armies and religious organizations. How does the network as a social practice relate to the co-op as a legal form? This type of strategic thinking makes it possible to free ourselves from the 'reticular pessimism' that accord-ing to Alex Galloway, claims 'that there is no escape from the fetters of the network'.[40] 'Networks are a mode of mediation, just like any other', he concludes. Let's, therefore, zoom in on the unforeseen organizational possibilities that lie ahead – inside and outside the network. Let's re-position ourselves on its edges, to understand net-works as new institutional forms.

— 1 —

WHAT IS THE SOCIAL IN SOCIAL MEDIA?

Headlines for the Few: 'Next time you're hiring, forget personality tests, just check out the applicant's Facebook profile instead.' – 'Stephanie Watanabe spent nearly four hours Thursday night unfriending about 700 of her Facebook friends – and she isn't done yet.' – 'Facebook apology or jail time: Ohio man gets to choose.' – 'Study: Facebook users getting less friendly' – 'Women tend to have stronger feelings regarding who has access to their personal information. (Mary Madden) – 'All dressed up and no place to go.' (*Wall Street Journal*) – 'I'm making more of an effort to be social these days, because I don't want to be alone, and I want to meet people.' (Cindy Sherman) – '30 per cent posted updates that met the American Psychiatric Association's criteria for a symptom of depression, reporting feelings of worthlessness or hopelessness, insomnia or sleeping too much, and difficulty concentrating.' – 'Hunt for Berlin police officer pictured giving Nazi salute on Facebook' – '15-year-old takes to Facebook to curse and complain about her parents. The disgusted father later blasts her laptop with a gun.'

The use of the word 'social' in the context of information technology dates back to the very beginnings of cybernetics. A sub-field called socio-cybernetics was created inside of sociology to study the 'network of social forces that influence human behaviour', able to optimize or modify information systems.[1] With the production of software well underway, the social pops up in the 1980s emergence of 'groupware'. In the same period, Friedrich Kittler from the materialist school of German media theory dismissed the use of the word 'social' as irrelevant fluff (computers calculate, they do not interfere in human relations, so we should stop projecting our mundane all-too-human desires onto electronic circuits, etc).[2] Meanwhile, holistic hippies of the Wired school ignored such cynical machine knowledge from Old Europe, celebrating instead a positive, humanistic approach that worshipped computers as tools for personal liberation, a mentality later turned by Steve Jobs into a design principle and marketing machine. Before the dotcom venture capital takeover of IT in the second half of the 1990s, progressive computing was primarily occupied with making tools, and focused on collaborations between two or more people; not for 'sharing', but for getting work done. The social, in this context, meant exchanges between isolated nodes. Owing partly to its 'alternative' beginnings, the Californian individualistic emphasis on cool interface design and usability was always supplemented with 'community' investments in networks. But this Californian 'social' just means sharing amongst users. It doesn't get close to anything like collective ownership or public utility.

Computers have, in fact, always been hybrids of the social and the post-human. From the beginning of their industrial life as giant calculators, the linking up of different units was seen as both a possibility and necessity.[3] In his never-published essay, 'How Computer Networks Became Social', Sydney-based media theorist Chris Chesher maps out the historical and interdisciplinary development – from sociometry and social network analysis (with roots going back to the 1930s) through Granovetter's work on 'weak links' in 1973, to Castells' *Network Society* (1996) and the current mapping efforts of the techno-scientists who gather under the Actor Network Theory umbrella – of an 'offline' science that studies the dynamics of human networks. The conceptual leap that is most relevant to grasp is the move from groups, lists, forums and communities to the empowerment of loosely connected individuals in networks. This shift had already begun in the neoliberal 1990s, facilitated by growing computing power, storage capacity and internet bandwidth, alongside simplifying interfaces on smaller and smaller (mobile) devices. This is where we enter the Empire of the Social.

If we want to pose the question of what this 'social' in today's social media really means, a possible starting point could be its disappearance, as described by Jean Baudrillard, the French sociologist who theorized the transition of the subject into a consumer. According to Baudrillard, at some point the social lost its historical role and imploded into media. If the social is no longer the once dangerous mix of politicized proletarians, frustrated unemployed and dirty *clochards* that hang out on the streets, waiting for the next opportunity to revolt under whatever banner, then how do social elements manifest themselves in the digital networked age?

14

The 'social question' may not have been resolved, but for decades in the West it has felt as if it was neutralized. In the post-World War II period, instrumental knowledge of how to manage the social was seen as necessary, to the extent that thinking about 'the social' in an intellectual and technical sense was delegated to a somewhat closed circle of professional experts. Now, in the midst of a global economic downturn, can we see a return or even renaissance of the social? Or is all this talk about the rise of 'social media' just a linguistic coincidence? Can we speak, in the never-ending aftermath of the 2008 financial crisis, of a growing social and class awareness, and, if so, can this spread into the electronic realm? Despite the hardships of unemployment, increasing income disparities and the achievements of the Occupy protests, a globally networked uprising that scales up quickly seems unlikely. Protests are successful precisely because they are local, despite their networked presence. 'Memes' are travelling at the speed of light, spreading basic concepts. But how can the separate entities of work, culture, politics and networked communication in a global context be connected in such a way that information (for instance, via Twitter) and interpersonal communication (email, Facebook) can have an effect on the actual organization of world events?

Here we must reframe considerations of the social into a larger, strategic context than the typical 'social media question' poses. Maybe all these neatly administrated contacts and address books at some point spill over and leave the virtual realm, as the popularity of dating sites seems to suggest. Do we only share information, experiences and emotions for the mirroring sake of it, or do we also conspire, as 'social swarms', to raid reality in order to create so-called 'real world' events? Will contacts mutate into comrades? It is clear that social media solved some of the organizational problems of the social that the baby boom / suburb generation faced fifty years ago: boredom, isolation, depression and desire. How do we come together, differently, right now? Do we unconsciously fear (or long for) the day when our vital infrastructure breaks down, and we really need each other? Or should we read the Simulacrum of the Social as more like organized agony – confronting the loss of community after the fragmentation of family, marriage, friendship and so on? With what rationale do we assemble these ever-growing collections of contacts otherwise? Is the Other, relabelled as 'friend', going to be more than a future customer, or 'lifesaver' only of our business dealings in precarity? What new forms of social imaginary already exist? And on the other side of these questions, should solitude as a response to the daily pressures of the 'social' be promoted as *Kulturideal*, as the likes of Nietzsche and Ayn Rand also proposed?[4] At what point does our administration of others mutate into something different altogether? Will befriending disappear overnight, like so many other new media-related practices that vanished into the digital nirvana, such as Usenet forums, telnet log-ins to servers, or our once wide-spread HTML coding of our own websites?

The container concept 'social Web' once described a fuzzy collection of websites from MySpace, Digg, YouTube, Flickr to Wikipedia. Five years later, the term was broadened to include a wider range of soft and hard devices (including not only PCs and laptops) and rebranded into 'social media'. There was very little that was nostalgic about this project, no revival of the once dangerous potential of 'the social' along the lines of the angry mob that once demanded the end of economic inequality. Instead, to remain inside Baudrillard's vocabulary, the social was reanimated as a mere simulacrum of its own capacity to create meaningful and lasting social relations. Roaming around in virtual global networks, we believe that we are less and less committed to our roles within traditional communities such as the family, church, political party, trade union and neighbourhood. Historical subjects, once defined in terms like 'citizens' or 'members of a class', carrying certain rights, have been transformed into subjects with agency: dynamic actors called users, customers who complain, and prosumers. The social is no longer a reference to society even – an insight that troubles us theorists and critics whose empirical research still proves that people, despite all their outward behaviour, remain quite firmly embedded in certain cultural, local and especially hierarchical structures. Stripped of all metaphysical values, the social is becoming a placeholder for something resembling inter-personal rubble, the leftovers after the neoliberal destruction of 'society', a loose collection of 'weak ties'. As a concept, it lacks both the religious undertone of terms such as 'community' and the retroactive anthropological connotation of the 'tribe'. To put this in marketing terms, the current 'social' is just that which is technical and vaguely 'open' – the space between you and me and our friends.

Accordingly, the social no longer manifests itself primarily as a class, movement or mob, nor does it institutionalize itself anymore, as happened during the post-war decades of the welfare state. Even the postmodern phase of disintegration and decay seems over. Nowadays, the social manifests itself in a network form. Its practices emerge outside of the walls of the twentieth-century institutions,

16

leading to a corrosion of conformity. The network then becomes the actual shape of the social. What counts, for instance in politics and business, are the 'social facts' as they present themselves through network analysis and its corresponding data visualizations. The institutional part of life takes shape as another matter altogether, the banal disappearing base of social data that quickly falls into the background of discussion, into some distant universe of concern. It is tempting here to remain positive and insist on the portrayal of a synthesis, farther down the road, between the formalized power structures inside institutions and the growing influence of the informal networks. But there is little evidence for this pleasant Third Way approach being either useful or realistic. The PR-driven belief system that social media will, one day, be integrated into functional institutions and infrastructures may be nothing more than New Age optimism in an age of growing tensions over scarce resources. Within this tension, the social can appear like a wonder glue, used to either repair or gloss over historical damages, or it can quickly turn into explosive material. A total ban on this explosiveness is nearly impossible, not even in authoritarian countries. Ignoring social media as background noise also backfires. This is why institutions, from hospitals to universities, hire swarms of temporary consultants to manage social media for them.

Social media fulfil the promise of communication as exchange: instead of forbidding responses, they demand replies or at least a technical notion of reciprocity. Similar to how Baudrillard outlined earlier media forms, today's networks are 'reciprocal spaces of speech and response'[5] that lure users into saying something, anything ... Later on, Baudrillard changed his position and no longer believed in the emancipatory aspect of talking back to the media. Restoring the symbolic exchange wasn't helpful – meanwhile this feature is precisely what social media offer their users as a gesture of liberation. For the late Baudrillard, what counted was the superior position of the silent majority.

In their 2012 pamphlet, *Declaration*, Michael Hardt and Antonio Negri avoid discussing the larger social dimensions of community, cohesion and society. What they witness is unconscious slavery: 'People sometimes strive for their servitude as if it were their salvation.'[6] It is primarily individual entitlement that interests these theorists in social media, not the social at large: 'Is it possible that in their voluntary communication and expression, in their blogging and social media practices, people are contributing to instead of contesting repressive forces?' For us, the mediatized ones, work and leisure can

17

no longer be separated. But why didn't Hardt and Negri express interest also in the equally obvious fact of a productive side in being connected to others?

Hardt and Negri make the mistake of reducing social networking to a media question, as if the internet and smart phones are only used to look up information. Concerning the role of communication, they conclude, 'Nothing can beat the being together of bodies and the corporeal communication that is the basis of collective political intelligence and action.' Social media links are probably nothing but fluff here, a veritable world of sweet sassiness. In this way, the true nature of mediated social life online remains out of sight, and thus unscrutinized. Social meets media doesn't have to be sold as some Hegelian synthesis, as a direction in which World History necessarily evolves; still, the strong yet abstract concentration of social activity 'out there', on today's platforms, remains to be well theorized. Hardt and Negri's (hopeless) call to refuse mediation does not address the problem. As they say themselves, 'We need to make new truths, which can be created by singularities in networks communicating and being there.' We need both networking and encampment. In their version of the social, 'we swarm like insects' and act as 'a decentralised multitude of singularities that communicates horizontally'.[7] But the actual power structures and frictions that emerge from – or alongside – this constellation have yet to be addressed.

While tarrying with the social online, it seems a brave but ultimately unproductive project to look for relevant remains from nineteenth-century European social theory. This is what makes the 'precarious labor' debate about Marx and exploitation inside Facebook so tricky.[8] What we need to do instead is take the process of socialization at face value and refrain from well-meaning political intentions (for instance, exaggerating the significance of 'Facebook revolutions' in relation to the 2011 Arab Spring and the movements of the squares). The workings of social media are subtle, informal and indirect. How can we understand the social turn in new media, beyond good and evil, through both its coldness and its intimacy, as Israeli sociologist Eva Illouz has described this terrain in her book *Cold Intimacies*?[9] Literature on the media industry and IT tends to shy away from the complexity of these questions. Virtues such as accessibility and usability do little to explain what people are looking for 'out there' in the network. There are similar limits to the (professional, neoliberalized) discourses of trust that also try to bridge new informalities with increasingly legal logics of rules and regulations.

While sociology as a discipline is still with us for now, the above-described 'obliteration of the social' has contributed to a downgrading of the importance of social theory within critical internet debates. Against this tendency, a web-based sociology that frees itself of the real–virtual dichotomies, and refuses to limit its research scope to the 'social implications of technology' (for example, studying internet addiction), could play a critical role in exploring how class analysis and mediatization are, more than ever, intertwined. As Eva Illouz wrote to me, regarding this issue: 'If sociology has traditionally called on us to exert our shrewdness and vigilance in the art of making distinctions (between use value and exchange value; the life world and the colonization of the life world, etc.), the challenge that awaits us is to exercise the same vigilance in a social world which consistently defeats these distinctions.'[10] The Amsterdam pioneer of web sociology and editor of SocioSite, Albert Benschop, proposes to overcome this real–virtual distinction altogether. Adapting the Thomas theorem, a classic in sociology, Benschop's slogan is: 'If people define networks as real, they are real in their consequences.' In other words, for Benschop, the internet is not only some 'second-hand world'. Its material virtuality influences our reality. The same applies to the social. There is no second life with alternate social rules and conventions. According to Benschop, this is why there is, strictly speaking, no additional discipline necessary.[11] The discussion about the shape of the social relates to all of us and should not be cooked up – and owned – by geeks and start-up entrepreneurs alone.

Here we are confronted with the main difference between old broadcast media and the current social network paradigm. Social media eliminate old media's human curators and require our constant involvement in terms of clicking, but machines will not make the vital connection for us, no matter how much we delegate thought or affects, or try to inflate social capital. We switch into a state of 'interpassivity' here, as discussed for instance by Pfaller, Žižek and van Oenen.[12] But this concept is still mostly descriptive and analytically not useful. It cannot question the current architectures and cultures of use of social media. Further, criticism of these aspects is not only motivated by some hidden, oppressed offline romantic sentiment. There are quite justified feelings of overexposure at play, not just to information in general, but also to others' lives, as much as this is the compulsory-'opt in' part of participatory media. We all need to have a break from the social circus now and then (though who can afford to cut off ties indefinitely?).

19

The definition of the personal in relation to the social is accordingly being reworked. The 'social' in social media asks us to experience our personal history as something that we have reconciled ourselves with and overcome in order to participate at all (think of family ties, the village or suburb, school and college, church and colleagues from work); at the same time, we are supposed to perform pride in present and historical forms of the self, to represent – and even to love to show off – ourselves. Social networking is experienced in terms of an actual potentiality: I could contact this or that person (but I won't). From now on, I will indicate what my preferred brand is (even without being asked). The social is the collective ability to imagine the connected subjects as a temporary unity. The power and significance of what it potentially could mean to connect to many is felt by many.

Martin Heidegger's 'we don't call, we are being called' runs empty at this point.[13] On the Net, bots will contact you directly, and the status updates of others, relevant or not, will pass by and filter through, regardless. On Facebook, it is impossible to have a solitary life. You will receive 'friend' requests without meaning. For the passive receiver, filter failure is real. Once inside the busy flow of social media, the Call to Being comes from software and invites you to reply. This is where the cool and laid-back postmodern indifference as a quasi-subversive attitude comes to an end. Because it is just as meaningless to not be bothered. We are not friends anyway. Algorithms have decided this for us. So why stay on Facebook? Forget Twitter. Delete WhatsApp. These are cool statements – but beside the point. The user is no longer in a nineties regime. No one can take the dumb sovereign position to be indifferent to the social anymore. The silence of the masses Baudrillard spoke of seems itself a strange utopia. Social media has been a clever trick to get people talking, without end. The addictive side of social media cannot be denied. We have all been reactivated. The obscenity of common opinions, and the everyday prostitution of our private details is now firmly embedded in software and engaging billions of users who do not know how to exit. Is there a way to exit the social without anyone noticing?

The example of exit that Baudrillard used back then was the opinion poll undermining the authentic existence of the social. Thus Baudrillard replaced the sad vision of the masses as an alienated entity with an ironic and object-centred one. Nowadays, thirty years deeper into the media era, even this vision has become internalized. In the Facebook age, surveys record our preferences continuously without people's direct participation, through elaborately coded data mining. These algorithmic calculations run in the background and log everything emerging from single clicks, keywords and even touches of the keyboard. For Baudrillard, this 'positive absorption into the transparency of the computer'[14] is something worse than alienation. The public has morphed into a database full of users. The 'evil genius of the social' has no other way to express itself than to go back to the streets and squares, guided and witnessed by the multitude of viewpoints that tweeting smart phones and recording digital cameras produce. The 'subject as user' has even fewer options: you can insert what feels like speech into the comment section, or continue as a lurker, while the occasional deviant personality appears as a troll. Much in the same way as Baudrillard reinterpreted the outcome of opinion polls as a subtle revenge of the common people on the political/media system, we should now question the objective truth of big social data operations, originating as they do from 'the stacks', a shortage for Microsoft, Google, Apple and Facebook, suggested in 2012 by Bruce Sterling.[15] Users are assisted by an army of dutiful, hard-working software bots, and surrounded by massive amounts of fake and inactive accounts. A lot of the traffic is between the servers themselves, without any user component. This is what object-oriented philosophy has yet to come to terms with – a critique of useless and empty contingency.[16]

The social media system no longer 'plunges us into a state of stupor', as Baudrillard described the media experience decades ago. Instead, it shows us the way to cooler apps and other products that elegantly make us forget yesterday's flavour of the day. We simply click, tap and drag, before turning the whole platform aside, and finding something else to log on to to distract us. Online services very suddenly are deserted, within weeks – we have forgotten the icon, bookmark or password. We do not have to revolt against the new media of the Web 2.0 era, leaving them in protest because of alleged intrusive privacy policies. We more often leave them confidently, knowing that they will remain out there like the good old HTML ghost towns of the nineties, raising paradoxes of eternal return.

Baudrillard phrased the beginnings of this situation for the old media days: 'This is our destiny, subjected to opinion polls, information, publicity, statistics: constantly confronted with the anticipated statistical verification of our behaviour, absorbed by this permanent refraction of our least movements, we are no longer confronted with our own will.'[17] He discussed the move towards obscenity that is made in the permanent display of one's own preferences

21

(in our case, on social media platforms). There is a 'redundancy of the social', a 'continual voyeurism of the group in relation to itself: it must at all times know what it wants. ... The social becomes obsessed with itself; through this auto-information, this permanent auto-intoxication.'

The difference between the 1980s, when Baudrillard wrote those early theses, and thirty years later, is the opening up of all aspects of life to the logic of opinion polls. Not only do we have personal opinions about every possible event, idea or product, but these informal judgments are also interesting for databases and search engines. People talk about products on their own initiative; they no longer need incentives from outside. Twitter captures the entire spectrum of uncoded life when it asks 'What's happening?' Everything, even the tiniest info spark provided by the online public is (potentially) relevant, ready to be earmarked as viral and trending, destined to be data-mined and, once stored, waiting to be combined with other details. These devices of capture are totally indifferent to the content of what people say – who cares about your views? In the end it's all just data, becoming their data, ready to be mined, recombined and flogged off for a profit: 'Victor, are you still alive?'[18] This is not about participation, remembrance and forgetting. What we transmit are the bare signals that we are still alive.

A deconstructive take on social media need not bother itself again with rereading the friendship discourse ('from Socrates to Facebook') or taking apart the Online Self. The 'interpassivity' concept might similarly encourage focus on breaks and time-outs ('book your offline holiday now'), but these are all critiques that very predictably played themselves out. Instead, we need bold 'cybernetics 2.0' initiatives, along lines that follow-up the original Macy conferences (1946 to 1953) where cybernetics were first discussed, to investigate the cultural logic inside social media, re-assert self-reflexivity in code, and ask what software architectures could be proposed to radically alter and reorganize online social experience. We need input from critical humanities and social sciences that enable dialogues with computer science on an equal basis. Are 'software studies' initiatives up to such a task? Time will tell. Digital humanities, with its one-sided emphasis on data visualization, working with computer-illiterate humanities scholars as innocent victims, has so far made a bad start. We do not need more tools for the ignorant, but a new generation of humanities that are technically skilled. What is required are research programmes that put critical theory and cultural studies in the driver's seat, managed by programmer-theorists, philosophers and art critics who have finally moved beyond painting and film. Concurrently, the submissive attitude towards the hard sciences and industries in the arts and humanities needs to come to a close. Humanities should not submit themselves in a masochistic manner to the digital regime. We need a bold counter-strike. But that's not going to happen if we continue to look away.

How can philosophy contribute to such a movement? The Western male self-identical subject no longer needs to be taken apart and contrasted with the liberated cyber-identity a.k.a. avatars that roam around the virtual game worlds. For this, an IT-informed post-colonial theory of embodied networks and organization is overdue. What is the role of affects in this? To speak directly of theory, we need to extend Derrida's questioning of the Western subject to the non-human agency of software (as described by Bruno Latour and his ANT followers). Only then can we get a better understanding of the cultural policy of aggregators, the forgotten role of search engines and the never-ending edit wars inside Wikipedia.

Thinking with the sociologists, the emphasis on Big Data as the 'renaissance of the social' is clearly a 'positivist science of society'. As of yet, however, there is no critical school in sight that could help us to read properly the social aura of this citizen-as-user. The term 'social' has effectively been neutralized in its most cynical reduction to data porn (and its discontents). Reborn as a cool concept for pro-prietary platforms and, in turn, corporatized Anglo media studies, 'the social' manifests itself neither as dissent nor as sub-cultural. The social organizes the self as a techno-cultural entity, a special effect of software, and real-time feedback features prove addictive for many users. In today's discussions of the internet, the social makes no refer-ence to the Social Question nor any hidden reminder of socialist thinking or socialism as a political programme.

Simultaneously, thanks to Facebook's simplicity, the online experi-ence is one that is deeply human: the aim of this human is the Other, not information. Ideally, the Other is online, right now. Communica-tion works best if it is 24/7, global, mobile, fast and short. Most appreciated are instantaneous exchanges with befriended users at chat-mode speed. This is social media at its best. We are invited to 'burp out the thought you have right now – regardless of its quality, regardless of how it connects to your other thoughts'.[19] The social presence and operational style of young people is the default (accord-ing to the scholarly literature). We create a social sculpture, and then, as we do with most conceptual and participatory artworks, abandon it, leaving it to be cleaned up by anonymous workers. This is the faith and fate of all social media, which will be remembered as (also) a historically particular form of non-togetherness in the post-9/11 decade, happily forgotten as the next distraction consumes our perpetual present.

It is said that social media grew out of virtual communities (as described by Howard Rheingold in his 1993 book with the same title), but how much should we care about reiterating the most correct genealogical picture? Many doubt whether Facebook and Twitter, in their current manifestations as platforms for the millions, are still generating authentic online community experiences. What counts are the trending topics, the next platform and the latest apps. Silicon Valley historians will one day explain the rise of social networking sites out of the remains of the dotcom crisis when a handful of survivors from the margins of the e-commerce boom and bust reconfigured viable concepts of the Web 1.0 era, stressing the empowerment of the user as a content producer. The secret of Web 2.0, which kicked off in 2003, is the combination of (free) uploads of digital material with the ability to comment on other people's efforts. Interactivity always consists of these two components: action and reaction. Chris Cree defines social media as 'communication formats publishing user-generated content that allow some level of user interaction',[20] a problematic definition that could already include much of the earlier computer culture. It is not enough to limit social media to uploading and self-promotion. Social media tend to be misunderstood if they are merely considered as one-to-many marketing channels; one-on-one personal feedback and small-scale viral distribution elements cannot be left out.

As Andrew Keen indicates in *Digital Vertigo* (2012), the 'social' in social media is first and foremost an empty container. The internet, in his exemplarily hollow phrasing, is 'becoming the connective tissue of twenty-first century life'. According to Keen, the social here is a tidal wave that is flattening everything in its path. Keen warns that we will end up in an anti-social future, characterized by the 'loneliness of the isolated man in the connected crowd'.[21] Confined inside the software cages of Facebook, Google and their clones, users are encouraged to reduce their social life to 'sharing' information. The self-mediating citizen constantly broadcasts his or her state of being to an amorphous, numb group of 'friends'. Keen is part of a growing number of (mainly) US critics who warn us against the side-effects of extensive social media use. From Sherry Turkle's rant on loneliness, Nicholas Carr's warnings against a loss of brain power and concentration, to Evgeny Morozov's critique of the utopian NGO world, and Jaron Lanier's concern over the loss of creativity, what unites these commentators is their avoidance of what the social could be alternatively, if not defined by Facebook and Twitter. The problem here is the disturbing nature of the social, which returns as a revolt with an unknown, and often unwanted, agenda: vague, populist, Islamist, driven by good-for-nothing memes.

The Other as market opportunity, channel or obstacle? You choose. Never has it been so easy to 'auto-quantify' one's personal surroundings. We follow our blog statistics, our amount of tweets, followings and followers on Twitter, check out the friends-of-friends on Facebook, or go on eBay to purchase a few hundred 'friends' who will then 'like' our latest uploaded pictures more reliably than real ones can, and start a buzz about our latest outfit. Listen to how RSS-inventor and ur-blogger Dave Winer sees the future of news in this realm:

> Start a river, aggregating the feeds of the bloggers you most admire, and the other news sources they read. Share your sources with your readers, understanding that almost no one is purely a source or purely a reader. Mix it all up. Create a soup of ideas and taste it frequently. Connect everyone that's important to you, as fast as you can, as automatically as possible, and put the pedal to the metal and take your foot off the brake.

This is how programmers these days glue everything together, connecting users to data objects to users. This is the social today.

— 2 —

AFTER THE SOCIAL MEDIA HYPE: DEALING WITH INFORMATION OVERLOAD

'You can't get a house mortgage from your Facebook reputation.' (Jaron Lanier) – Understanding how to Ignore Requests – 'What I often do at 3 AM, exhausted, yet unable to sleep, I sometimes browse on my twitter, reading banal nonsense to further raise my ire for the human race and listen to Tom Waits to restore my faith.' (Mickey MacDonagh – Government of Temper) – 'I'm no prophet. My job is making windows where there were once walls.' (Michel Foucault) – 'Bullshit is the new wisdom.' (ProfJeffJarvis) – 'I know how it ends: one day I will be declared "web-hostile" and liquidated. God, why is so much Internet theorising so awful?' (Evgeny Morozov) – Cataclysmic Communications Inc – Growing irrelevance of iEnhancement – 'Facebook to Tell Users They Are Being Tracked' (*NYT*) – 'My data is bigger than your data.' (Ian Bogost) – 'Forums are the dark matter of the web, the B-movies of the Internet. But they matter.' (Jeff Atwood) – The inevitable 'haven't we done this seventeen times already?' thread – 'Since the world is evolving towards a frenzied state of affairs, we have to take a frenzied view of it.' (Jean Baudrillard) – Hunter marked it as 'to ignore'.

Public debate around 'social media' is moving away from discussions and studies of side effects, such as loneliness (Sherry Turkle), stupidity (Andrew Keen) or brain alterations (Nicolas Carr), towards ethical design questions. In other words, how to manage our busy lives.[1] The Foucaultian turn to ethics and technologies of the self happened when we left behind the initial stages of hype and mass uptake, and started to consider seriously the role platforms will play in the long run. Can we live a meaningful life with a smart phone, or is our only option to switch it off and forget about it? Must we be bothered for the rest of our life by retweeting each other's messages? Can we call the Valley to ask: When will the social fad be over and done with? We seem almost ready to move on to a next phase. Time for a last #lolcat picture.

Familiar tropes of the Decline of the West get engaged here, a century after Spengler's Faustian processing of World War I (but this time accurately described by economist Dambisa Moyo[2]). With access to social networks no longer scarce, theories that continue to make utopian and democratic claims for them have to be adjusted. Where was the internet in Syria in 2012? Internet networks facilitated rather than stopped the rise of Islamic State in 2014. Meanwhile, mainstream internet discourse has fallen flat. Remember the good old days of those 'useful idiots' like Steven Johnson, Clay Shirky and Jeff Jarvis? How did Evgeny Morozov fight against them to gain meme supremacy over the American liberal opinion space? Where have all the tech evangelists gone? It seems the internet has become almost everything no one wanted it to be.[3] Is social media the nail in the coffin of the op-ed class that is being pushed aside amidst all the shit storms? For sure, social media contribute to the erosion of mainstream-styled credibilities:[4] 'Twitter is a vast confusion of vows, wishes, edicts, petitions, lawsuits, pleas, laws, complaints, grievances' (James Gleick).[5] Who will guide us in our current search for the rules, duties and prohibitions of digital, networked communication? Where is the stoic calm in this sea of populist outrage?

The internet and smart phones are here to stay and smoothly blend into the crisis-stricken neoliberal age, characterized as it is by economic stagnation, populist anxiety and media spectacle. The question is no longer what potentials 'new media' have and what impact on society they might enable, but how we can cope with the reality of this surreality. This is not the Foucault of surveillance and punishment, but the later Foucault, the one who wrote about the ethical care of the self. How to shape the 'art of living' with so much going on simultaneously? Blog research has already emphasized Foucault's genealogy of confessional form, analysing Web 2.0's user-generated content as a self-promotion machine. Critical 'selfie' research points to a similar 'culture of narcissism'.[6] After an early emphasis on the network's 'empowerment' potential, attention shifted towards the aesthetics of mental and physical sanity. Can we speak of a 'virtue of networking' that guides us in what to say and when to shut-up, what to save and when to join-up, when to switch-off and where to engage? How can everyone's life become a work of art in this age of standardized commodities and services?

Whereas most artistic, activist and academic work emphasizes social media as series of technologies of domination, the authors that

I discuss in this chapter explore the possibility to alter lifestyles. Hippies design therapies, hipsters write apps, while the sovereign attitude of ignoring the busy signals of our techno everyday is clearly not an option for everyone. Further, distraction is also not 'all bad'. As an animal residue inscribed deep in our human system, it helps us to focus on potential dangers from different sources. Can we still regard it as a gift to be able to focus on our multiple tasks simultaneously? Baby-boomer thinking rears its head here, but some of the thoughts are very serious indeed.

Let's focus on Europe, dive into history and discuss the work of the German literature scholar Petra Löffler, whose history of attention in the twentieth century was published in 2014 (in German). She approached this question less from the media archaeology angle than from hermeneutic discourse analysis. In her work, the supposed decline in concentration and today's inability to read longer, complicated texts are starting to affect the future of research as such. Social media only make things worse. Humankind is, once again, on its way downhill, this time busily multitasking on smart phones. While the education sector and the IT industry promote the use of tablets in classrooms (with MOOCs – massive open online courses – as the most current hype), there is only a handful of experts that warn against the long-term consequences. The absence of a serious discussion and policy approach thus gives way to a range of popular myths. Quickly, the debate gets polarized, and any unease is reduced to generational debate and accusations of technophobia. Yet among millions of computer workers, apparent diseases vary and multiply, from damaged eyesight, ADHD and related medication problems (Ritalin), Carpal Tunnel Syndrome and RSI, to bad posture from badly designed peripherals, leading to widespread spinal disc problems. There is talk of mutations in the brain (see, for instance, the work of the German psychiatrist Manfred Spitzer). Within this worrying spread of postmodern diseases, is there any space at all for the 'healing effects of daydreaming'? The surprising bit of Löffler's research is that writers such as Krakauer and Benjamin were in fact in favour of distraction. Michel de Montaigne very early recommended diversion as a comfort against the suffering of souls. In Löffler's analysis of early cinema, we see the emergence of entertainment as a right of the working class and part of the necessary reproduction of the workforce. Distraction was seen as a very real class-based demand, not only as a conspiracy by the hegemonic forces to 'fool' its subjects. From this perspective still, attention becomes a disciplining force. In an interview I did with Löffler, she stated:

'Following philosophers like Kant or psychologists like Ribot I believe that a certain level of distraction is not only necessary for life balance, but also a common state of body and mind.'[7] For Löffler, we live in an uncertain period of transition:

> That's why formulas that promise easy solutions are highly welcomed. Neurological concepts are often based on one-sided models concerning the relationship between body and mind, and they often leave out the role of social and environmental factors. From historians of science such as Canguilhem and Foucault, one can learn that psychiatric models of brain defects and mental anomalies not only mirror social anxieties but also produce knowledge about what is defined as normal. And it is up to us as observers of such discourses to name those anxieties today. Nonetheless, I would not signify distraction as a metaphor. It is, in fact, a concrete phase of the body, a state of the mind. It's real. You cannot deal with it when you call it a disability or a disease and just pop pills or switch off your electronic devices.

The question on the table then, thinking again with Foucault, is how to minimize domination and shape the new technologies of the self. The question as to why the internet industry has bred its own monsters of centralization and control (through the cartel of Google, Facebook, Apple, Amazon) while promising their opposite remains unanswered for now. Understandably, the internet's paternal founders remain silent on the issue, and are not scrutinized over their direct responsibility for their industry's trajectory either. We know they are part of the problem, not part of the solution. What bothers more is our own survival in terms of spaces of thought and agency. Which techniques are effective in reducing the social noise and permanent data floods that scream for attention? Which online platform types facilitate lasting forms of organization? We're not merely talking here about filters that delete spam and 'kill' digital traces of your ex. As the state of the art of internet discussion shows, it is all about habit, training and repetition (as Aristotle already emphasized). There is no ultimate solution. We will need to work constantly on our mental conditions to focus while remaining open to new currents and historical leaps sideways that question the very foundations of our path. This is not merely a question of a fair distribution of concentration. When do we welcome the Other and when should the Alien be jammed? When do we stop searching and start making? There are times when all real-time communication weaponry should be fired up for mobilization and temporary domination of the spectacle, but the evening must set in when it is time to chill out and open other doors of perception. But when do these times ever clearly arrive?

It has been proven by now that criticizing the Facebooks of this world in public is not in itself enough. There is a hope that boredom amongst youngsters will prevail, with users moving on, forgetting current social media platforms altogether within weeks or months after their final logoff (as happened to Bibo, Hyves, StudiVZ, Orkut, MySpace). It is not cool to be on the same platform as your parents, family and teachers. The assumption is that the heroic gesture of the few that quit will eventually be followed by a silent exodus of the multitudes. While this may be inevitable in the long run, the constant migration from one service to the next does not take away any of the collective feeling of restlessness, nor our sensitivity to ongoing, manufactured ignorance and culturally induced doubt. According to Belgian pop psychiatrist Dirk De Wachter, author of *Borderline Times*, Western citizens are struggling with a chronic feeling of emptiness. His German companion would be the psychiatrist Manfred Spitzer, who, in his book *Digital Dementia*, argued that the use of tablets and social media in school would lead to decreased social skills and depression. Intense social media use thus becomes part of a larger societal analysis, connecting networks to ADHD and globalization. Instead of reading social media as a Zeitgeist symptom of some singular untouchable evil, we must approach the Internet Question here as an interplay between cultures of use and the technical premises of both founders and coders of these systems.

There is a need to design daily rituals of network sovereignty. We must not get lost anymore in endless browsing, surfing and searching. That seems more like nostalgic nineties behaviour by now (keep up!), but there is a danger of 'rienisme' (nihilism) when the techno-social routines become meaningless, and there is even nothing left to report: where we can no longer separate boredom and technology. Aimless swiping on your phone in the elevator, or at the platform waiting for a train. That's the moment when you need to come up with passionate forms of disengagement from the virtual world. The question is: how to lose interest in something designed to be vital? The issue here is different from the late twentieth-century dialectic between memorizing and forgetting. There is nothing to remember on Facebook that is so socially eventful (mostly break-ups and divorces). What sticks more is the micro-trauma: the wrong remark, the encounter with your ex, the stalker and bully, the embarrassing picture. In the end, it is all nothing but traffic. For such a cybernetic environmental history, how to manage eventless events, like sitting on the banks of a cyber-river, staring at the water passing by, remains in question.[8] Social media are fluid also because of their 'tyranny of informality', too secondary and unfinished to be properly stored, and thus also to be remembered. Viktor Mayer-Schönberger, author of *Delete: The Virtue of Forgetting in the Digital Age*, may be right in arguing all digital information can and will be stored, and will not so easily be lost. However, the architecture of today's social media is developing simultaneously in the opposite direction. Good luck finding that one tweet or email or that one Facebook status update that seems suddenly essential from five years ago. As only temporary reference and update systems, difficult to access with search engines, the streaming databases are caught in the Eternal Now of the Self.

If we limit our scope to internet debates, we know the New Age tendency that dominated the roaring 1990s is slowly losing supremacy. The holistic body and mind approach has been overruled by waves of conflicts in society. The New Age faction shied away from negative critique, in particular of corporate capitalism. Nevertheless, Google still (apparently) can't be evil. We still utilize technology with the aim of 'thriving'. According to the collective oracle Wikipedia, 'thriving is a condition beyond mere survival, implying growth and positive development'. In the persistence of this positivism, our will is supposedly strong enough to 'bend' the machines in such a way that they will eventually start working for us – and not the other way round. Therefore it is not the IT world that has to change: it is all our fault! In this model of tech, we are told as conscientious citizen-customers to flock together, and the business community will follow suit. There is no conspiracy of Facebook (for instance their collaboration with the CIA and NSA), as 'we' *are* Facebook. We are its employees, investors, first adaptors, app developers, social media marketers and so on. We can be truly (momentarily) upset about the NSA, but suspicion about the business model of internet start-ups is somehow a non-conversation.

In this context, those who support the malignant social media cause, which they naively believe to be a most accessible force for good, are kept busy thinking they have signed up for a self-improvement course. The user is busy trying to 'thrive' in a constant stream of tweets, status updates, pings and emails until it is time for the next gadget. Responding from the self-help shelf to this misguided optimism are books like *The Information Diet* (2012) by Californian IT professional Clay Johnson, who writes about information obesity and how to recognize its symptoms.[9] Johnson discusses the ingredients of a 'healthy' information diet, and how we can develop a data literacy that helps to (also) access information. Information obesity arises when the consensus in a society over what is truth and what is not diminishes, and any odd piece of information can obtain (apparent) vital status as 'knowledge'. For Johnson, the parallels between food and information consumption are real and go beyond metaphor. There is no such thing as information overload; it is all a matter of conscious consumption.

Dealing with the full power of distraction without getting sucked into the self-help shelf requires more nuanced thinking. Indeed, why should we think of our life as something that we need to manage in the first place? Is it not the point that we want to observe our work, lives and selves adding up to something, still?

We can read as many facts as we like, but they often refuse to become a system. Some speak of online mental processes involving a kind of protective shield that bounces off the information that approaches us, making it hard for most info bits to be properly digested. Jean Baudrillard, during his lifetime, celebrated this composure, calling it 'passive indifference'. It has now become the cultural norm, and the result is more often a kind of 'epistemic closure'. Constant exposure to real-time interactive media results in a poor sense of time and attention fatigue. Johnson noticed a loss of his own short-term memory. Constant overconsumption of specialized knowledge can also lead to a distorted sense of hyper-reality. The info-vegan way out would be to work on willpower, which is an executive function that can be trained, the goal being to increase one's attention span. Some install RescueTime on their desktops: software that tracks what you pay attention to and every week sends you a productivity score.

The bigger issue is a kind of training, as Peter Sloterdijk already noticed in his 2009 book, *You Must Change Your Life*.[10] What is most weird and radical about the anthropo-technology approach, as Sloterdijk calls it, is its distinction from the rational IT world of the engineer, because of being cyclical, so neither linear nor disruptive. Sloterdijk is less about concepts and debugging than genuine workouts. Self-improvement has to come from inside this whole (techno) cultural gymnasium. Physical exercises need to be repeated on a regular basis. Otherwise they are useless. If we want to survive as individuals and in social relations while maintaining a relationship of sorts with (potentially addictive) gadgets and online platforms, we will have to get into a genuine fitness mode – and stay there. Visiting a Social Media Anonymous group might be helpful in extreme cases, but what average users need are undramatic triggers to instigate ongoing, ordinary moments and processes of release from and better engagement with gadget worlds.

The logic of repetition as a way to learn and improve tends to be considered conservative and anti-innovative in environments where constant improvements and paradigm shifts happen overnight, and planned obsolescence is the rule. Still, Sloterdijk's emphasis on exercises and repetition, combined with Richard Sennett's arguments (in *The Craftsman*) for skills, help us to focus on tools (such as the diary) that enable us to set goals in the morning and reflect in the evening on the improvements that we made during the day. The disruptive nature of real-time news and social media must find a place in this model. It is clear that Sloterdijk has remained ambivalent about the use of information technology. Remarkably, it is hardly on his mind. In his 2012 diary notes of 637 pages called *Zeilen und Tage*, covering the years 2008–11, I counted precisely one short entry that deals with the internet, in which he describes it as a universal bazaar and Hyde Park *Gemüsekiste* (vegetable crate). The same could be said of Slavoj Žižek, who admits that he is not the world's hippest philosopher.[11] Even though both use computers, the internet and Wikipedia intensely, the internet has not (yet?) been a serious object of inquiry in their work.

Beyond symbolic negations, drop-out privileges and good-looking slogans, there are no easy fixes for the current data crisis that we face. How to deal with data relativism, mental exhaustion and back problems each day? Downloading anti-stress apps such as Stay-Focussed and Freedom ('designed to keep a computer user away from the internet for up to eight hours at a time') is one approach. But we cannot solve this problem by simply downloading more apps. What we need to overcome is not technology as such but actual installed habits, especially relating to time-consuming popular applications. Unlike knowledge, which we obtain or run into and then store, interpret, spread and remember, our attitude on how to deal with info overload and multitasking needs to be worked on constantly. Otherwise, we lose our 'condition' and fall back into previous modes of panic and indifference.

For Howard Rheingold, this is not a new topic. He explicitly discusses the balance between mental awareness and clever dealings with our computer desktops. In his book *Net Smart: How to Thrive Online* (2012), he borrows from early 1970s brain research and 'neuro-linguistic programming' to argue against being captured by our flows of status updates, and to create a mental distance from the scene instead.[12] It is all about feeling back in control, gaining confidence and accessing independence again. There is a movement of tactical detachment at play; the addiction metaphor is misleading in this context. It is not about total involvement followed by complete withdrawal. With social media, the latter is often, for social and economic reasons, not possible. Who can afford to endanger his or her social capital? Rheingold knows this and offers his readers a range of practical guidelines on how to master the master's media. He is not a brilliant polemicist, and his discussion with the current US techno-pessimist wave is not convincing (after all, he spent most of his life in the Bay Area exploring the spiritual and collective dimensions of online communication). But he identifies some useful digital literacies.

What makes *Net Smart* and the online video lectures that Rheingold has produced on the topic over the past years so compelling is their relevance to the ordinary everyday, refraining from both pure utopian thinking and merciless deconstruction of the corporate agendas of the Silicon Valley giants. Rheingold is neither a hardcore Silicon Valley visionary *à la* Kevin Kelly or Stuart Brand, nor a Continental European critic. As a technology writer, he did not have the classic American career of an academic, even though he has been giving classes at Stanford in recent years. He is a brilliant, while nuanced, instructor, who believes in 'internal discipline, not ascetic withdrawal'. *Net Smart* is essentially a pamphlet in favour of public education. Self-control, along with other social media literacy, needs to be taught. We're not born with these skills, so we need to learn how to practise 'real-time curation'. Following Daniel Sieger, author of *The Mindful Brain*, Rheingold argues that we have to wake up from automatized life. As Sieger puts it, we need to do more than just be aware: 'It involves being aware of aspects of the mind itself. Mindfulness helps us awaken.' How many of us prefer this state of mind over the pleasures of distraction is another issue. Killing time by using escapist social media, in non-spaces, surrounded by non-people, is widespread, and loved, as we all know. This is the cynical reasoning behind 'I am aware of not being aware.' What Rheingold teaches us are tricks to train the brain, for instance through breathing exercises, and then turning them into habits. The book concludes that 'the emerging digital divide is between those who know how to use social media for individual advantage and collective action, and those who don't'.

The most significant sections of *Net Smart*, in my view, are where Rheingold talks about 'Crap Detection' and where he zooms right in on his desktop. 'Crap Detection' is a 1960s term that certainly deserves a renaissance and stands for a critical attitude towards information. What is the political, religious and ideological background of the person who's talking? Let's do some fact-checking. These days, there are numerous online tools available, but few of us are aware of their existence. The widespread lack of search engine literacy is a major but classic problem. Ernest Hemingway and Neil Postman both argued in favour of everyone (ideally) possessing a built-in crap detector. In this age, with a ten-fold employment of PR agents and communication advisors compared to journalists (who traditionally were supposed to do fact-checking), internet users must increasingly do all their own homework. For an expanding group of users, it is a somehow new insight that one cannot always believe what one reads. How to dissect pseudo-information from think tanks, copy-editors and consultants? Other sections of *Net Smart* espouse old-school values concerning media manipulation, but couple this with a sophisticated knowledge of how to manage a range of online research tools, in terms both of their functionality and of interface usability. Rheingold fully reveals his desktop: his screen is large; there are a lot of menus open at the same time, yet he is in charge. This is called personal dashboard design – and we don't hear enough about it, because the organization of one's desktop is supposed to be a private matter, even shameful. He talks about desktop management using the term 'infotention', which he defines as 'synchronising your attentional habits with your information tools', the aim being to 'find, direct and manage information' better.

Social media are often portrayed as necessary and unavoidable channels. For Rheingold and Johnson, they are here to stay. The outgoing baby-boom Europeans may perceive these platforms as nihilist vehicles, drugs that promote the feeling that we are being left out and are about to miss the boat. Linking, liking and sharing prolong the systemic boredom and 'rienisme' that is experienced as a consequence of the exaggerated and commodified 'event' culture that we all experience. It therefore comes as a surprise to read Tom Chatfield's *How to Thrive in the Digital Age*, a booklet in Alain de Botton's School of Life series that claims to reinvent the genre of the self-help book.[13] No more moralistic warnings and well-meaning tips, such as the one from Evgeny Morozov who used to hide his smart phone and internet cable in a treasure chest when he had a deadline. Chatfield's way out is, surprisingly, to politicize the field in the spirit of the Arab Spring, Occupy, Wikileaks, Anonymous, pirate parties and demonstrations in favour of online anti-copyright peer-to-peer exchanges. We have received enough tips on how to carve out time by not using our smart phones. Offline romanticism as a lifestyle solution is a dead horse.[14] Even 'slow politics' has more to offer in this respect than delusionally post-digital pastoralism. It's liberating to let go of all those accelerating events, not do anything for a while, experience the downfall, pretend to live in agreement with nature and enjoy a well-deserved break. But then what? What interests us are (still) new forms of collective lives. We suddenly find ourselves dragged into events, stories, situations and people that make us forget all the yelling emails, Tumblr image cascades and business-as-usual on Twitter. When will the Long Wait be over?

It is worth circling back to Petra Löffler here, whom I asked about Adorno's moralistic stand and his rejection of media as a light form of entertainment. If he were still alive, I asked her, what do you think he would say about the internet? Löffler replied:

> For Adorno's thinking of negativity, art is an autonomous and alterna- tive sphere of society. And it's art's alterity and autonomy that is the condition for its power to undermine the capitalistic order. That's why, for these thinkers, it's not a matter of morality to reject popular mass media of entertainment. It's an 'ontological' question, because these media give no room for reflecting the mode of existence in capitalist society.

However, Löffler discovered, Adorno's position is not so definite as it seems at first sight:

> I was surprised reading in *Dialectics of Enlightenment* that according to Adorno and Horkheimer a total excess of distraction comes, in its extremity, close to art. This thought, it occurs to me, resonates with Siegfried Kracauer's utopia of distraction of the 1920s in dealing with modern mass media, especially cinema. In this passage Adorno and Horkheimer are saying, and this is revolutionary for me, nothing less than an accumulation and intensification of distraction is able to fulfil the task of negation that was originally dedicated to art, because it alters the state of the subject in the world completely. With this thought in mind, it would be really funny and, in the end much less elitist, to speculate about what Adorno has to say about the Internet.

— 3 —

A WORLD BEYOND FACEBOOK: THE ALTERNATIVE OF UNLIKE US

Geek quotes for a post-geek culture: 'Soldiers at government checkpoints, as well as at Islamic State checkpoints, commonly demand Facebook passwords" – "Das Ich ist nicht zu retten' (The subject can't be saved) (Ernst Mach) – 'I fear the day when the technology overlaps with our humanity. The world will only have a generation of idiots.' (Albert Einstein) – 'I can buy a Ford, Toyota, BMW or Smart car and drive on the same roads and use the same fuel. Everything is interchangeable about them except the key that gets me in and starts the engine. It's a good model for how our communication systems should work, at all levels.' (Dave Winer) – 'Take a position, be an author.' – 'The idea of splitting the social between "collaborative" and "individual" sounds to me like splitting the animal realm between "ants" and "pumas".' (Hellekin) – 'It is a small step from distribution to dispersion ...' – 'Most wheels need reinventing.' – 'Neither information nor a drug fix ever gives any happiness when you have it, but will make you miserable when you don't.' (Michel Serres) – 'I've violated my own privacy. Now I am selling it all. But how much am I worth?' (Federico Zannier) – 'I am not anti-social, I am just not user-friendly.' (Geek phrase)

Whether or not we are in the midst of yet another internet bubble, we can all agree that social media dominate the use of internet and smart phones. The emergence of apps and web-based user-to-user services, driven by an explosion of informal dialogues, continuous uploads and user-generated content, have powered the rise of 'participatory culture'. A handful of social media platforms dominates the information age.[1] Tensions are on the rise regarding what to make of the influence and impact of 'social media'. Whereas the original internet ideology still promises open, decentralized systems, why do we, time and again, find ourselves locked into closed, centralized walled gardens? Start-ups no longer threaten the monopolies, as they are all eager to sell out early. Why are individual users so easily lured into such platforms, then finding them so hard to quit? Is this human nature or simply the wrong design by naïve hippies turned conservative power-mongers? Do we understand the long-term costs that society will pay for the ease of use and simple interfaces of beloved 'free' services?

This accelerated growth of social media is unprecedented and remains the main reason for the profound state of confusion amongst geeks, artists, scholars and activists alike. We are all (still) busy befriending, ranking, recommending, retweeting, creating circles, uploading photos and videos and updating our status.[2] Despite this massive user base, the phenomenon of online social networking remains fragile and secondary in nature. The social is fluid and so easily vaporizes into the Great Nothingness. Just think of the fate of the majority of social networking sites. Who remembers Friendster? The sudden implosion of MySpace[3] was phenomenal and timed with the parallel demise of Bebo in the UK, Hyves in the Netherlands, StudiVZ in Germany. It is still presumed that the fall of Google, Twitter and Facebook is only a masterpiece of software away – and the advocates of 'alternative' social media options still take this idea as their premise. The 'protocological' future was not supposed to be stationary: the internet is expected always to allow space for us to carve out a variety of techno-political interventions. Instead of repeating the entrepreneurial-start-up-transforming-into-corporate-behemoth formula, it has always been urgent to continue reinventing the internet as a truly independent public infrastructure that can effectively defend itself against corporate domination and state control. The political agenda of social media critics is, however, ambivalent. The dominant platforms have to be studied and criticized, but not necessarily regulated. There's no evidence that Brussels is willing to do this in any case, within the period in which it will be effective. However, other cultural patterns can be counted on: at some point boredom will set in, and the end of the befriending craze will be in sight. Indifference is the great motor behind liberation. It's already a subversive thought that friends and family will have to come up with new ways to monitor your life. After so many updates, one's status in society still hasn't improved, and the urge is suddenly there to waste our time elsewhere.

How to study semi-closed ephemeral spaces? I observe Ph.D. students making gains from new insights produced by the recently established 'software studies' discipline. They nevertheless face the risk that their object of study will already have vanished before they hand in their thesis. It is one thing to formulate a 'black box' theory[4] to study the algorithmic cultures of such social networking websites – but what happens if the algorithms indeed remain a black box for us non-geeks? Will internet studies become synonymous with small talk, chasing negligible impacts, ending up as a subsection of cultural studies? This may happen, not only because of the computer science deficiency amongst arts and humanities scholars. We are also running up against very real corporate secrets, blockages, and related patent wars. To a large degree, social media research is still dominated by quantitative and social scientific endeavours, which play with data available through application programming interfaces (APIs) and visualizations based on those data.

In the first phase of social media research, a social science focus led by US scholars such as danah boyd and Lisa Nakamura came together through the scholarly Association of Internet Research. Research projects focused, for example, on everyday racism online, or the moral panic around young people using social media, and dealt with gender, privacy and identity theft. The studies often used the (dated) self-representation theories of Erving Goffman, Michael Foucault's concept of the technologies of the self, and graph-based social network analysis, which continues today, to focus on influencers and (news)hubs. What was missing in this early stage was the willingness to look elsewhere for knowledge and analytical tools, and to organize encounters with the strengths of the humanities, including arts and design. There was almost no attention given to the political economy of emerging social media giants – let alone the techies in their own universe, and the Internet Society that only dealt with technical, regulatory issues. The different approaches of social science and technology studies never really met – a missed opportunity to create a multi-disciplinary tradition of critical internet research. The clear beneficiary of this non-meeting was Silicon Valley itself, which, instead of having to face a critical public, much rather preferred the exclusivity of TED conferences and similar business networks, while propagating itself in 'local' meeting places.

Dismissing social media studies as just 'supplementary' to critical media studies and debates is as implausible as considering social media entrepreneurs the baddest boys of capitalism. Even if Twitter and Facebook disappeared overnight, befriending, liking and ranking would only spread further as habits, embedded in software. The beauty and depth of social media lie in the fact that they call for a new understanding of classic dichotomies such as commercial/

political, informal networks / public at large, users/producers, artistic/ standardized, original/copy, democratizing/disempowering. Instead of taking these dichotomies as a point of departure, let's scrutinize the social networking logic itself. Why value the network? Is it a primal need to create a social safety net around us, to fight against isolation? Or is it a more immanent tendency to grow our list of friends, potential clients and other social circles? Is the network the new church, our unique version of the village tribe? What else is it?

Today's social media platforms are too big and too closed for anyone to do proper independent research on them outside of existing proprietary organizations of data. In other words, we are dependent on the companies and marketing companies for this. But what we need to do is develop ways to capture specific processual flows and turn them into proper stories. Remember, there is no psychoanalysis without the explanatory power of the case and its material base. So the problem is not only the mutation of the object of study but the actual disappearance of matter. Before we've gone through the litera-ture, theorized the field and developed specific critical concepts, written down methodological considerations and compiled datasets, the object of study has already changed dramatically. Research runs the risk of producing nothing more than historical files filled with network assessments and other ethical considerations.[5] In a variation of Einstein's quantum theory, we could say that it is not because we observe them that objects change, but because we research them. But even this inverted idealistic notion is not the case. The main reason for research futility is our collective obsession with the impact of technology rather than its architecture. This happens as often with simplified, easy-to-use informal network sites as with complex systems. At first glance, social media present themselves as the perfect synthesis of nineteenth-century mass production (in this case of networks) and history in the making (see the 2011 Arab Spring). There is surprisingly little 'différance' at work here. In this sense, these are not so much postmodern 'machines' as straightforward modernist *products* of the 1990s wave of digital-globalization-turned-mass-culture.

Discussing the latest research trends, we can see a growing tiredness with the 'exploitation' thesis of social media in favour of quantitative analyses, including those of the 'like economy'. The powers of monopoly and their related control and paranoia are becoming too obvious and banal to present as research findings. Power arrangements in the IT industry, from IBM and Microsoft to

Google and Facebook are becoming well known. Ordinary users do not want to risk social death and cannot afford to be left out in this informal reputation economy – this is why they feel forced to follow the herd. We all still have to get used to the two faces of networked reality: networks are ideal to scale up quickly so that early movers can create new publics; and, cashed up with venture capital, a technology or application of supposedly public networks can be taken over by monopoly forces in no time. In contrast to this reality of speed and size, there is also the distributed and decentralized, informal quasi-private side of networks. Lately, social media companies have emphasized the first and neglected the second, obsessed as they are by hyper-growth at all costs.

As I make clear throughout this book, the massive popularity of social media should not be seen as a 'resurrection' of the social after its death. The online system is not designed to encounter the Other (despite, or evidenced by, the popularity of online dating sites). We remain amongst 'friends'. The promise of social media (if there is one) is rather to design and run defensive systems that can recreate the community feelings of a lost tribe, in computer-generated informality. The social – that once-dangerous category of class societies in the process of emancipation – has now gone defensive, is facing massive budget cuts, privatizations and the depletion of public resources. The critique mode of the Situationists is running empty here. In this society of the query, Facebook is anything but spectacular. It's neither tragic nor scandalous. At best, it is cute and pathetic.

In the closed-off social media sphere, the critical apparatus of representation theory only has a limited range. Instead, we need to radicalize further what Jean Baudrillard wrote about the 'death of the social'.[6] The implosion of the social in the media as he described it, happened twenty to thirty years before the birth of Facebook: in moves away from the messy and potentially dangerous street life of the crowds into the regulated traffic flows of the last vestiges of public space, and towards post-Fordist interactivity inside the confined spheres of apartments, cafes and offices. The renaissance of the fashion concept 'social' in Web 2.0 was not part of a retromaniac effort to revive the twentieth-century Social Question in the twenty-first century. There is no class struggle here. The very idea of social media is not to return to an Omega Point of History, circumventing Hiroshima and Auschwitz while continuing the Human Story at some convenient or deluded other point. This kind of idea of the Social is produced for no other reason than to extract value. The Social Media

Question circles around notions such as aggregation, data mining and profiling, while confirming Hannah Arendt's observation that the Social Question expresses itself as a political factor in the concept of exploitation.[7] The algorithmic exploitation of human–machine interaction consciously wagers that the dark elements of the social (mob behaviour, but also system suicides) can be managed.

Considering the wide-ranging and ambitious efforts that are made to build alternatives, it seems important to narrow down what precisely is meant by the term 'social media'. Some would go back to the days of early cyberculture and stress the public-domain aspect of 'virtual communities'. This somewhat Catholic term lost its hegemony in the late nineties when start-up firms, backed-up by venture capital and 'silly money' from investment banks and pension funds, flooded the scene. In the Golden Age of Dotcom mania, the emphasis shifted away from the internet as a public domain towards the image of an electronic shopping mall. Users were no longer seen as global citizens of cyberspace and instead addressed as customers. This came to a sudden halt in 2000/1 when the dotcom crash unleashed a global financial crisis. Coinciding with the surveillance crackdown after 9/11, this history has had major implications for internet freedom.

To reconstitute its dominance in the world IT market, Silicon Valley was forced to re-invent itself and unleash a renaissance movement called Web 2.0. This reincarnation of American entrepreneurial energy put the user in the driver's seat only once companies had benefited most from the crucial 'mainstreaming' phase of internet culture, riding on the roll out of broadband and the arrival of mobile internet. The central slogan of the Web 2.0 era was 'user-generated content'. With Google as the main player, profits shifted away from the production and purchase of paid content towards the exploitation of user data. From blogging to photo sharing and social networking, the idea was to reduce complexity and user freedom in exchange for easy-to-use interfaces, free services without subscription, and larger databases with free content for users to browse through.

The Web 2.0 ideology celebrates 'variety' in the proliferation of start-ups, tracking them on popular news sites from the US West Coast – think of TechCrunch and Hacker News, but also Slashdot, Wired, Mashable and ReadWriteWeb, alongside the various activities of O'Reilly publishers and conferences such as SXSW (Austin), LeWeb (Paris) and The Next Web (Amsterdam). But the actual term 'social media' marks media change characterized by consolidation and integration. When we talk about social media, we essentially refer to players such as Facebook, Twitter, Tumblr, Instagram and Pinterest, LinkedIn (for professional networks), Google+ (for professionals) or Academia.edu, and post-blogging platforms such as longreads.com and medium.com. This reduction is done in an unconscious manner, which perfectly illustrates (corporate) desired agreement on a common standard of communication, which is still not possible in this dynamic environment.

Social media indicate a shift from the HTML-based linking practices of the open web to liking and recommendations that happen inside closed systems. The indirect and superficial 'like economy' keeps users away from a basic understanding of what the open web is all about. With info acts such as befriending, liking, recommendation and updating, social media introduce new layers of invisible code between you and others. The result is the coded reduction of complex social relationships, and a flattening of social worlds (see Zadie Smith in her *New York Review of Books* piece[8]) in which there are only 'friends'. Google+ was initiated in response to the possibilities of this New Age worldview, as programming without antagonism. This is the contradiction of the democratized internet: whereas many benefit from simplified technology, we all suffer from the cost of the same simplicity. Facebook is popular *because* of its technical and social limitations. We clearly need a better understanding of interfaces and software, and of how our data are stored in the Cloud. We cannot access the code anymore, which is a problem identified by movements that consider themselves to be at 'war on the general purpose computer', as described by Cory Doctorow at the 28th Chaos Computer Congress in Berlin (December 2011).[9]

While we continue to demand open data, use open source browsers and argue over net neutrality and copyright, 'walled gardens' like Facebook close off the world of technological development and move towards 'personalization' in which messages outside of your horizon will never enter your information ecology. Another important watershed that moved us from Web 2.0 to social media was the arrival of smart phones and apps. Web 2.0 was still entirely PC-based. Social media rhetoric emphasizes mobility: people have their favourite social media apps installed on their phone and carry them around wherever they are. This leads to info-overload, addiction and a further closure of the internet that only favours real-time mobile applications, pulling us further into accelerated historical energy fields such as the financial crisis, the Arab Spring and the Occupy movements.

In July 2011 the Unlike Us research network was launched, dedicated to social media monopolies and their alternatives, and founded by the Institute of Network Cultures in collaboration with Korinna Patelis (then Cyprus University of Technology, Limassol). The launch event took place on Cyprus on 28 November 2011. A 2½-day conference with workshops followed in Amsterdam, 8–10 March 2012, with #3 one year later, also in Amsterdam.[10] The Unlike Us Reader came out in February 2013, followed soon after by a special issue of the online journal *First Monday*. The classic Unlike Us-era campaign is Europe versus Facebook, coordinated by the (former) Viennese law student Max Schrems.[11] The Snowden revelations, in June 2013, impacted heavily on efforts to promote alternatives in social media at this time. The agenda of geeks and activists broadened drastically, from individual apps and software initiatives to the future of the internet as such.[12] Not only did alternatives have to be decentralized and non-profit, from now on they had to have crypto privacy protection on all levels as well. Technically speaking, this was almost too much to ask from such a dispersed bunch of hacktivists being brought together by a European applied research centre. Over time, the Unlike Us community became reduced to sporadic yet interesting debates on the mailing list, proving that we had nowhere near reached the social media vanishing point.

Parallel to social science efforts such as Christian Fuchs' (Marxist) analysis of the political economy of social media,[13] Unlike Us has been primarily interested in a broad arts and humanities angle, incorporating 'web aesthetics' (as described by Vito Campanelli[14]), and activist use of small peer-to-peer architecture. In this context, critique and alternative media debates are both guided by an aesthetic agenda.[15] No matter how understandable the need for practical how-to information is for those who remain inside the corporate silos,[16] critical research cannot stop here. Another Social Network is Possible. Should we reassess the semi-centralized model of a global 'federation', or continue to argue for radically decentralized models? Can a 'federated social web' ever be any more than some sort of half-baked Third Way alternative?

The best-known social media alternatives include Lorea, which was widely used in 2011 amongst the Indignados activists in Spain, and NY start-up efforts such as Diaspora, which ended quite disastrously after successfully raising $200,000 in development funds through Kickstarter, but failing to gain widespread traction among activists, and suffering an overall implosion after one of its founders committed suicide. It took several years for Diaspora to reconstitute itself as a platform after the code of the project was made open source and handed over to the community. Furthermore, as April Glaser and

Libby Reinish note in a recent *Slate* column, most social media alternatives still 'use centralised servers that are incredibly easy to spy on'.[17] Other initiatives such as Crabgrass, Friendica, Libertree, pump. io, hyperboria, GNU Social, the Dark Web Social Network and the IndieWeb tool kit have been around for a while (in different iterations), yet none of them reached critical mass, not even in the activist community.[18]

The uptake of commercial initiatives such as Instagram (now a subsidiary of Facebook) and Snapchat did not weaken the overall position of the big players. Most American social media start-ups did not distance themselves from venture capital and were forced into the same old business model of fast growth, and surveillance of user data. This was also the case with Ello, which attracted momentary hype as a potential Facebook alternative with its anti-ads principle: 'We believe a social network can be a tool for empowerment. Not a tool to deceive, coerce, and manipulate – but a place to connect, create, and celebrate life. You are not a product.'[19] At least it had a slick design, something that most alternatives did not pay any attention to.[20] The 'Richard Florida' thesis – that services picked up first by countercultural, artistic and gay and lesbian scenes, 'the canaries of the creative economy' will be mainstreamed soon after – proved no longer the case. Christian Fuchs added to the debate:

> Being ad-free is not enough – the point is that you have to be non-capitalist in order to be an alternative to Facebook. Ello nowhere says whether it is a for-profit company, a hobby project of a bunch of artists or a co-operative. It seems to conceal its legal status, and that's a problem. Ello says it is 'a public network'. You are only truly public if you are either a public service or commonly owned. It is unclear what Ello is – and that it is not communicating its legal status and what its relationship to capitalism is, is troubling.[21]

Daily Dot asked the obvious question: 'What if a social network's purpose was actually social networking instead of just making money?'[22] Within weeks, for most on the Unlike Us list, Ello was a forgotten chapter. It eventually got venture capital,[23] and after a year in operation succeeded in attaining 1-million-plus sustainable users.

Scaling up to the level of Facebook will only work if new initiatives are willing to import entire address books (if possible, behind the backs of its new users) to secure hyper-growth. If this is not desirable, we'll have to downsize the expectations of alternatives and focus on the specific impacts of the newly formed networks, instead of capture and quantity (clicks per 1,000 impressions, likes). To be able to migrate all personal data such as photos, updates, in a seamless way from Facebook is a necessary yet unrealistic demand. It might be a much more appealing and liberating gesture to start all over again and forget Facebook entirely.

Despite the sense of stagnation, 2013–14 saw lively exchanges about social media ubiquity. Focus moved from 'friends' to 'interests',[24] and a growing investment in 'contextual networks',[25] comparable to the 'organized networks' focus discussed in the final chapter of this book. Could forum software be an alternative? At the same time, the 'privacy' concerns related to Facebook and Google started to go mainstream.[26] The list of alternative apps and social network tools of varying sizes has grown. Examples include the Hater App ('instead of posting things you like, you post things you hate'), the EFF test for the cyber security of mobile chats, and the commercial Firechat app that was used for nearby communication during the 2014 Hong Kong protests.[27] Free software initiatives strengthened during the year, from the creation of the GNU Consensus project, to the NoisySquare Assembly during the hackers camp Observe.Hack. Make, culminating in the You Broke the Internet workshops[28] during the 30th Chaos Communications Congress in Hamburg.[29] Beside further privacy intrusions, attention turned to addressing Facebook's ICT for development, 'venture humanitarianism', alongside the internet.org initiative, with its aim of giving access to limited web services in non-Western countries – for instance, through balloons or networks of wi-fi towers.

Do we have a political programme here? How do we deal with the political realm of regulation? We often like to walk away from it, while at the same time demanding (of whom?) that something needs to be done to stop the erosion of the independent internet. Think of the post-Snowden slogan: 'We Need to Fix the Internet.' But who is the 'we' and to whom is this demand addressed? This issue builds on the moral bankruptcy of the internet governance models that have been around for the past twenty-five years. If we leave it to the engineering class, we get centralized monopolies: technical governance bodies such as Internet Society, IETF and ICANN. They have all, in the end, facilitated censorship, filtering and monopolistic 'markets', and ennobled the centralized infrastructure of cables and data centres that normalized surveillance, from ad agency scales to the NSA. It would be too kind to say that the liberal struggle for an open internet failed. Some other form of regulation will need to happen. The engineers cannot walk away from the job and say: we had nothing to do with it. No one from their camp tried to stop Facebook. Their blind belief in 'net neutrality' fooled even the libertarians. Without going as far as setting up an international criminal tribunal, these questions need to be addressed, and first of all researched in an independent manner. This is also the case if we want to build alternatives. We can't do things the old way anymore. It is no longer a question of developing superior code. At the same time, we also need to understand that regulation without ideas is not a viable option either. We can blame Brussels for acting too slowly, but that becomes a token gesture if we stand there with empty hands, without answers to the question 'What other internet is possible?' Without alternative concepts and blueprints, we cannot regulate the internet industry. We need to work through the digital: there is no safe outsider's position in this case. But this can only be done if we see our work as a political project, in dialogue with the political realm. As Carlo said on the Unlike Us list: 'We no longer wait for the tech people to come up with something as that may be like waiting for Godot.'[30]

4

HERMES ON THE HUDSON: MEDIA THEORY AFTER SNOWDEN

Words of advice for young people: 'Hope is the mother of fools.' (Polish saying) – 'Views stated in this email are not my own and cannot be used against me.' (Footer) – 'The No-Excuses Truth to Understanding Anarchism' (Book title) – Tame Your Junk (3-day course) – 'Hardwired for Nonsense' – 'Make the most hegemoney with a career in Gramscience.' (Ian Bogost) – 'Why [popular technology] is [unexpected opinion]' (4chan) – 'On Encountering Algorithmic Flags on Content' (paper sub-title) – 'Not just anti-aesthetic, but anaesthetic.' – 'You restored our world.' – 'Why I stopped coding and focus more on my blog' with 39,123 comments – 'Please note: I am not checking my spam folder anymore. If your message is not answered soon, please rephrase and resend.' – Happy Dark Ages – 'I have seen dancing soldiers on Facebook' – 'Modest and quiet cryptographers have superior ethics over word artists.' (John Young, nettime) – 'Man plans, and God laughs.' (Yiddish expression) – Online petition to Google shareholders: 'Be Sociable, Share!' – 'You sound like the drunk guy who won't put down his bottle as though it's stuck in his hand all the while calling alcohol bad and terrible.' – 'We don't need your aid, please fund our budget deficit.' ('African saying') – 'A fool is bad news, and it rubs off – don't let it rub off on you.' (WB) – 'My God: dead. My expertise: wasted. My Skype: on. Hire me to talk to your class.' (Nein)

Enlightenment not only promises new knowledge – it also shatters mythologies. The Snowden revelations in June 2013 mark the symbolic closure of the 'new media' era. The NSA scandal put to rest the last excuses for cyber-naivety and lifted the Internet Issue to the level of world politics. The integration of cybernetics into all aspects of life is a fact. The great values of the internet generation have been dashed to pieces: decentralization, peer-to-peer, rhizomes, networks. Everything you have ever clicked on can and will be used against you. We've come full circle and returned to a world before 1984. That was not only Orwell's year, but also the moment Apple launched the Mac, and personal computing hit the mediascape. Until 1984, a small conglomerate of multinationals such as IBM, Honeywell-Bull and GE defined the public imagination of computers with their sterile, corporate mainframes, which processed punch cards and stored data on tape. Until 1984, computers had been used by large bureaucracies to count and control populations and had not yet shaken off their military origins. The radical critiques of personal computing at the time aimed at the totality of the machine. We were all hooked on our terminals, connected to a Big Daddy Mainframe.[1] Now, thirty years later, the computer is once again the perfect technical instrument of a cold, military security apparatus that is out to allocate, identify, select – and ultimately destroy – the Other. The NSA, with the active support of Google, Facebook, Microsoft and allied secret services, has achieved 'total awareness'. Precisely at the moment when the PC is disappearing from our desks, large and invisible data centres replace them in the collective techno-imaginary. Welcome back to the Mainframe.

The Turkish-American web sociologist Zeynep Tufekci reflects on the new state of affairs: 'Resistance and surveillance: The design of today's digital tools makes the two inseparable. And how to think about this is a real challenge. It's said that generals always fight the last war. If so, we're like those generals. Our understanding of the dangers of surveillance is filtered by our thinking about previous threats to our freedoms.'[2] She calls on us to update our nightmares. Let's take this call seriously. In what ways can we still read our terrifying dreams with (Freudian) tools based on ancient Greek myths? In what ways can't we? In the age of smart phones, archetypal layers have been rewired and have mutated into a semi-collective techno-subconscious. We never dream alone. The digital is being pushed into the realm of the subliminal. The subject-as-user, the one that takes selfies, can indeed no longer productively distinguish between real and virtual, here and there, day and night. What is citizen empowerment in the age of the driver-less car?

In late 2013, the University of Chicago Press released the third volume of its Trios series. *Excommunication* includes three extended essays written at the brink of the Snowden affair by New York-based new media scholars Alex Galloway, Eugene Thacker and McKenzie Wark – theory royalty who belong to the digital nineties generation.[3]

Their co-authored introduction to these 'three inquiries in media and mediation' opens with the wider shared discontent that 'new media' has become an empty signifier: 'One of the things the trio of us share is a desire to cease adding "new media" to existing things.' As the nineties slogan says: new media are tired, not wired. Or, to put it in eighties theory jargon: new media have moved from the schizoid, revolutionary pole to the paranoiac, reactionary pole. Fashion over, next hype? If so, how do we deal with the remnants of the Media Question, knowing that it is 'over' but has never gone away? Have traditional media been neutralized, *kaltgestellt*, and no longer form a threat to the ruling classes? Have they lost their aura now that everything is digital? Is content only a concern for Islamist Jihadists who attack media outlets such as *Charlie Hebdo*? What does it mean to 'publish' into a presumed public realm, when all we do is press a 'submit' button that saves our file directly to a private database? In short, what do we gain when we drop the media concept and replace it with, for instance, the network?

To put this in the German context, what's media theory after Friedrich Kittler? This question has been with us for some time. It is not enough that the historical wing of the question, Media Archaeology, is doing well as a disciplinary frame. Can we speak of a next generation that grew up under postmodernism, matured in the post-Cold War era of digital networks, and is currently taking over? Taking over what? There is a lot to say for the thesis that the height of speculative media theory so far was reached in the 1980s. The rest has been about possible implementation – cue boring and predictable collisions with the existing political economy of global capitalism. What is the mandate and scope of today's media theory (if there is anything left of it)? Siegfried Zielinski has been one of the few theorists to take seriously the implications of what it means for media theory to have lost its object of study.[4] Are we ready to hand over the 'new media' remains to sociologists, museum curators, art historians and digital humanities officials? Can we perhaps stage more imaginative and generative acts of appearance and, as the trio argues, disappearance? Are we ready for other kinds of *détournements* and disguises amidst the new normal?

There are many ways to read *Excommunication*. One way would be to see the trio's coming together as itself a possible trend. Are new media theorists ready to become the next generation of public intellectuals, following the example of Evgeny Morozov? It is difficult, though, to speak of an 'emerging' New York School of Media Theory. It would be cool, but that's not really what's happening.

What ingredients do we need in order to speak of a school? A programme? Large quantities of research money? Institutional power? Influential academic positions, such as chairs? None of these seems to be present now. Instead of endlessly comparing New York to LA, London, Paris or Berlin *vis-à-vis* silly (neoliberal University) city marketing logics, it makes more sense to return to the eighteenth century model of philosophy as correspondence – happening now through email lists, forums, blogs, Twitter. Pick your platform and start to follow the ideas in this trio's print collaboration across the digital domain.

Is it the task of media (theory) to explain the world? The New York three seem to have given up on this idea. Not only do they doubt the very possibility of communicating their research, there is also a growing uncertainty that theory can unfold the truth about our technological objects and processes – now that the user as datapoint can no longer distinguish between human flesh with its metaphysical layer and networked machinery. What does it mean in the context of 'new media' that hermeneutics is, as Alex Galloway writes, in a crisis? 'Why plumb the recesses of the human mind, when the neurological sciences can determine what people think? Why try to interpret a painting when what really matters is the price it demands at auction?'[5] As was already noted in the 1990s, most media theory was speculative in nature and projected its concepts into the future in the hope of cashing in, or up, at some stage. Already, two decades ago, much writing on media was incapable of theorizing chips, computer code and related interfaces (with the odd exception of Friedrich Kittler and a few others). The inability of theory to take apart the prime drivers of our civilization has caused a self-marginalization of the arts and humanities.

So, what if we've lost our faith in media's future, and are left to our devices in the cold storage of Big Data? The contrast with 1980s film analysis, dominated by semiotics, postmodern philosophy and psychoanalysis, couldn't be greater. New media were, and still are, speculative, and not hermeneutic. New media (arts) search constantly for devices and services that can be revolutionized (drones, 3D printing, bio tech, RFID chips). Fetishizing attention to devices connects to the difficulties of laying out the object of study. We must put computer code, network architectures, user interfaces and so forth on the dissection table, and rearrange them towards material readings of a bigger picture. The Will to Exegesis might still be there, but the black box is resistant to dissective readings. *This* is the real hermeneutics crisis. It happens because theorists have not learned to programme, and also because the object of study is simply no longer available (think of all the corporate algorithms, increasingly out of reach).

A narrative reconstruction of deeper meaning is hard to perform in the digital media age, not least because in this McLuhan era, no one walks into the trap of content analysis. The message of the medium is its underlying structure. It is from this background that the 'Greek turn' emerges in New York media theory, in which the internet gets interpreted through comparisons to Hermes, Iris and Fury (as well as through fashionable channels such as Badiou, Laruelle, Nancy and others). As Wark summarizes: 'Hermes stands for the hermeneutics of interpretation, Iris for the iridescence of immediacy, and the Furies for the swarm of the distributed network.'[6] Thus, *Excommunication* takes the freedom to step back from the political everyday of the Snowden scandals and turn to a highly coded language that uses Greek mythological names to speak to the revolutionary few. According to Leo Strauss, persecution gives rise to a peculiar type of literature 'addressed to trustworthy and intelligent readers only'.[7] Is this the form and address that Wark, Galloway and Thacker had in mind? Are they under surveillance and in danger? Do they encrypt their conversations to protect themselves from both the NSA and the constant barrage of banalities on Twitter and Facebook? Who knows. The suppression of independent thought through self-censorship has a long history, as Strauss explains. Could we call it a voluntary act of self-marginalization? Or, rather, a desire to be accepted by established philosophers? Is it the overflow of social media that urged these authors to 'combine understanding with caution', or are the stakes of ostracism being performed 'as if'? Whatever the case, the question remains of what kind of discourses can revitalize freedom of speech in a digital age. I don't want to read between the lines. With so much at stake, instead of dragging this text into a pool of misinterpretations, I propose to open up the debate. Can we even say that media theory as such is suspect to the majority? Because of the growing gap between usage of computers (and similar devices), and the stagnation of new media theory coming from academia, we need to take this question seriously.

In terms of 'Greek' references, I missed Michel Serres' impressive work on Hermes. Ulysses does not run through my veins. German academic authorities fail to invest in translating their main works into English so that a proper international dialogue can take place. A pressing example would be Friedrich Kittler's last study, *Music and Mathematics* (2 volumes), in which he exclusively positions his ideas inside ancient Greek philosophy. Contemporary German theorists are still rare in international discourse, and are usually in their fifties and sixties before they get translated, or are being forced to write directly in English (as has already been the case for decades in the Netherlands and Scandinavia). To dismiss the New York trio as would-be Continentals who speak in Greek tongues avoids the debate that is at stake here: kill all your darlings, or, 'how to say farewell to new media'.

In a climate of urgency and stagnation, rage and depression, people are caring less and less about newness. The trend across media theory to move away from its object of study can be traced back to a variety of sources: from Neil Postman to Adilkno's Unidentified Theoretical Objects in their 1998 *The Media Archive* collection, and George Steiner's *Real Presences*, to Fuller and Goffey's ambivalent *Evil Media* strategies and Florian Cramer's *Anti-Media*, Lüneburg's Post-Media-Lab (a collaboration between *Mute* magazine and Leuphana University with its *Provocative Alloys: A Post-Media Anthology*), and comparable incarnations of the 'post-digital' concept in the arts. As one of the promoters of such moves, Florian Cramer explains: 'Anti-media is what remains if one debunks the notion of media but can't get rid of it.'[8] The New York trio remark that 'they pursue not so much a post-media condition but rather a non-media condition'.[9]

For these three co-authors, the key question is: 'What is mediation?' Posing this question means imagining the opposite: there is no communication without excommunication. What if we stop mediating? Instead of digging into the ongoing rise of the connected world, the authors favour studying the 'insufficiency of mediation', and 'modes of mediation that refuse bi-directionality, that obviate determinacy, and that dissolve devices entirely'.[10] Not everything that exists has to be represented and mediated. Let's look at the great beyond.

To what extent is this different from the traditional deconstruction agenda, from a glitch aesthetic *à la* Rosa Menkman, or from even the 'exploit' philosophy as formulated by Galloway and Thacker themselves? Already there, the authors argued in favour of counter protocols, an 'anti-web' approach or – to put this in philosophical parlance – an 'exceptional topology'. If we exclude offline romanticism, how could we translate this analysis into a workable political programme? It is one thing to imagine a specific aesthetic. There are multitudes of artists working in this direction. In the post-Snowden age, it is no longer sufficient to call for open source alternatives that merely copy the corporate premises of the dominant platforms (the 'friend' logic, and so on). The logic and order of the social graph itself is being interrogated. Can we bring together a collective intelligence that is capable of formulating the very principles of another communication order?

Excommunication is not just a reference to a world after media, to the post-digital or post-media, as some characterize this next phase. It shows we must also perform a literal reading of acts of power. We are excommunicated from the new media paradise and suddenly confronted with the cold logic of Big Politics. A generation or so ago, people thought it was possible to refine the very terms under which they were communicating. One impulse, Do-It-Yourself, brought together punks, geeks and entrepreneurs. Our radical disillusionment after Snowden could be classified as a secular version of the late-nineteenth-century discovery that God is Dead. However, the ecclesiastical censure of this age is non-technological in nature. We have not been expelled from the networks. Smart phones and tablets have not been confiscated. The problem is neither increasing censorship nor advanced filter techniques that we are only half aware of. Technological blockades can be circumvented. We can armour ourselves with layers of crypto-protection. But the problem goes much deeper than this. What the NSA revelations have unleashed is the existential uncertainty that comes along with the fact that 'everything you say can and will be used against you'. The long-term implications of such a radical destruction of informal exchange are yet unknown. Will online communication become more formal? Will there be fewer trolls? In short, will new cultures of conflict arise, be suppressed, or not even turn up in the first place?

What does it mean to excommunicate, to be excommunicated? We are not excluded from the communion of believers here. Rather, we remove ourselves because the consensual thrill has dried up. Our discontent tells us to move on. Many feel the social pressure of Facebook and Twitter and withdraw, or mute themselves while staying fearfully half-logged into the 'participatory culture', its silent nightmare of presence. When community becomes a commodity, we should not be surprised that we burn through these platforms quickly and abandon them so easily, as recently happened to the secure Facebook alternative, Ello.

Social media without its full libidinous drive is a deadly boring routine. It feels like work. Work for whom? The playful dialectics between anonymous voyeurism and the exhibitionist display of the selfie are still driving social media, but that's likely to stop. Once this productive couple becomes a routine, user statistics tumble and mass migration to the next platform sets in. This has now expanded from email and linking to the social media realm. What happens when re-tweets and the like dry up and the frantic 24/7 obsession becomes meaningless? It has proven to be not enough to follow and have followers. The act of following remains passive and invisible as long as there is no communication, while to refrain from commenting equals social death. The crisis caused by Snowden is of an entirely different nature from this. To submit emails to a non-responding, deserted cyberspace might be death – but the dominance of a non-responding Big Other is Hell.

There is an emerging consensus that 'the internet is broken' and needs to be fixed. It is becoming harder for the Googles and Facebooks to go back to business as usual. In this historical moment, it is of strategic importance to hear the voices of technically attuned public intellectuals. Slavoj Žižek, with all his shortcomings, is able to raise some of the issues in the cases of Pussy Riot, Occupy Wall Street and Snowden, and on demonstrations in Bosnia. However, when it comes to dealing directly with the (new) media, he inevitably falls back into a 1980s film analysis of Hollywood. Jodi Dean does a better job with her analyses of blogging and 'communicative capitalism'. In the Snowden era, another generation of internet studies has arisen, this time rooted in social science, emphasizing quantitative research into 'big data' on the one hand, and 'digital ethnography' on the other. Researchers are covering a range of issues critical to 'media and society', while shying away from theory as practised for decades by the humanities. They ask: why is theory so important? After all, it is only text. But theory's power and potential lies precisely in its capacity to travel – between contexts and continents, organizers and practitioners. Unlike academic research outcomes in closed journals, it is also less likely to get stuck speaking to one discipline.

Overall, it is clear that speaking truth to power has become an unfamiliar gesture – not because scholars grew more conformist, but because the consensus on how to express dissent, mediate and organize it, fell apart ages ago. The proliferation of news websites, blogs, social media platforms and online journals (closed and open) has been so rapid that it has become difficult to identify how academics can change the public discourse. The state of radical disillusionment we find ourselves in also calls for a reassessment of the role of theory. Any quick survey shows that the role of the theorist has been taken over by commentators and journalists. As in most countries, there is only a weak institutional representation of media theory in the US, and the fact that most internet critics in that country are not (established) academics (Carr, Lanier, Keen, Morozov, Pariser, among others) says it all. It is possible to make similar observations about the new media (arts) programmes and festivals that are disappearing. It is not hard to see that traditional film and television programmes have won the game. Digital Humanities won't help us out here. Neither will 'Communication Science' with its applied PR knowledge. In this context, perhaps we need to go back to the classics and read the Greek gods as an allegory of the 'faith' of media theory.

The post-media tendency results in a withdrawal of theory in favour of largely uncritical tools and methods that are eagerly being implemented by mainstream social science, on the lookout for new fields of employment. Digital Humanities can be seen as a distraction – a pragmatic but desperate gesture to uphold the disappearance of the humanities. Digital potency is not a unique selling point for shrinking disciplines such as history, philosophy and literature. Nor is it the task of media theory to build visualization tools that prove the usefulness of scholars' ideas. Rest assured that the Big Data wave will be over soon, while related issues will remain: the Quantification of Everything will continue quietly, in the background. In the meanwhile, internet research faces a theory crisis. The situation is much like what Niklas Luhmann noticed in the opening page of his *Social Systems* (1984), where he observes that empirical research, 'though on the whole successful in increasing knowledge, has not been able to produce a unified theory for the discipline'.[11] As a consequence, Luhmann continues, 'those interested in theory return to the classical authors. Then the task becomes one of dissecting, criticising, and recombining already-existing texts. What one does not trust oneself to do is assumed to be already at hand.' How to prevent a situation like this happening in the context of internet studies?[12]

Why hammer out concepts, be they speculative, critical or pragmatist, if there is a meta-authority overseeing it all? Why conspire in the light? To riff on the spirit of Pink Floyd: We don't need no Second God. Multiple versions and loci of Big Brother have arrived and are here to stay, unless we have the collective courage to dismantle their installed technical infrastructure. We need to develop dissident knowledges on how to bring down drones, detect sensors, hack servers, distort GPS signals, disrupt the Googles by fooling their databases and calling for the socialization of all data centres. Forget the next innovation cycle. If the common hacker's paranoia informs us correctly, we lost that war years ago and are surrounded. Soon we will be called to surrender, one by one.

To put it in Deleuzian terms, is it still our task to create concepts, or do we switch to spending our time destroying worlds? Over the past decade, the affirmative, light part of this French philosopher has been emphasized. Now the pendulum is swinging belatedly to his dark side.[13] Are we in the process of un-becoming, disassembling identities, withdrawing from the overexposed public realms, unfolding the networks, interrupting the flows of links and likes, putting the joyous production of signs on hold?

The NY trio rightly states that what's at stake is the destiny of media theory *an sich*. Old or new, visual or literary, digital or post-digital, what media theory invites you to do is read the past in a different way. But why must it be the case that if we merge media with theory, we're inevitably drawn into the past? We may as well posit the thesis that the media angle results in speculative tinker toy theory, rather than theory being a critical tool for dissecting the present.

'Media is foreign to us', it says in the introduction to *Excommunication*. How should we read this? Have we come full circle from, say, the Romanian December 1989 'television revolution' to which the slogan 'the media are with us' was later attached?[14] Apparently, that politicized vitalist impulse has left the media sphere. Media are dead, long live pure and direct experience? Have the three removed themselves from the scene? I beg to differ. After all, they wrote a book, they tweet, and so forth. Exodus is no withdrawal. Dionysian darkness helps us to step out of the unbearable lightness of transparency. Theory and criticism need to claim their own space in the debate, next to Reddit, Hacker News and Verge, where ZDNet, Wired, Slashdot and TechCrunch were in the past. Would Longreads and Medium, the newest startup by the Twitter founder, be a gesture in this direction?

Theory can potentially always spin off into its own realm, and lose touch with the current issues that cry for critical interventions. But media theory cannot afford to withdraw. As we speak, there is an assault on media theory happening in the form of Big Data hype, which threatens to marginalize both speculative and critical approaches. Why study concepts and their origins if you can indulge in a sea of data? In a coming Methodenstreit 2.0, we should go beyond the pitiful bourgeois defence of 'liberal arts' and 'humanities' and demonstrate that there is no software without concepts, and no concepts without mediation. Where are software studies and their philosophies of practice now that we need them?

Bernard Stiegler's pharmacological approach seems capable of counterbalancing the exodus sentiment concurrently. Despite his dark analysis, Stiegler remains one of the few contemporary thinkers who works in both philosophy and digital media, without trying to construct artificial synergy between the two. Likewise, Evgeny Morozov, the Eastern European migrant to the United States who refuses to submit to the American Dream, has written about Silicon Reality and its alternatives, which are all presumably infected by hegemonic concepts, including NSA backdoors. His uncompromising attacks have had an impact, and the wide uptake of his recent term 'solutionism' is quite remarkable. Digital disgust is out there, and the impulse of offline romanticism is widely felt. But for the NSA these are irrelevant sentiments. The security complex is agnostic about our movement back and forth between the online and offline worlds.

From Gezi Park in Istanbul to the June 2013 riots in Brazil, and Maidan in Ukraine, we are indeed turning into waves of furies and delinquent packs (to use McKenzie Wark's terms). Theory's quandary – or one of them – is widely debated: are the uprisings occurring despite or because of social media? Zeynep Tufekci advises that the 'State-of-the-art method for shaping ideas is not to coerce overtly but to seduce covertly, from a foundation of knowledge'. How can theory play a role in this seduction? A temporary pause might seem inevitable, to break routines. *Excommunication* as a strike of meaning, a boycott of messaging. Zeynep Tufekci explains: 'Internet technology lets us peel away layers of divisions and distractions and interact with one another, human to human. At the same time, the powerful are looking at those very interactions, and using them to figure out how to make us more compliant.'[15] These days we are torn between the seductive aspect of coming together and the fear that we are consciously producing evidence that will be used against us. Let's move away from the binary logic of online/offline, of participation/exodus, and instead design other forms of social interaction and organization together, based on sustainable exchanges, strong ties, and a sensual imagination that allows us to transcend the given cultural formats (from the edu-factory to Facebook).

What we need now are philosophical responses to the cult of the selfies; more interventions into the moral panic over the loss of attention and the presumed distraction epidemic; further investigations into the dialectics of attention, distraction and the 24/7 economy of sleep deprivation (with Jonathan Crary's essay as a brilliant start[16]); a head-on confrontation with the contemporary arts system over its digital blindness; a further strengthening of New Materialism and similar investigations into hybrids of the real and the virtual; drone aesthetics; Internet of Things politics; sophisticated, gendered theories of programming; more! It is not enough to 'master' the social media in a massive training programme, Sloterdijk-style, if we leave out all of these critical chapters of our ever-mediated life. We need to make software features visible, make their workings public and politicize the hidden infrastructures. How can media theory jump over its own shadow? *Excommunication* is an attempt to find new inroads. If there ever was a Media Question, it is now reaching its existentialist moment.

— 5 —

INTERNET REVENUE MODELS –
A PERSONAL ACCOUNT

The German poet Heine warned the French not to underestimate the power of ideas: philosophical concepts could destroy a civilisation. ... Our philosophers seem oddly unaware of these devastating effects of their activities.

Isaiah Berlin[1]

Unfortunately for the creative industries, there's money and prestige to be gained from promoting the baffling child-like view of the free. The funds that cascade down from Soros' Open Society Initiative into campaigns like A2K, or from the EU into NGOs like Consumer International, or even from UK taxpayers into quangos like Consumer Focus, all perpetuate the myth that there's a 'balance' – that we'll be richer if creators are poorer, that we'll have a more-free society if we have fewer individual rights, and that, in the long-term, destroying rewards for creators is both desirable and 'sustainable'.

Andrew Orlowski[2]

'Content for all, revenues for some'. How ordinary this has become. Net criticism of the free extends back as far as to the late 1990s[3] and has become louder and more pronounced over the past years.[4] After the global financial crisis, with increasing attention on the role of debt in the neoliberal economy, the free remained the operating default but lost its aura of invincibility. 'If you're not paying for it, then you are the product' is now a common insight, shared frequently in Facebook debates. But critiquing the 'free' and 'open' business model that proclaims its intrinsic progressiveness and subversive value is a tricky business.[5] If you want to make enemies quickly, this is the way to go. Usually, you will end up either defending the existing intellectual property regime or questioning the worthy personal motives of those who defend the unrestricted exchange of information. The choice is set up as one or the other, and both positions are perfectly legitimate, in their own way, especially for those who like to mire in contradictions. It never made sense to me, however, why it is fair to pay a monthly subscription fee to your ISP to get access to the internet, but not for the online magazine that you read daily.

The most novel operations of the free have arrived with the platform, where the free becomes fundamentally speculative, based on an imagined timeline and covenant that gears all parties towards a future in which promised revenues and profits materialize. This 'free' ushers in a new form of anticipatory capitalism that builds up user profiles over time. The platform tries to steal market share from other platforms, but only to create its own internal market. 'If you build it, business will come', is the mantra of anticipatory monopoly capitalism. Every builder is *technically* capable of accessing a majority share of the market in this monopoly-style democracy. Complaining is for losers; subscriptions and other revenue models only slow down the desired hyper-growth. Growing a start-up like this, of course, is not do-able without venture capital. Once the monopoly position is reached, the 'winner takes all'. The ideal of every successful platform is a mass of platform-dependents – hooked users who are locked in via emotional ties, and who feel from now on they've got nowhere else to go. The logic of fair play and consumer trust gets left behind from this point, and platform owners start doing serious business, including going to the stock markets and acquiring other networked assets. (And once the 'free' has done its work, it can even be abandoned.)

This ideology of 'free content' first and foremost benefits the venture capitalists who back first-movers who themselves aspire to become monopolists. The VC construction makes sure there is enough investment to knock out competition through the use of cynical tools (labelled 'creative' for the benefit of outsiders) such as viral marketing, creative bookkeeping (assisted by auditing firms) and internal management tricks, often to get rid of the first generation that built up the firm. To get the highest market share as soon as possible, several rounds of investments are necessary to scale up cloud infrastructure, marketing departments and global presence. In 2008, Wired's editor-in-chief Chris Anderson summarized the free ideology just before it lost its innocence and its seductive side, when it could still be presented as the 'inevitable endpoint' of technological development.[6] That there is no alternative to the speculative 'free' has been the ideology of platformed times.

The good news is that since the global financial crisis of 2008, fierce public discussions of free content, alongside other 'free' ideologies of online culture – the muted position-taking of Creative Commons and the Free Culture movement, the politics of crowd funding, and the weird hoarding tendencies of Bitcoin – play out more openly. The dismal payments from music streaming sites such as Spotify are now mainstream news, courtesy of Taylor Swift. Even the broad neoliberal consensus that 'free' and 'open' are by definition worthy goals may have fallen apart. But where do we go next? Is the monetization of more aspects of a creatively lived life the way to go, or is what we actually want a fair way to redistribute income? How are creative workers going to make a living otherwise? As deregulated bartenders and supply teachers? Doing their creative work on the side? Through guilds or new unions? What if you're trying to tour the country and give concerts? Where are today's creatives able to get any 'real capital'? Before we look into alternatives, let's recap these debates.

The questions raised in the 'free' debate go to the heart of what it means (or doesn't) to work in media and culture industries. When should we embrace and promote the free, and when should we be sceptical? What is the difference between free and open as these words are used by creators, designers and workers, and how do our preferences and distinctions compare or get us beyond, for example, the late nineties Stallman–Raymond controversy between free software and open source? Can we learn anything else from the political concept of openness articulated so forcefully by Karl Popper?[7] Are there other historical examples of so-called 'open societies', with an actual common wealth or resources, that we can draw from to answer these questions? Is the distinction between 'commons' and 'common' yet another English language game? (Is the first really ideal? The second too ordinary?) Or is there something dialectical at work here? Last but not least, what's the difference between common and communism?

Moving the questions closer to the economy of our own industry: how do we situate unpaid, crowd-sourced content in relation to the profits made by intermediates and aggregators such as Apple, Google or Spotify? How 'common' is it these days for content to originate from waged employees working for mainstream outlets or labels, as opposed to from independent cultural producers? The stats are needed. Is a resource still 'open' if a user's unwaged attention is quantified and sold off to advertisers? Is openness an absolute (either/or) concept, or does it make sense to think of openness in degrees, or on a spectrum, depending on the project that we are involved with? Alternatively, is it possible to develop an ethics of relative closure, in contrast to openness, where specific cultural contexts require this? Would a situated ethics apply? One thing is certain: there is no way back to the old intellectual property rights regimes. How can we create sustainable sources of income for 'digital natives'? How do we reconcile the diverging interests of professionals and amateurs? And how do we adjudicate the differences of values – ourselves, collectively and strategically – within and beyond monetary terms?

It is important that the inevitable critique of 'free' and 'open' concepts in the post-intellectual-property world be transformed into actual sustainable economic models. If the arts and humanities, theory and criticism see a pivotal role for themselves in shaping network societies, they are obliged to construct revenue models too – otherwise, critical practices will vanish (or never emerge to start with). A first step would be openly to confront the free culture and software gurus (like Stallman) who show zero interest in how artists are going to make a living in the internet age. But, further, we must be clear that it is of strategic importance, a conscious choice, for these people to state that the free they mean connects their 'gratis' to your 'free beer'. Stallman wants to change the dictionary, to get a bit away from the present history. He should abandon his crusade, and enter more contemporary debates – for example, on how free software and crypto-currencies might try to relate to each other (and in ways that also benefit content producers, not just programmers).[8] This is not a 'personal' provocation. The point is just what the free software movement has totally failed to see: the fact that income, for millions of people, increasingly comes through software, through IT architectures. Geek cultures have always wanted some weird 'proper' separation of these two worlds: 'I am cool, but I am not going to tell you how I am making a living.' We've passed that station now. The medium of your private income is political, and cyber-currencies will be an important step in that direction.

'Only craftsmen copy: artists create' – Isaiah Berlin again. The political economy of the internet, analysed from a critical cultural perspective, remains an under-researched topic. This is not merely a question for the business model of start-ups but goes to the heart of software architecture and mediated life. The cult of 'free' has been a dominant *a priori* concept since the late 1980s. Being 'free' and being 'open' have been presented as self-evident elements of the medium itself. They came with the internet, so there is no choice here. The PC, multi-media and internet grew so rapidly because the industry did not have to worry about its content whatsoever. Apple grew large on its corporate slogan 'Rip "n" burn'. A more recent example of the celebration of the free would be Chris Anderson's *Free: The Future of a Radical Price* (2009) that draws heavily on the philosophy of open source – celebrating (again) the fight against record labels and copyright holders, yet refusing (again) to examine the issue of paying for actual cultural production. The non-programme it outlines for post-sales musicians is to focus on live concert revenue. We continue to pay for access, for hardware, software, but not for content. Content is never on the table for discussion. Time and again, hackers have looked angrily at me when I broke the taboo and asked why ISPs got money for monthly access and associated artists didn't. We needed a slogan better than 'access for all' (the open demand); it was always access to something. There was no such thing as access to *rien* (nothing). Were employees at ISPs paid because they worked harder, or because their work was invisible, vital or a service? Why wasn't the internet being maintained as a public infrastructure, as it was in the very beginning? Why didn't we see geeks working in supermarkets alongside their artist friends and doing their free coding in the evenings? And if this whole set-up was skewed in the first place, why didn't we struggle to change that architecture at the time when it was still relatively easy to do?

From free software to free music, a copy culture has established itself, making it difficult for cultural content producers to make a living from direct sales. Jochai Benkler, in *The Wealth of Networks* (2006), announced the limits of his own open source philosophy – it celebrates the fight against record labels and copyright holders, yet refuses to look into the issue of how cultural producers are going to make a living. In his words: 'From the perspective of a society's overall welfare, the most efficient thing would be for those who possess information to give it away for free – or rather, for the cost of communicating it and no more.'[9] The question of who, in the end, benefits financially from the 'wealth of networks' was not raised at all. Could the answer perhaps be that it is those who provide access and aggregate the information? Benkler didn't say. The reference to Adam Smith's *The Wealth of Nations* (1776) runs empty; there is no formulation of a political economy, let alone a critique of one, in this mimesis of a wealth conversation.

Contradictory forces are clearly at play where short-term freelance work is simultaneously denounced as neoliberal exploitation and praised as the freedom of the individual creative worker. The rise of Web 2.0 and associated economic models has greatly complicated the status of creative labour. One end of the apparent spectrum of options, exemplified by Wikipedia, is informed by the belief that information should not be commodified, and is directly connected to the Free Culture movement. While this model has been very effective in certain standout projects, it relies almost entirely on voluntary work and thus offers no model for sustaining creative labour. The other end of the spectrum, exemplified by Red Hat and Ubuntu is informed by Eric Raymond's Open Source Initiative and is focused on turning the voluntary inputs of users, eventually, into new commodities. Also with these initiatives it is rare for revenues ever to be distributed among those who produce the content.

Critics of the second mode of production have pointed to its similarity to the immense dependent outlay of free labour that goes into platforms such as YouTube or Facebook, whose 'harnessing value' is considered parasitical. A related issue is the blurring of traditional categories of labour and play, where online platforms are promoted as sites of leisure, but their outputs are turned into commodities and serious income for speculating hyper-leisure classes. This ambiguous form of value creation not only offers no form of remuneration for 'creative outputs' but also complicates the very idea of a (professional) creative artist. Lawrence Lessig and Axel Bruns have celebrated the rise of creative amateurs while simultaneously pointing out that the blurring of work and play is a central component of new forms of exploitation. Why are amateurs so much more important in these discussions than emerging artists? The different intensities of creative work (casual, sustained, professional) in relation to value creation require further attention.

The Personal is Financial

'The personal is political.' This 1970s adagio of the feminist movement has rarely been applied to our financial situation. Money was always a private fate ('doomed if you have it and doomed if you don't'). But 'making money', more literally, is a capacity that only the fast boys of Wall Street possess, while speculating with other people's savings – the rest of us are busy scraping coins together.[10] With the recent decline of middle-class incomes, everyday finance is becoming politicized. Debt is now a public affair. After 2008, we can hardly say: 'Wir haben es nicht gewusst' ('We didn't know'). Can we finally speak of an emerging 'virtual class'-consciousness?[11] With resource sharing becoming a financial, political and ecological necessity, the currencies through which restructuring is happening are on the radar of a growing number of geeks, artists and activists. We need also to talk about the aesthetics of post-credit money. But before we do this, I want to go back and offer up the insights and impasses from my own personal-political engagement with the net economy – as one narrative of how culture and financialization came together over the past decades, and also to reflect on why Silicon Valley has so far stopped us from using tools that redistribute resources.

In the midst of the never-ending economic malaise of the 1980s, I went through an existential crisis of sorts. In 1983, I graduated in political science with an MA thesis on financing alternative projects. It included as a case study (written together with Eveline Lubbers) the squatters' weekly newspaper *Bluf!*, which I co-founded in 1981 and ran for 1½ years, reaching a national circulation of approximately 2,500. Like others of my generation, I was living on social welfare, making my home in squats, and hitchhiking between Amsterdam and West Berlin while being confronted with the neoliberal backlash of Reagan and Thatcher. Witnessing the sad decline of the autonomous movements I had been involved in, having said farewell to academia after grad school, there were few professional opportunities for us post-hippies (or pre-yuppies). I felt too much of an independent intellectual to identify with journalistic role models or the bureaucratized NGO activists. From mid-1987, I decided to call myself a 'media theorist' (wherever that would take me). I had recently joined the Amsterdam free radio movement with my weekly theory show at Radio 100 and later Radio Patapoe, set up an alternative publishing house called Ravijn, and practised my theory aspirations as a member of the Adilkno collective (a.k.a. Foundation for the Advancement of Illegal Knowledge). The 'mass psychology' programme called the Kurt Baschwitz Institute,[12] where I studied, had just closed down in 1985, and its remains dissolved into the newly established Media & Communication programme, dominated by behaviourist social scientists. Despite all the riots and autonomous movements (in which I was involved), we were acutely aware that the 'roaming crowds' were no longer considered dangerous. There was no local branch of German media theory either. The German programme was retro-hermeneutic in nature and focused on German literature from a historical perspective. How was a 'media theorist' going to make a living? Video art, underground culture, digital utopias and hackers' conventions were showing the way.

Five years later, I had still not improved my job situation but I quit the dole anyway, as I started to sell essays in the media arts context, give lectures, and do organizing work in the Amsterdam cultural scene (then already dominated by baby boomers) while working part-time at the Dutch national broadcaster VPRO. In 1992, I earned $700 (US) a month, barely more than a social security cheque. Post-1989, the world had tumbled into yet another recession. Regardless, 'new media' started to boom under speculative rubrics such as 'multi-media', 'virtual reality' and 'cyberspace'. In early 1993 I obtained internet access. With the help of my hacker friends, I uploaded my archive of digital texts, which was already considerable since I had started using a PC in 1987. It was in this context that I pressed forward with the first public discussions about the absence of an 'internet economy'. I was told excitedly, and often, that content was going to be 'free'. Users had to pay an ISP to gain access and would also continue to purchase and upgrade their hardware such as PCs, screens, printers and modems. In the case of software, the situation wasn't as clear-cut. From early on, there were shareware and free software vs corporate proprietary versions; games were another grey zone. How to navigate this?

My hacker friends told me: 'If you're not into old media or aca-demia, try to find an arts grant or a job in the cultural sector, but do not expect the internet to provide you with an income.' I disagreed but took their advice anyway: 'Find a day job and express yourself the way you want to at night. Set cyberspace on fire. That's the destiny of writing and all art forms anyway.' Or, 'Become an entre-preneur and start your own business. Retrain and learn to code and become one of us.' In 1993, serious money could be made with web design, but then again, that wasn't content either and looked like a hyped-up, temporary opportunity. Writing, be it journalism, fiction, poetry or criticism, would still only be financed through cultural funds or traditional publishers, and so would be increasingly de-professionalized – or 'democratized', to put it in more friendly terms. Clearly, the internet was going to disrupt all businesses, and 'text' was its first victim – a Napster moment *avant la lettre*.

The mid-nineties is a crucial period in the 'dotcom' saga. Its liber-tarian spirit was captured well by Richard Barbrook and Andy Cameron in their seminal piece 'The Californian ideology' from 1995. A few critical elements were missing, however, including the economy of the 'free' and the role of venture capital and the IPO (Initial Public Offering) in the dotcom business plan. Internet start-ups all follow the same scheme: the main one being to attract a criti-cal mass of users in a short period of time. Market share is more important than a sustainable revenue stream. In this cynical model, it is basically accepted that most start-ups fail, and losses are made up for by the promise of one or two success stories that reach the stock market or can be sold to large players such as Google or Facebook.

It took us years to decipher the Wired ideology (sold and *kalt-gestellt* in 1998). Around 1997, when the initial role of arts and culture declined and business took over, Red Herring and Fast Company magazines finally started to provide straightforward pieces on what the economic premises of the dotcom craze were all about. There were hardly any books about this then, and the critical literature was almost non-existent – then, by late 2000, before we knew it, the market had all but collapsed. It was time for G. W. Bush and 9/11. The roaring nineties were over, the millennial party its turning point.

A classic study of how the internet ruined San Francisco, which is still worth reading, is Pauline Borsook's *Cyberselfish*, which came out in 2000.[13] Borsook should be considered a first-generation Californian net critic, writing a decade before Carr, Lanier, Keen, Turkle and Morozov took the centre-stage. Much like scattered initiatives such as *Bad Subjects*,[14] and individuals such as Steve Cisler, David Hudson and Phil Agre (just to mention a few names), Borsook was an independent writer and Bay Area insider, closely connected to Wired founder Louis Rosetto, and one of the first to criticize the libertarian tendencies that were driving Silicon Valley.

Hilarious accounts of the rise and fall of dotcoms soon followed, many published on the Fucked Company website. Our only academic guardian at the time was Saskia Sassen, who linked global finance with computer networks. Alongside her complex macro analyses, together with Manuel Castells' sociological account of the 'network society', solid overviews were starting to emerge – however, none of these projects dealt directly with the madness of dotcom culture. From 1997 to 2000, billions of dollars flowed from pension funds, mutual funds, etc., into internet ventures. Only some of these investments ended up as fake e-commerce companies, such as pets.com and boo.com. A great deal more of the institutional investments disappeared into fibre-optic infrastructure. None had any revenue; all were based on future hyper-growth schemes, fuelled by venture capital. In the golden days of neoliberalism, tens of thousands of designers, musicians, engineers and social scientists had quickly retrained as HTML coders, communications and PR officers and IT consultants – only to find themselves unemployed again a few years later when the bubble burst. Can we call this an economy?

One way to counterbalance the ruthless waves of privatization and the stock market craze was to hold on tight to the idea of the internet as public infrastructure. The internet, against its military and academic background, should guarantee 'access for all'. 'We want bandwidth' was the slogan of the Hybrid Workspace project's one-week-long campaign at Catherine David's Documenta X of 1997.[15] The same group, coordinated by the Waag Society in Amsterdam, where I worked part-time as a Fellow in that period, designed a similar 'Free for What?' campaign out of the Kiasma museum in Helsinki in late 1999, as an early attempt to analyse the role of the 'free' in the wider political economy of the net.

Delays in perception concerned me just as often then, in the 'roaring' nineties, as they do now. Who benefits when we are not quick to understand Facebook's business model? Which factors turn us from heroic subjects into grumpy consumers who merely click? Even if we try very hard as individuals, and collectively in networks and research groups, why can we only understand the dynamics of contemporary capitalism retrospectively? Is this the real reason we lack avant-gardes? These days it seems we can only fight the causes of the last recession. As I write, we are still processing the fallout of the 2007–8 crisis so many years afterwards. A basic understanding of derivatives and high-frequency trading has started to spread (thanks to Scott Patterson, Michael Lewis, etc.); meanwhile, unemployment caused by the Euro crisis remains at unimaginably high levels, stagnation becomes permanent, and budget cuts ravage infrastructure, healthcare and culture. The economy (and its discussion) as a whole remains stagnant: we seem to be waiting for a recovery that never arrives.

Ever since initiatives such as the nettime mailing list took off (in 1995), collective efforts have been made to develop a political economy of the internet, drawing from cultural, political and economic perspectives from both inside and outside academia. In February 2000, right after the victory over the millennium bug and the announcement of the merger of AOL and Time Warner, the dotcom bubble burst. A belated attempt to analyse the 'New Economy' and bring together critical voices from both sides of the Atlantic was the Tulipomania Dotcom event (Amsterdam/Frankfurt, June 2000), held right after the NASDAQ crashed (mid-April 2000). The histories of the first stock market craze in the early seventeenth century, the South Sea bubble, and the crash of 1929 are well known. Here, it happened again right under our own eyes, in our own sector, causing so much destruction.

Projects like Tulipomania Dotcom directed us to look at the larger picture of global finance: Wall Street, hedge funds and high-speed trading. Why was it impossible to imagine sustainable sources of income for the non-technical workers who were so directly involved? Why did IT consistently exclude artists and content producers and only reward a handful of entrepreneurs and technicians? With perhaps the exception of a few years during the boom, nothing had changed much over a decade. This Is Not an Economy. In fact, soon after the explosion of the 'dotbombs', armies of web designers and project managers lost their jobs and returned to their hometowns and former professions. Still, the poverty of the 'precariat' was about to get worse. In 2002, I eventually moved into academia after two decades of working as a free-floating theorist, getting a Ph.D. in Melbourne based on my work on critical internet culture. 'Sexy but poor' used to be the Berlin slogan. But what critics like myself experienced in the 1990s soon spread to neighbouring professions such as theatre, publishing and film criticism, as well as investigative journalism, photography and independent radio; all joined the impoverished, globalized 'creative class'. With state subsidies withdrawing from smaller and more experimental initiatives, the remaining paid jobs shifted to advertisement and PR.

After finding a research job back in Amsterdam – a career move that many of my fellow critics and artists were forced to make – I was able to kick off the Institute of Network Cultures in 2004. After the considerable reduction in the amount of jobs in the internet industry after 2000, the idea of employing an in-house theorist wasn't realistic. Instead, the emphasis was on marketing and usability. The first big event of my newly established research unit at the polytechnic Hogeschool van Amsterdam (HvA) was 'Decade of Webdesign' (January 2005), an event that looked at the shifting economics of this young profession, followed by MyCreativity (November 2006), which discussed the misery of the 'creative industries' policies that had recently reached Europe from the UK and Australia. The internet was no longer associated with millionaires, but with a fast-growing culture of precarity.

Due to the rise of blogs and 'template culture' in the immediate aftermath of the dotcom crash, it was no longer necessary to build a website from scratch. The price of web design had plummeted, and bots started taking over simple editorial tasks as well. Geek inventors of blog software had, once again, failed to build a monetary plan into their systems, and soon the hobbyists of 'participatory culture' fell prey to the same old free-culture logic, this time led by visionaries such as Henry Jenkins, who was opposed to professionalizing (that is, paying) net-based writing, and instead praised the democratic nature of 'Web 2.0', which could be so easily exploited by intermediates. On the iDC list, the mechanisms were described as follows: 'The Silicon Valley ideology around web 2.0 has always had two aspects fused together: open systems, on the one hand, and a recognition that "users add value", on the other. Yes, users add value, and their labor is free, but they add even more value if you can monetise the data you collect on their behaviour.'[16]

A handful of bloggers was eventually able to make a living from the syndication of their content, combined with web banners and micro-revenues through click rates to Amazon and Google's AdSense and AdWords. Others' prominent contributions to networks ended up being taken over by some of the old media industries, with the Huffington Post remaining one of the more interesting cases: its reputed online commentary community went to court against its founder, Arianna Huffington, when she cashed in 315 million dollars-worth of their volunteered labour from the sale of 'her' site to AOL.[17] If they had built up the Huffington Post with their content work, why indeed shouldn't they be entitled to a fair part of the sales price? The free had publicly started to lose its innocent face.

The period that follows, in which 'Web 2.0' consolidated into 'social media', has been characterized by the victory of this 'winner takes all' logic erected by the previous decades' venture capital-backed dotcoms. The internet economy turned out not to be a free market but a breeding ground for monopolies, with libertarian cartels carefully governing and manipulating the Silicon Valley Consensus. The real estate and financial services driving the 2007–8 crash did not affect the internet economy. Rapid growth continued, this time fuelled by new users in Asia and Africa, and the rise of smart phones and tablets. The internet economy, originally based on IT and the media industries, started feeding into other economic sectors, from retail and services to healthcare, logistics and agriculture. The *Vergesellschaftung* (becoming society), as this process is called so neatly in German, turned the internet into a general processing machine, based on largely unknown protocols that reproduce, still, the ideology of the free. No single individual or profession, no matter how traditional and off the map, has been able to escape its influence. Criticism of the range of 'parasitic' strategies has now hit the surface of a generalized culture. 'If you are not paying, you are the product' is no longer an exclusive insight of the few but a collective awareness amongst the online masses.

71

In the early 1990s, I envisioned an internet-enabled audience reading online or downloading my essays for a small fee, using a built-in peer-to-peer micro-payment system, designed according to the distributed nature of the computer network. If data could flow in a decentralized manner, then why couldn't small digital payments systems be attached to this? A variation on the direct payment method could be a subscription model or a card system with small credit storage capacities. A group of hackers and crypto-experts in Amsterdam were working on this very idea. I visited a number of presentations by David Chaum, the American founder of Digi-Cash, who was at the time based at the UvA Centre for Mathematics and Informatics (CWI) in the east of Amsterdam, one of the early internet nodes in Europe. In 1993 I produced a one-hour radio show with Chaum, in which he explained his struggle against the US credit card companies, banks, the patents involved, and the importance of anonymous, encrypted data for future online payment systems.[18]

The challenge is how to build and implement peer-to-peer internet revenue models for culture that combat exploitation and work towards a more egalitarian (re)distribution of the wealth that is generated by it. A system that allows those who do the actual work to attain a decent income is urgently needed, and the system itself cannot be skewed to the greater benefit of its founders and early movers. One thing is clear: the time for merely complaining about one's precarity is over. We not only need to demand to be paid, we need to push for drastic measures in changes of governance, on top of, and in combination with, new models for small (networked) units to generate income. Debt strike/forgiveness projects do not question the dominant definition of money and how it functions. Most users now understand the cynical logic of the free in which they're caught. This is the age of monetary experimentation. By 2015, cyber-currencies and the public outrage over austerity in the age of too-big-to-fail banks are no longer separate trains of practice and thought.[19]

THE MONEYLAB AGENDA:
AFTER FREE CULTURE

The best way to rob a bank is to design a currency.

Johan Sjerpstra

The digitization of the world is complete. Its logic has taken over all sectors of society, including finance. Meanwhile, actual networked subjects are left to their own devices, having to generate revenue themselves and create something out of nothing, from zero to one. Neoliberal subjects find themselves in permanent start-up mode. The content potlatch is over. You can share – but who cares? The copy is neither the problem nor the solution and tends to postpone rather than speed-up the decisions that lie ahead. In times of advanced stagnation, we cannot count on subsidies nor investments provided by the traditional world of finance. Welcome to digital realism: the 99 per cent have all become survivalist artists in large-scale austerity networks, subjected to rolling crises amidst never-ending economic decline. Interest, loans, savings, investments are no longer solid but can vaporize overnight.

The search for new modes of value extraction intensifies. Even the classic distinction between the idealistic hacker and the opportunistic start-up entrepreneur has begun to blur. It is no longer clear whether genuine alternatives are unfolding, or we are simply witnessing incident after incident of creative destruction without rational cause or end. The latest ubiquitous technology is financialization itself. In this not-so-brave new world, conflict – even as a concept – risks being reduced to, or superseded by, competing economic visions, articulated through software. The volatility of this climate, however, means also that currencies and payment models are no longer a given. Finance technologies and related design seem increasingly up for grabs. The spectacle of Bitcoin has captured everyone's attention. IT heavy-weights have been busy reimagining themselves as financial services and payment providers for the online masses, while banks are catching up quickly. How long will this last? What do we already know about where things might end up, as opposed to where we might want them to?

MoneyLab is a network of artists, activists and researchers, founded in mid-2013 by the Amsterdam-based Institute of Network Cultures. The initial 'MoneyLab: Coining Alternatives' conference was organized in March 2014 in Amsterdam and focused on the Bitcoin debate, first steps in crowdfunding research, mobile money in Africa, and artistic responses to the 2008 global financial crisis – its ongoing recessions, foreclosures and insolvencies. A second conference, 'Economies of Dissent', happened in December 2015, also in Amsterdam, with themes ranging from investigative journalism into (illegal) money flows to block chain theory.

In line with the analyses of this book, MoneyLab takes off from the dominant economic model of the outgoing neoliberal internet era of the free, a default mode that has lost its aura of invincibility.[1] The project takes up the possibility and urgent challenge of collectively researching, discussing, designing and experimenting with (alternative) internet-related revenue models. This also means working actively against the commonly shared insight that 'If you're not paying for it then you are the product', and the cynical logic in which such a net culture is caught up. Consensus on the Free collapsed once internet- (algorithm-) generated forms of income finally became a political issue, but this issue has mostly played out in conversations around debt. Since the global financial crisis, debt is no longer experienced as a personal issue but as an effective prison sentence to lock-in citizens into the capitalist everyday and its depressive logics.

Thanks to the success of David Graeber's bestseller *Debt*[2], and related anti-debt movements that arose in the aftermath of Occupy, public concern around the mounting debt problem of students, home owners, teenagers and other members of the declining middle class is widespread. MoneyLab recognizes, however, that in this raised consciousness of finance, activistic outright disgust with money keeps us away from asking questions and proposing models for how we can imagine redistributing wealth, rebuilding public infrastructures and designing new models of value creation. In times of economic crisis, we do not merely need more money; we need to push for drastic measures in large-scale changes of governance, on top of, and in combination with, new models for small (networked) units to generate income. Debt strike/forgiveness is (otherwise) not questioning the dominant definition of money and how it functions (and it is a facile romantic notion that the poor are happy because they're not yet encapsulated by the debt system). How do we generate value now, in an economy that is designed against us? After the copyright regime lost its legitimacy ages ago, how will creative workers make a living? This is the central question I deal with here, through MoneyLab's own research agenda.

Welcome to the Algo-Wars

Imagine how different the frontier mentality of earlier phases of 'new media' would have looked if it had paid serious attention to internet banking. Out there, there is no community, no collaboration, no anonymous exploration of multiple selves (just an army of outsourced IT jobs). Online banking never took place in some adventurous virtual world and was never progressive since its inception. Instead, we see user accounts linked to real identities supported by hard documentation. These are websites that function to support utterly mundane financial tasks. Security – of selves and infrastructures – is a central concern. The goal of the internet banking experience is seamless functionality and ease of transfer, devoid of any unforeseen potentialities. Financial subjectivity is quietly fostered through the routine browsing, clicking and scrolling through of one's meaningful numbers.

Large portions of the web have now been recast via this standardized imagination of internet banking. But, at the same time, the converse is also true. Contemporary banking has been folding in logics of socialization and personalization, recommendation and advertising, and is starting to borrow from design techniques pioneered in social media and other commercial platforms. Internet banking has started to feel like a genuinely individual, unique experience. Online statements are now riddled with promotional material and questionnaires. User accounts come with money management dashboards that categorize and visualize spending and saving habits, or lack thereof. And, of course, banks have entered the data profiling game.

In this highly aesthetic terrain, we need to keep asking: what defines global financial operations today? A key feature is transaction speed. Real-time flows, measured in milliseconds, reflect the technical infrastructure they are conducted on. Screen interfaces, information visualizations, financial models and trading algorithms comprise the media ecology of contemporary financial practice, organizing routine operations and guiding decision-making process in a probabilistic fashion. Noting the complexity of the situation has become a common trope of government regulators seeking to 'simplify the system'. The minimalism and vagueness of our knowledge of the 'deep waters' and 'dark pools' of finance is itself a concern. Most people will only be confronted with the realities and processes of a crash months, if not years, after the event. The initial crash happens in a matter of minutes, but billions feel the consequences.

Attempts to 'democratize' old-school finance through electronic markets and high-speed trading platforms in the name of transparency and openness, turn out to be nothing more than a libertarian dream of programmers who, in the end, only seem to contribute to secretive 'algo wars' – for instance, between competing high-frequency trading systems, run by hedge funds and banks. Struggles over who might author the singularly perfect and heroic algorithmic solution leave only the biggest, most sophisticated, connected firms to compete seriously. As a result of this, Scott Patterson speaks of 'an algorithmic tragedy of the commons, in which all players, acting in their self-interest, spawned a systematically dangerous market that could threaten the global economy'.[3]

Financial technology (fin-tech) experts work as almost a separate class in a space of 'known unknowns', trying to counter future market uncertainty (via derivatives, etc.). Models have come to replace the seer, and strategy takes the specific form of game theory. However, the forgotten classic in this context is Rudolf Hilferding's 1910 *Das Finanzkapital*, at the time considered the necessary additional volume to Karl Marx's *Das Kapital*, in describing the growing autonomy of financial markets.[4] After serving as one of the Weimar Republic's ministers of finance, Hilferding was murdered by the Nazis in a concentration camp. When I came across his work for the first time in the late 1970s, *Finance Capital* was considered obscure, if not futuristic. For obvious reasons, his body of thought did not enter any of the twentieth-century currents in Marxism, notably not Europe's social democracy – because that's what Hilferding belonged to in the first place. Would the world have been a different place if Tony Blair had urged his Labour party in the nineties to study – and upgrade – *Finance Capital*?

In global finance, electronic trading has taken over the spectacle of the trading pit and its 'market makers' that had already started to be replaced back in the 1980s. The floor-trading profession was the first to be wiped out by computer networks. As anywhere, computational processes are fully integrated, and, because of this, economic practices develop computational characteristics. Consider how automated high-frequency trading co-emerges with a distinct form of technical accident. The so-called 'flash crash' of May 2010, which reportedly wiped 1 trillion US dollars of wealth, was the catastrophic result of algorithms working as designed but in conditions unforeseen. The computational glitch, similarly, takes on decidedly financial traits (and ramifications). Indeed, flash crashes have become increasingly regular in high-frequency trading and are analysed in detail on websites such as Zero Hedge. A decade ago, it was cool for traders to look down on small investors and the pension savings of ordinary citizens who could not keep up, creating a 'hunter-seeker battlefield' that fed Uncle Joe and Auntie Millie to the sharks. Growing public awareness around toxic financial products and high-frequency trading has turned against autonomous computer systems themselves, identified as the source of so much trouble. Either these financial weapons will be decommissioned altogether, ending the arms race (including their dedicated fibre-optic cables, for instance between New York and Chicago), or we will see desperate attempts to reform the industry.[5]

Thomas Piketty is not our Hilferding 2.0, so who will be? We urgently need to get a better understanding of the dark world of finance – and high-speed trading in particular. Journalists like Michael Lewis and Joris Luytendijk raise public awareness, but in the end only spread hear-say knowledge. This is a systemic issue. What's needed right now is programmers who work(ed) in 'fin tech' and can grow into the role of public intellectuals – sufficiently verbose technical philosophers who can effectively communicate 'what is to be done'. A great example of such a public communication approach was Charles Ferguson's *Insider Job* documentary. We need a new category for this kind of work or role: the whistle-blower-mediator, a most dangerous figure who speaks out in public, like an Assange or Snowden of Wall Street and the City. In a rather different register, the work of the literary critic Joseph Vogl is also relevant in this context, coming as it does to analyse financial crisis out of the tradition of German media theory traditions linked with humanities.[6] My previous work has built on that of Saskia Sassen, who, already in the early 1990s, drew convincing lines of dependencies between electronic trading, global cities, social movements and internet cultures. Current technical approaches in the humanities come from 'software studies', an emerging field of studies that emphasizes the importance of understanding the role of algorithms and bots in contemporary media power. However, software studies has yet to hit the surface and deal with 'fin tech' directly.[7]

Yet another trajectory – the one that interests me most in this chapter – focuses on the development of alternative forms of money and finance outside of the mainstream banking system, as a possible answer to the current/currency crisis. The second reason for doing this is because, often, alternatives are useful mirrors through which we can study the technics of the mainstream. Micro-credits and barter, crowdfunding, peer-to-peer (P2P) banking, time-banks, mobile money and crypto-currencies are examples of these parallel strategies. We can ask ourselves how these financial alternatives are positioned in relation to the broader critique of global finance, and also whether it is possible to operate autonomous systems outside of the influence of national banks, the US dollar and credit card companies. If there is 'no right life in the wrong one', as Adorno stated, how should we read these exercises, presuming that they are not aiming merely at proto-capitalist libertarian innovations?

Tales from Crypto-Land

Alternative forms of exchange emerge for a number of reasons, including structural failure, group marginalization, and more strategic, proactive identifications of social need. Digital money is no exception. In the 1980s, Michael Linton developed a computerized system for the facilitation of LETS (Local Exchange Trading Schemes), which he named LETSystem. This system sought to 'marry the efficiency of commercial barter with the liberatory potential of counter-cultural exchanges'.[8] In the 1990s, David Chaum's DigiCash was thought to be the game changer. Working out of the computer science department of the University of Amsterdam, Chaum was a pioneer in applying cryptographic techniques to currency, effectively turning money into a cryptographically encoded string of numbers. In 1994, Steven Levy wrote a feature article in Wired that detailed this Dutch project and others of the day in what we now understand to be the first serious flirtations with digital crypto-currency. After DigiCash, there was Mondex and MintChip. Is there anything we can learn from these historical forerunners?[9]

More recently, soon after the 2008 financial crisis, Bitcoin was launched. Was this precise timing perhaps because the 'free' exchange consensus had finally broken down? Is it that Levy's words (and Chaum's sentiments) suddenly rang more true as the reality of the Big Data Society unfolded before us (again)? Bitcoin realizes the crypto-libertarian dream of the global private market: that is, a market that does not depend on state facilitation and regulation. Through the use of public key encryption technologies, combined with distributed P2P software architectures, Bitcoin enables the semi-anonymous transferal of funds between users. Early on, the most visible antagonistic capacity of this new currency was its facilitation of illegal marketplaces (the sale of illegal goods), most notably drugs on Silk Road.[10]

What happens to tax when a critical mass starts operating in a private economy? The simple answer is that governments would prefer never to let such a situation develop. And isn't it a nineties dream to see cyberspace as a separate cosmos with its own laws? But the most disruptive potential of Bitcoin might very well be its range of less controversial and more pragmatic functions. It could be used, for example, as a default currency for remittances, greatly reducing if not eliminating the fees associated with sending money across borders. Here, the otherwise antagonistic and disruptive capacities of Bitcoin come to resemble the more palatable Schumpeterian creative destruction, in which the hegemonic economic order is overturned (outcompeted), but only in such a way as to reaffirm its overall logic.

As with the current economic order, Bitcoin, too, privileges specific forms of exchange and social relationship. It is currency as *Weltanschauung* (comprehensive worldview), and, like any other system, it will produce its own animal spirits. To come to terms with Bitcoin, we must account for its value, but also its 'values', reading these through economic sociology and anthropology. In fact, these two notions – money and value – need to be reunited. What, for example, are the social values that underpin the design of Bitcoin to give its currency value? Besides the thrill of financial speculation, can we speak too of a certain geek-cool, of a hacker geek value, or of something else?

Bitcoin is underpinned by public key cryptography – a technique of privacy specific to the realm of communication. As Jean-François Blanchette has recently put it, cryptography is a form of communication that takes place 'in the presence of adversaries'. But cryptography is more than the communication of secrets. It is not equivalent to a whisper. Rather, it is privacy that resides in public, 'in the presence' of others.[11] We might equally refer to it as the persistence of privacy in a world defined by open communication. The question is, however, whether and how the cryptographer's imperative shapes Bitcoin, in addition to the very fact that it makes it possible. Is there any relation between the politics (or privacy) going in (to design) and out (in use)? Other than supporting the dream of a private market, what are the concrete new practices that are emerging through this currency system? One thing that has become very clear is that it is now possible to see money as an artifact of design. No longer is it imagined as a universal commodity (gold), or as the monopoly creation of governments (by fiat); basic questions about the function, source (of value) and purpose of money are once again on the table. Perhaps it was the recent existential crisis of the fiat monetary system and its failure in hiding its designed existence – whether it be quantitative easing or selective bailouts – that somehow led to this situation. Whatever the case, these basic questions will have to be addressed by every experimental currency, not just at the level of discourse.

AdVentures in Crowdfunding

New creative projects have long relied on either venture capital or grants from governments, foundations and other third-sector institutions. Workers in the creative industry more generally hold on to the dream of permanent, well-paying, creativity-quenching work, but sustain this dream through a patchwork of one-off projects, forced voluntarism and underpaid and supplementary gigs. They are caught in the precarity–idealism nexus: the dream job is just around the corner ... soon they'll give me a permanent contract. These issues were explored in detail by the MyCreativity network of the Institute of Network Cultures from 2006 to 2008. Since then, a range of networked funding initiatives has emerged, holding new promises for the creative class that one day there will be Content Justice. In the short run, prospects remain bleak.[12]

Whereas crypto-currencies focus on payment after the fact, crowdfunding aims to resolve the income issue straight-up and beforehand, much like film financing and the advance system in trade publishing. Crowdfunding platforms assume many forms, but the model usually looks something like this: a person or group needs money to fund a project; they pitch the project on a website, inviting the 'crowd' to contribute funds; the pitch will include a specific project quote (e.g. $10,000) and a deadline by which the quoted figure must be met. If enough people 'pledge' money and the target figure is reached, the project becomes active, and the pledged funds are collected. If the figure is not reached, the 'pledged' funds remain with the funders. The 'all or nothing' model is used on sites like Kickstarter and Indiegogo. Project funding also often includes 'tiers', with the option to contribute a large or small amount of funds, with different 'returns'. Returns range from tokens of appreciation, the product itself (if there is one), to exclusive or 'individualized' versions of the product for the higher-tier contributors.

For workers in the creative economy, the difference with crowdfunding is that it represents a viable alternative to investors and (research/cultural) grant models, enabling autonomy from foundations and the state, cutting out a whole chain of potentially parasitical intermediaries and forces. Inside actual autonomous movements, crowdfunding had existed for decades (e.g. benefit gigs, redistributions of venue profits, etc.). Today, digitalized and socially networked crowdfunding is a business concept in itself. Promotion takes the form of blogging, (Facebook) liking and tweeting. Popular projects rise to the top and enjoy increased site visibility. 'Interesting' projects find themselves on site-sanctioned curated lists. Some appear on 'featured' pages. Kickstarter sends updates on 'projects we like' to site subscribers. Popular projects make headlines. All this, of course, increases the chance of funding success. The Silicon Valley logic becomes apparent: it is not the democratic thriving of many, but the filtered heights of the few that the model truly values. One Culture.

It is still early days for crowdfunding research. As usual, we are not asking the critical questions. Crowdfunding platforms make new funders the priority, not criticism.[13] Cultural workers are focused on unlocking the secrets behind successful projects, using quantitative techniques that function through correlation and pattern detection. The number of friends on Facebook, the inclusion of a video excerpt in the pitch, the geographical location of the project, the pitch duration (shorter is better), and being 'featured' on the funding platform, all correlate with success. To maximize your chances, be popular and live in a cool city.[14] The more important research question is how the mechanics of crowdfunding shape the process, in ways that allow for projects to differ from the projects of older funding models. I'm thinking here of Inge Sørensen's comparative investigation into funding for documentary films in the UK.[15] Unsurprisingly, her study identifies clearly that different funding models favour different documentary genres. Why and how do some projects circulate like memes and attain their funding goals many times over? What does the long tail of failure look like? We might equally ask more radical questions, such as whether or not crowdfunding could become a machine for producing the commons, or how private inputs are translated into common outputs. Would that leave less room for, or interest in, the Warner Bros. of the world? Kickstarter is the most visible crowdfunding site so far, but what are the alternatives and local analogues, and how do they differ in terms of design and output? Would it be better, for example, to have dedicated funds that specialize in theatre, development aid, documentary films or neighbourhood projects?

Beyond these structural inquiries, we must also consider the experiential and psychological aspects of these new funding models. What would the early twentieth-century money theorist Georg Simmel make of all this? Is this the way to become truly independent? No more sponsors, no more state (but you still need that crowd). Or would crowdfunding be better understood as the 'democratic distribution' of the mindset of the financier, and therefore as an intensification of the logic of finance? How can art be free if it is tied to the tastes of an over-identifying mob? What is the effect of turning funding into an act of web browsing? Or of design interfaces and 'user experience(s)' becoming such key criteria in funding outcomes? Ian Bogost thinks sites like Kickstarter are instead better understood within the trajectory of reality television. Focusing on the products (outputs) misses something crucial:

> When faced with the reality of these products, disappointment is inevitable – not just because they're too little too late (if at all) but for even weirder reasons. We're paying for the sensation of a hypothetical idea, not the experience of a realised product ... For the pleasure of desiring it. For the experience of watching it succeed beyond expectations or to fail dramatically. Kickstarter is just another form of entertainment.[16]

Entertainment it may be, but we might also ask why people are willing to pay for a 'hypothetical idea'? It's not just a hypothetical product we are investing in, but also a clearly viable hypothesis of 'funding by other means'.

Mobile Money in Africa

Whereas in the West, US-American credit card companies such as MasterCard and Visa remain in control when it comes to internet payments, elsewhere in the world things look different. Over the past few years, alternative payment methods using mobile devices have grown at exponential rates across many parts of the so-called 'developing worlds'. At a time when traditional banks are less and less interested in customers, full stop, let alone catering to the poor, mobile phone carriers started taking over this job, expanding their initial monetary system for purchasing airtime, ringtones and SMS credit to an expanding range of services, from peer-to-peer payments to water and electricity bills, school fees and transportation. Bascially, users pay all sorts of bills with their phone credit. Today, mobile money is front and centre in development discourses. It is tied to a new understanding of development, one which eschews outdated notions like charity and instead seeks to foster the entrepreneurial spirit of the poor while making a buck along the way. Mobile money is positioned as a way to solve the problem of 'unbanked' people's capacity for economic participation, while fostering new financial literacies in the management of money. Meanwhile, those who have made profits (or missed out on them) from the set-up of small-scale mobile exchange systems are looking for ways in and out. As the mobile money industry matures, new telco-banking arrangements are being forged, and local state regulation is being rewritten. Underpinned by the new narrative of development as commerce, these processes are further legitimized by the eager participation of NGOs, which have equally bought in to the idea that 'there is a fortune at the bottom of the pyramid'.

The question of who, in the end, will dominate the mobile money space remains open. Will it be the Asian and African telcos or rather Visa (which currently owns much of the underlying software that mobile money companies utilize)? Will large global banks one day wake up and buy themselves into this market? From a different angle, what about the proposition of a Bitcoin clone developed for P2P mobile money payments? The strength of the existing platforms is precisely that they are making use of the existing national currencies (and treasuries that issue them) and are not tempted to go in the 'virtual' direction of parallel currencies. Policy-wise, this is also what the term 'financial inclusion' seems to suggest and demand. No exodus and no outside. With an estimated 80 per cent of adults in Africa still unbanked, the potentials are obvious. Around 3 billion people worldwide lack access to formal financial services. Are there lessons to be learned from the micro-finance sagas? We also need to consider the wider position of mobile money in relation to new media of exchange unfolding 'at the top', designed by Microsoft, Google, Apple (and Ubuntu?), which will all have their own strategies for how to integrate monetary transactions into future smart phone architectures. Will the telcos and their mobile money initiatives eventually fold into the existing banking system or will they team up with Silicon Valley? They might also be left alone and build up a 'third space' of their own.

Who is in charge of what, and where should we go to make our demands? Is it justified to expect that we will have to develop our own alternative money flows? Hack the code ourselves and just start? Is barter the way to go? How can we build a larger demand to redistribute wealth into such obvious system changes? Can we disarm the online traders, taking away the toys from the boys? Is there such a thing as 'slow money'? How do alternative visions of finance, such as P2P banking, sit within these developments? These are big questions.

If we turn to the troubled cultural sector, we can see that the last few decades of the creative industries have not offered up any concrete revenue models for artistic and cultural production besides corporate sponsorship and the (morally) bankrupt model of intellectual property. In this time of economic crisis, we can no longer only criticize financial capitalism but need to imagine, and practise, alternatives. What are the long-term prospects of crowdfunding platforms, beyond the hype? Is there a way for precarious cultural workers to earn money directly, cutting out intermediates, through a P2P economy, using bitcoins? It is not hard to see that the free and open as facilitating ideologies of the 1990s no longer play a dominant role in this new landscape. If there is anything in need of disruption, it is the global finance sector itself.

MoneyLab in the Picture: Coining Alternatives

In the US, the East–West division of powers is shifting. The visions and aspirations of Wall Street and Silicon Valley are slowly merging. Whereas one part of the industry is still struggling with paper cheques, credit cards and legacy systems of ancient IT investments dating back to the 1980s, the other is preparing for the mass introduction of Bitcoin-styled blockchain technology. Increasing numbers of start-ups are looking to innovate at the level of money, payment, and funding, while financial companies innovate through technology. Finance is more and more (still) where the geeks end up: mathematical modellers, machine learning experts, physics majors and so on. And their target is increasingly the 'data flows' of social media and related platforms. Front-end financialization of the web coincides with the discovery that the web can be used as a financial resource. Wikipedia page edits can be used to predict stock movements. Social media platforms are machine-readable, and the content of these 'flows' is reflected in fluctuating stock values. Any difference engine can send out signals that the finance networks can read as possible indicators of future movements.

We must not fear finance as such. This point has been made most clearly by financial activist Brett Scott.[17] His technique is to approach the world of finance through the mindset of the hacker-activist. We might equally ask what other strategies of engagement are possible. After the global uprisings of 2011 – in particular, Occupy – we know that our post-2008 foci did not deal enough with hardcore finance. The movement quickly turned inward-looking and got obsessed with its own democratic rituals. Occupy not only showed how mainstream the discontent with global finance had become (later called the 'Piketty effect'), but also demonstrated the need for alternative views on money, capital, income and finance – as well as how primitive and minimalistic 21st-century bohemia's concepts of these things had become. There is a growing awareness of 'dark pools' and other absurdities, but how can all this evidence be turned into an organized outrage and translated into policy? Many fear that regulation alone will not do the job. It is no longer enough to condemn the IMF as an imperial tool. The neoliberal austerity policies are now imposed on all and are imposed well beyond the Global South. It might be too late to decommission financial tools. In his highly recommended *The Quants*, Scott Patterson discusses critically certain public proposals to ban quants[18] from Wall Street. To him, 'that would be tantamount to banishing civil engineers from the bridge-making profession after a bridge collapse. Instead, many believed the goal should be to design better bridges – or, in the case of the quants, more robust models that could withstand financial tsunamis, not create them.' But what's better 'design' in the age of algo wars? Saskia Sassen points to a too-real Theatre of Cruelty, the neoliberal revenge on the poor, as a result of the 2008 financial crisis. Her book *Expulsions* is another post-2008 classic. Her ambitious, stats-based argumentation so clearly shows the deliberately hidden costs of the crisis and its long-term fall-out zone. The autonomy of the 'money that went to heaven' is relative. As we know from our youth, not even a game of Monopoly is innocent and without consequences.

Is Bitcoin the better bridge? What does it mean merely to improve systems when we have clearly reached the end of the liberal market illusion? There will always be 'new insiders'. Will it be Apple, Google and Facebook this time? Or should we expect the telcos to become the new banks? A global ban on high-frequency trading, hedge funds or derivatives will not prevent a next crisis, and might only be put in place in retrospect of an nth disaster. Besides a General Theory of Global Finance for the twenty-first century, we also need blueprints for how money should be generated in this age of digital networks. In fact, these are one and the same.

The simple and most challenging question arising from this period of history and its critique is: how did the neoliberals emerge from the crisis stronger than ever? This is Philip Mirowski's important line of questioning in his highly recommended book *Never Let a Serious Crisis Go to Waste*, from 2013. MoneyLab needs to open up and further this line of critique. What if all these well-meant, constructive alternatives have only strengthened or made no difference to neoliberal policies, benefitted the parasitic 1 per cent? Or, worse, what if the very alternatives proposed are themselves somehow neoliberal? Should we go on an alternatives strike and even refuse to formulate any form of criticism? What's the deadliest form of negativity for the world of finance?

The questions Mirowski asks eventually culminate towards querying the organizational strategies of adversaries as part of a 'sociology of knowledge'.[19] On the positive side, initiatives such as MoneyLab can also come together in larger organized networks and flip into a Thought Collective (as Mirowski calls it), an eventually global initiative that can review and distribute alternative seeds of presents and futures. Mirowski asks, 'What would a vital counter-narrative to the epistemological commitments of the neoliberals look like?'[20] Can we make so bold as to answer: the MoneyLab organized networks? If the 'major ambition of the Neoliberal Thought Collective is to sow doubt and ignorance amongst the populace', as Mirowski continues, what role can internet-based research networks such as VideoVortex, Unlike Us and MoneyLab play? Should these units be smaller, or rather bigger? What do we gain from 'pop-up networks'? What forces are benefitting most from all the lost experiences when networks disappear? If, as Mirowski states on the same page, 'true political power resides in the ability to make the decision to "suspend" the market in order to save the market', is it enough for oppositional forces to make entrepreneurial myths uncool again, and break the spell of the unchallenged capitalist realist consensus? Why should radical movements regress and defend the market in their critique of the monopolies? We can surely "do better than that.

So far, the left has mainly defended mid-twentieth-century models of the welfare state and demanded the redistribution of money, instead of considering a radical reinvention of money itself. Alternative, complementary and local currencies have remained at the margins. It is one thing to conclude that the think-tank model itself is an outmoded organizational form with which to do research and make policy. The professionalism of the NGO model is too dull, too slow for this fast-moving world of continuous events, wars, climate disasters and political ruptures. In this light, Mirowski asks the 100.000 Bitcoin question: 'Is there a coherent alternative framework within which to understand the interaction of the financialisation of the economy with larger ebbs and flows of political economy in the global transformations of capitalism?' One possible direction that needs to be discussed is the issue of financialization from below. So far, financialization has only been understood as a move from trade and commodity production to profits from financial channels. Is the monetization of services that were once free of cost (or that did not exist in the first place) changing this picture?[21]

Are initiatives like those that gather underneath the MoneyLab umbrella ready for the financial state of emergency as predicted by populist websites such as Zero Hedge and Putin's satellite news channel RT, which hosts presenters such as Max Keiser who fiercely attack the devastating logic of global finance?[22] Do we, unconsciously, underestimate the urgency of the current situation, or rather enjoy the alarmist 'I told you so' position? According to Mirowski, this is precisely what defines the behaviour of financial elites: they know how to get ready for the next crash – 'Neoliberals may preach the rule of law, and sneer in public about the ineptitude of government, but they win by taking advantage of "the exception" to introduce components of their program unencumbered by judicial or democratic accountability. They know what it means to never let a serious crisis go to waste.' Are we ready? Are efforts to collectively imagine alternative, internet-based revenue models – for instance, for artistic and cultural production – decisive enough to act and take over after the Great Collapse?

In bringing together and reading as One these partial solutions of crowdfunding, digital and crypto-currency, mobile money services, micro-payment systems and other P2P experiments, MoneyLab asserts that it is naïve to treat these different phenomena as unrelated to each other, or to dismiss them offhand. Now, more than ever, we need constructive engagement with the hackers, entrepreneurs and other creators of economic alternatives, precisely because of the systemic stakes. We need audaciousness for times of austerity. But we need to do all this while continuing to generate the emergent maps of the present: what works and what doesn't? What is worth pursuing and what must we leave aside? What destabilizes the dominant ideology or strengthens the hegemon? Which histories are bearing strongest on the present? And what are the limits of our economic imagination?

The Dutch design collective Metahaven proposed that 'the faltering Euro currency [be] rescued by Facebook credits', and that Germany and Microsoft together launch a national virtual currency. Another of their speculative ideas is Facestate, the social superpower with an economy using social reputation as its currency. In this dystopia, as outlined by Metahaven, large corporations like Facestate have already appropriated unfolding socio-technological developments, as well as ones that may not yet exist.

One of the most explosive phenomena generating new concepts arises in the coupling of mobile phone and P2P technologies, as this is being employed in the Global South, where Western banking models (using ATMs, credit cards, local branches, online banking through PCs, etc.) are not dominating the economic flow. Of course, nation states and their taxation offices might ban such innovations – this is precisely what is discussed in the case of Bitcoin. Much like the crisis-mapping website Ushahidi – which, like the pioneer in mobile money M-Pesa, originates from Kenya – these are developments that reflect actual practices from the African continent. Through the development of new financial instruments for mobile phone platforms, the traditional banking scene is trying to keep control of the fast-growing P2P sector as it develops in various directions. The telecom provider is in charge here, not the banks. The base of it all remains the simple transferal, from one phone to the next, of purchased credit. This is a tech set-up, which, if implemented in the right way, could benefit artists, activists and other 'precarious' freelance workers who could then receive micro-payments themselves.[23] Ideally, mobile money would be an encrypted currency that makes optimal use of distributed and decentralized network architectures, enabling fast and easy exchanges of small amounts. So far, mobile money has not yet experimented with such a parallel cyber-currency of its own. In fact, development is currently going in the opposite direction. Mastercard and Western Union are getting more of a grip on the mobile money sector while other traditional banks and national regulators give out mixed signals about how they will relate to this rapidly growing payment system.

It is time to combine radical critiques of global finance with investigations into emerging revenue models, payment systems and experimental currencies. These trajectories should be linked and feed off each other. It is not enough to demand a reform of the financial sector and hope for a return to Keynesian employment policies. Our attempt at MoneyLab is situated inside contemporary network cultures. For the past few decades, the informal nature of networks meant that the buzzing communication sphere was perceived as an autonomous realm, a world apart from the 'official' reality with its formalized social and economic relations. The rise of high-speed trading over the past fifteen years has shown how fast niche software, still under development, can take centre-stage.

Until recently, if money circulated in the internet economy, it did so either through traditional direct purchases of goods and services (for instance, through e-commerce) or indirectly, behind the back of the user, through ads such as web banners and sales of private data. If we want to step up our critiques of 'the stacks' and their culture of organized cheating, it is not only important to make these economic dimensions of the digital and the social visible. And we can't stop at reclaiming the 'free' and 'open' and abolishing them from the marketer's vocabulary. The gesture of giving things, ourselves, away for free should once again become a genuine gift, not the online default, but the offline exception, with financial exchanges taking place on a peer-to-peer level. The larger question of the organization and the operation of value beyond the gift, however, has clearly become our research and activistic business, to share and pursue. It is time to reinvent money, and redistribute it, in the name of San Precario![24]

— 7 —

FOR BITCOIN TO LIVE,
BITCOIN MUST DIE

Why is it that we can communicate and exchange immaterial capital on a global level, but not simply pay someone? Here we must confront a glaring issue in the so-called 'political economy' of the internet.[1] While the net is more friction-ridden than we often make out (try emailing in Central Tanzania), higher degrees of ICT 'development' have made for reliably smooth communications through major nodes. Money transfers, in Western Europe at least, are similarly almost friction-less, and largely free of human labour costs. The reality is that everyday 'exchange' problems, and unrealized potentialities, reside much more with the banking system, wavering as it does on the verge of collapse due to its extreme (and excessive) financialization, than with existing payment infrastructures. If we were to run the infrastructure instead like any other utility, with costs borne out of public funds, it would be largely seamless and free of charge to users. But given how unlikely public banking looks in any conceivable future, all kinds of new, mostly net-born formats will continue to arise.

Bitcoin is just one of the first natively digital currencies, but, in playing this role, it has already made its mark. As one promoter sums up its impact: 'the technology behind Bitcoin cannot be legislated away'.[2] Until recently, you used your own computer to make a Bitcoin. The process was wholly virtual but still quite slow because of the fact that each coin must be algorithmically produced, registered and administrated individually. Every Bitcoin has a unique number. When one person pays someone, and the other confirms being paid, it is this reciprocal exchange moment that is automatically caught and minimally registered in the innovative blockchain technology –

there is no central authority needed to record payments otherwise. That is Bitcoin's point of difference: 'distributed trust' instead of 'contractual trust'. Governments and banks, among other 'real world' institutions, function on the basis of contractual trust, enshrined and enforced by way of charters, constitutions, laws and regulations, etc. Bitcoin believers want an alternative, disseminated form of trust, shared and borne by all the individuals involved, without 'political' interference. The tech difference is similar to that between broadcast (one-to-many) and narrowcast (one-to-one, many-to-many) polarity, the latter propelling the internet revolution of the 1990s.

The currency was launched on 2 August 2010, right in time to be considered the geek response to the 2008 global financial crisis. For the first couple of years, Bitcoins were one-for-one with the value of the US dollar (starting off at 6 cents, it began being indexed after one year, when it had risen to approx. US$1). It was not until 30 September 2013 that it spiked, when investors came in suddenly. The value went up rapidly from 1 to 1,000. Presently, it hovers around US$400 and there is also talk of forking the project (in the tradition of software forking: creating similar but different clones). How do we deal with this? We may hear rumours of Berlin shop owners hooking their businesses to Bitcoin, but for now this kind of optimism is well off the mark. The volatility of the currency means that there is no social trust in the value. That it reached $1,000 makes for a great story. The period of the spike was itself intense, with evangelists thinking this was nothing, and estimating 50,000 times the value. With a value of $1 for most of the time, then spikes, and drops back to $200, how do you plan incomings and outgoings if a currency is so volatile?

Alternative vs. Complementary Currencies

The difference between alternative and complementary currencies, though blurred by both operating outside the economic and financial mainstream, is essential to comprehend. They vary greatly in concept, aims and *modus operandi*, and tend to display radically different politics.

Complementary currencies largely focus on the local, which, depending on the prevailing circumstances, can substantially vary in size: the WIR bank in Switzerland, for instance, functions on the national scale; in other countries, specific local currencies have not transcended the level of a middle-sized town or province. Yet complementary currencies, by virtue of being local, are inclusive. As their name indicates, they have modest yet long-term ambitions; they are generally pegged to the 'real existing' money of account in their (national) sphere of circulation, which they do not intend to replace entirely (many provide for 'hybrid' payments, part 'local', part 'real' money). If used within an entirely 'closed' locale, their scope can be even more limited.

Alternative, crypto- and virtual currencies, on the other hand, potentially can function on a much larger, even global, geographical scale. But since the number of participants in the system is just as severely constrained with them also – by different measures – they are, *ipso facto*, exclusive. Bitcoin mythologizes itself as an alternative currency that wants to displace, and replace, the current monetary arrangements. In having this aim, it does not want to be limited in scope and reach, whether geographically or economically. But here lies its main strength-as-weakness: it does not have an 'authority' that can both (somehow) guarantee its value and compel its use by legal means. Bitcoiners insist that this constitutes precisely its main strength. It is a valid argument to promote while being a totally preposterous one on a 'real world' scale. Furthermore, a faction of the Bitcoin community is clearly emerging that wants recognition and certification by the 'system' (under-defined) – this is yet another example of the currency's 'open contradictions'.

(Re-)Occupation or Withdrawal? Having it Both Ways

The most contradictory aspect of Bitcoin's inception is its unimaginative modelling on the gold commodity. By definition, virtual mining could be limitless. But, like gold, Bitcoin's inventors wanted a limit upon the number of Bitcoins that are mineable. This programmes in artificial scarcity, which is why many commentators call Bitcoin a 'pre-71' project. Bitcoin essentially wants to reintroduce the gold standard into virtual space; with this, you couldn't just increase the amount of money in the world. Now, with quantitative easing, the Federal Bank and ECB artificially decide on and create the amount of dollars and euros that can circulate. This first paradox of Bitcoin's modelling means that the natively digital currency need not actually be digital. Or, in other words, instead of using colonized workers or machines to go mine real gold, in this choice it's just computers doing a similarly constructed job – making irrelevant the fictive nature of the 'material' resource. If Bitcoin is both a fantastic digital negation of the inflation/debt economy, and a fictional return to an analogue mode of production, what is it trying to be? Maybe its critical contribution lies just here – performatively lamenting the fact that the dire state of current economic modelling results from an economy that has been wholly disconnected from the earth.

The historical concurrence of Bitcoin and Occupy is, in any case, no accident. The internet crypto-currency expresses a longing for technology-mediated liberation from (inequitable) regulation. It grows out of a post-apocalyptic will to begin all over again, in-between financial crises of epic proportions, and to put an end also – symbolically as much as materially – to never-ending recessions. The enthusiasm for Bitcoin amongst geeks and IT entrepreneurs stems from wide-ranging popular disillusionment with the financial system in this sense. That disillusionment meets up with redacted versions of earlier Internet ideologies. Complexly so, because it carries all the contradictions of that earlier era. Bitcoin wants to have it both ways. And it is not surprising that its community of believers is strangely silent about the dual role, in their 'alternative' model, of the US dollar, which they accept as their currency's by-default reference – the US dollar is fiat money, partaking in all the sins lambasted by Bitcoiners, not least inflationary tendencies. On the other hand (but really the same), it is the 'imperial' currency of the United States of America, welcomed and used by the entire world. Still, it is subject to the sole decisions of the US Federal Reserve, which takes near-exclusive consideration of the political and economic interests of the USA. As both the instrument and the executor of the United States' 'structural hegemony', the US dollar thus has 'exorbitant privilege' attached to it. The position of Bitcoin in being hooked to such a dispensation system remains unclear, and unstated. Suffice to say that a truly sovereign currency would never refer itself to the US dollar (or the Euro, Yen or Pound for that matter).

In its eagerness to reassemble a next 'tech' elite subculture that might achieve escape velocity from the murky complexity of contemporary power, we can understand Bitcoin as an avatar of the privileged classes wanting to pull out of the grunge of everyday reality and its messy social sphere. This time – or so believers in Bitcoin maintain – the economy will be led by a tribe of techno-libertarians, not by a vile, corrupted dictatorship of banksters and politicians. This Bitcoin articulation of autonomy is more like 'sovereignty in one's own circle' (a Dutch religious-cultural classic, close to apartheid), doing away with social complexity and its large institutions. Crypto-money for us, and poverty for all. As the *Washington Post* once wrote: 'Bitcoin is a system to redistribute money among libertarians.' So far, it's been hard to falsify this statement. The 'ecology' of its users consists of just a minority of the world's population; we can safely guess the main players come from the mostly white, largely male, North American 'anarcho-geek' sphere,[3] with the rest being outliers scattered across the rest of the planet. Bitcoin is part and parcel of the 'Masters of the Universe' narrative played out by invincible hedge fund managers, as portrayed in Tom Wolfe's *The Bonfire of the Vanities* (1987) and Bret Easton Ellis' *American Psycho* (1991), only this time in its 'geek' declination. It cannot be considered as some subaltern, folkloric movement. Still, the Bitcoin ideology reflects a profound, and much more widely shared, distrust in existing organizational formats and practices. The overall direction is a structural withdrawal from society: it's 'our' currency, not theirs. Amidst the rubble of collapsing global capitalism, is there nothing else left to demand? And who or what, exactly, is supposed to be listening? How good is this as a blueprint for the next monetary system? Bitcoin architecture is not the only alternative possible. Everything is up for grabs, including the premises of the Bitcoin project itself. Let us confront directly Bitcoin's Ponzi messianism, its scale and its politics of scarcity, the obvious links of unregulated money to the free labour debates as instigated by Trebor Scholz and others, and the very different varieties of trust in techno-political solutions.

Trust vs Proof and Crypto Values

Scalability vs range and ease of exchange, alternative vs complementary systems. Behind these decisions, or contradictions, lie matters of trust and value, and their counterparts: responsibility, accountability and liability. Trust and value are complexly related. How to figure these two concepts when they overlap considerably and are each an outcome of the other?[4] The dilemma may appear arcane, but is fundamental to understanding the role of money as we know it, and hence the opportunities and limits of alternatives. So let us first look at those parts that do not overlap. Trust is mainly about the definition stage; there are splits between the different forms of money-related trust. We need to distinguish between 'contract trust', which, in the West, is the basis of formal financial relations, and 'distributed trust', the algo-based alternative system propounded by Bitcoin and all other digital crypto-currency systems so far. There is also a potentially far more important – i.e. socially meaningful – alternative to 'contract

94

trust', based on ex-ante verification, and thus on 'distrust by default'. Let's call this 'community trust', post-facto enforced, and hence a socially constructed security. Community trust has been, and still often is, the standard business practice in the East, where there is a remarkably low occurrence of financial delinquency. It is important to keep this in mind when figuring non-libertarian alternative currency schemes.

The self-determined, or trust-independent, part of money's value is the entirely subjective assessment of exchange 'once the deal is done'. In other words, there is no such thing as intrinsic value; money is primarily about exchange and transfer, movement. Considering various alternative monetary schemes through such a lens, we can observe that for many the money held in 'done deals' is relatively irrelevant and may represent no net worth – as is the case in so-called 'demurrage' currencies. A truly alternative currency would have parallel resolution instruments (a proto-sociality), rather than being just tokens of, well, value. The overlap between trust and value is, of course, the more interesting part of any design conundrum.

Advocates of crypto currencies maintain that 'human' trust can be effectively – and efficiently – traded for cryptographic proof. The disappeared Bitcoin inventor Satoshi Nakamoto was most succinct about this: 'an electronic transaction ... does not rely on trust but should be based instead on cryptographic proof'. In his view, social interaction is seen as an obstacle or weak link, something to be routed around or eliminated as much as possible. Unfortunately, Bitcoin's trust in post-human science does not seem to apply to the programmers themselves. All-too-human coders, miners and exchange-owners appear to be exempted from the rule. With faith set firmly in the algorithm, the phenomenon of Silk Road was considered to be the inconvenient main thing stopping believers from feeling legitimate in the critical public media sphere of the post-2008 economy. Soon after, growing pains were singly attributed to the Japanese Bitcoin exchange Mt Gox, which blew up and 'disappeared' the money of so many faithful investors.

While I write, it is the block size debate that threatens to pull Bitcoin apart from the inside into two factions, but no one knows how this is going to be played out. On the one side, you have the traditional programmers who have been with Bitcoin from day one. They want to grow the blockchain, which means that the number of transactions that happen inside this blockchain will be increased. If that happened, the number of transactions that the system allows would be raised. On the other side, there is a valid proposition to cut off mining and the blockchain from Bitcoin (as I and my collaborator on this research, Patrice Riemens, propose). The problem that will remain here is trust, because the blockchain – the distributed verification algorithm that vouches for the validity of Bitcoin transfers, guaranteeing that no Bitcoin is spent twice – is basically the nearest approximation to the Divine in the Bitcoin religion. In any case, if the foundation does split, one outcome would be that you would not be able to exchange one kind of new Bitcoin from the split-off other Bitcoin economy. To put this even more starkly, the human interactions that in the end cannot be eliminated are the ones that turn out to be paramount. This typically constitutes the ontological blind spot of all 'techno-solutionism', as Evgeny Morozov has defined this. Bitcoin's inflexible faith in algorithms and machines above the – always fallible, and crookedly inclined – human being is another reminder of its solidly 'Anglo' origins.

Morozov is an independent critic, not an academic; he has an Eastern European NGO source legacy and has extensively covered interconnected media, freedom and democracy issues, having worked for George Soros' Open Society Foundation. His first book, *The Net Delusion*, was about Iran and the green revolution, the failed 2009 revolt against the mullahs, and the ambivalent role of social media. His second, *To Save Everything, Click Here*, tackles directly his appraisal of the rise of 'solutionism' in the new economy – the idea that social problems can be solved with a technical idea. After the 2008 financial crisis, Morozov gained attention in the US press because he was one of the few accessible independent critics of Silicon Valley's role in the disaster. This was the first time that the Valley agenda started to be questioned in the mainstream media – up until that moment, it had held its ground as the shiny boy-child of capitalism itself. Or, in other words, it did not generate its own critics. The mainstream media have never invested anything in its coverage, either neglecting it entirely or just copy-pasting its hype. In the aftermath of the 2008 global financial crisis, as older mainstream newspapers started to ask serious questions about what happened and felt increasingly threatened by Apple iPad, Google and so on, Morozov grabbed their attention. For the most part, the author translates US media politics to Europe, and not much in the other direction, but he does have a lot of American outlets and coverage. He is also interesting for mainstream outlets because he does not originate from the small dedicated European net criticism circles.

In the 'fin-tech' context, we cannot underestimate the importance of Morozov's 'techno-solutionism' concept. Bitcoin embodies the idea that there will be a technical solution for the current economic crisis. Of course, Morozov is not saying that social and political problems aren't real, nor even that these couldn't benefit from technical and infrastructural applications. The key elements to his critique of 'techno-solutionism' involve, firstly, reappraising how problems become perceived as 'problems' (hypocrisy in politics is not eliminable); and, secondly, attending to the real costs of solutions conceived for problems that have been identified. Today, for example, it is not obvious to people that solving a problem by the means of an app is not the same as, say, regulating the laws of the food system. Morozov similarly understands Bitcoin to be offering an 'algo' solution for a political problem. Its inception is somehow based on the common conviction that 'politics sucks' and always will, and that technical solutions are always 'cleaner' and 'better' than social ones. 'Replace the messy social with the beauty of pure mathematics', as the saying goes.[5] Bitcoin believers hold that what really matters is mastering the technology, and that those who master the technology will rule (though rule what?) – by right. In other words, proof of the system's success makes the case for Bitcoin users to be in political economic command, instead of, for example, politicians. Morozov's superior *realtheorie* of this moment might very well arrive at a dead-end street, however. In terms of strategy, it is true that the currency gained momentum through truisms (and traumas) resulting from disappointment in all forms of power, leading to a 'been there, done that' brand of indifference and cynicism. But Morozov's argument does not open back up the conversation on these matters, either. Stated without much of an understanding of lived alternative practices, his calls to 'return to politics' away from the algorithm proves problematic, because it glosses over the moral bankruptcy of Western democratic procedures. His Continental European technology critique, in particular, pleases 'old media' liberal newspapers, and established publishing houses, whose business models are crumbling under the onslaught of the digital, social media, and the rise of intermediaries.

Ponzi Messianism and Trust in Algo Form

The sheer size of the speculative finance complex – the macro-economic background against which Bitcoin has emerged – is difficult to get one's head around. For quite some time now, monetary and fiscal balances have grown out of control, both in terms of quantity and in terms of the velocity with which they circulate, the former being also a consequence of the latter. For many, the relationship between the financial sphere and the 'real economy' has been lost; indeed, speculative finance operations dwarf the actual needs of the everyday, brick-and-mortar products and services-based economy. The factual problems with the narrative of a Bitcoin future arise when thinking financialization alongside Bitcoin's design, indexing and scalability. Bitcoin functions mostly in the sphere of small/micro payments. Perhaps counter-intuitively in this sense, it is scaled in opposition to speculative finance tools, while being conceived and developed by the same quant class. Simple math shows that Bitcoin in its current form cannot scale to make even a relatively modest alt-economic/financial system possible. This is precisely because of the limit put on the number of Bitcoins that are mineable: 21 million at the most, which, when fractioned by 9 positions behind the zero, gives a maximum of 220 billion units of micropayment (say, the equivalent of US1¢) at a very conservative valuation of Bitcoin at US$100 per unit. Going by the 1 Dollar – 100 cents division of currency, this results in a total maximum amount of 2.2 billion 'Bitcoin Dollars', a somewhat diminutive economy by all means … you can do the math yourself.

Price rises and monetary devaluation have a different impact, depending on societal/economic classes. The poor suffer at 'ground level' as price increases affect their consumption, and they must see how to make do day-to-day with their (low) earnings. But they do not hold wealth. The rich, and especially the super-rich, do hold (a lot of) wealth, but that is usually in the form of tangible assets or ownership deeds (shares, stakes in enterprises, etc.); monetary balances are secondary to them. It's the middle classes whose holdings (often in the form of savings, e.g. towards their pension) are the most at risk. We have observed this play out in past inflationary and hyper-inflationary bouts, when the nest eggs of the middle classes were wiped out, resulting in trans-generational trauma. The major difficulty with Bitcoin is that it does not correct this problem of the loss of the real economy, and even moves in the wrong direction. By any count, the maximum size of the potential circulation of Bitcoin is dwarfed, several times over, not only by the size of the current financial, speculative, balances, which form a recognised problem, but also by the amounts needed to run the 'real economy' itself. The fact that its base unit of measure can only be shifted nine decimal places reduces the usability of Bitcoin to that of a very local currency, not a planetary one. This is only one difficulty, but a very practical one, stopping Bitcoin from being a real alternative to our present global monetary dispensation. Bitcoin believers are fairly disingenuous in denying this reality. Despite the limited options Bitcoin offers as a financial instrument (basically only peer-to-peer transactions), its core members are absolutely convinced both of its superiority as a payment system and of its speedy adoption worldwide, and see its uptake alone as proof of its potential for liberation and large-scale takeover of the monetary/financial system, regardless of cultural and political issues and differences. Their argument hinges more on 'inevitability' logics than on structural analysis – this is the hallmark of any messianic religion. Cultish valuations of the currency play out in other immeasurable ways: in Bitcoin T-shirt trends, apps and glossy magazines, and in members' conspicuous off-loading of Bitcoins at gambling sites and so on.

If the scarcity of Bitcoin is designed in, not a bug, nor a technical limitation to be resolved in due time by more powerful computers, then we have to consider scarcity a feature of its paradoxical value/ valuation. Indeed, the pyramid set-up of Bitcoin turns, or has turned, early players into winners at the expense of gullible latecomers. This is hardly accidental: Bitcoin is a typical geek-meritocratic project. Indeed, one of the main critiques addressed towards Bitcoin is that it is designed like a Ponzi scheme. Believers' usual retort to this accusation is that these critics do not understand what Bitcoin really is – nor, for that matter, what a Ponzi scheme entails. The resemblances are so obvious that the 'Duck test' allegory comes to mind ('if it looks like a duck ...'). This constitutive limit on supply automatically pushes up Bitcoin's value over time. What is a payment system, let alone an alt.economy, that encourages speculative *refrain* from its use? The scarcity logic is predicated on a very retro-futurist desire amongst geeks to return to something like the dependable quality of gold – an objectified and materially timeless 'neutrality', but without gold's material disadvantages, easily abolished by the magic of the digital. Virtual gold? The peer-to-peer model is difficult to reconcile with this retro-futurist fantasy of scarce and invented pre-Nixon gold. It institutes a hoarding attitude, and exacerbates Bitcoin believers' ingrained fear of inflation.

The middle-class character of Bitcoin is demonstrated by this obsessive fear of inflation, and users' embrace of hoarding a currency that supposedly 'can only accrue in value'. It is crazy that 'hoarders give Bitcoin value'. The Bitcoin literature is replete with such conflicting statements and theories as this – all brought forward with the same enthusiasm.[6] If the original sin of fiat money is inflation, the original sin of Bitcoin is this hoarders vs spenders contradiction: the modalities of the system, as agreed by Bitcoin believers themselves, make it uniquely convenient for peer-to-peer exchange. But, for all practical purposes, this is an exclusive convenience. When Bitcoin increases in value, the incentive to spend it or sell it is simply not there, the moment never arrives. Only losers sell. Such contradictions are ostensibly not a problem for the Bitcoin community itself. You can have your cake and eat it too (and own the bakery in the process). This deflationary aspect of the Bitcoin model not only gives mainstream economists or politicians the creeps, it further reinforces believers' aversion to transactions – Bitcoin's principal *raison d'être* is that spending amounts to a distress sale. Here it falls victim to its origins in rugged individualism crossed with the anarcho-capitalist axiom that 'greed is good'. This has never made for a sound economic system in social exchange. The mining principle, Bitcoin's foundational myth and principal motor, points to a dark past, not a common future. A truly alternative currency would think with the conditions necessary for it to be used by billions of human beings. No one designs an alternative currency for best use by themselves and a few of their friends. This is a basic premise of economic exchange. On the other hand, slaves do not need Bitcoin; their life is totally subordinated to the economy already. Here, clearly, code is not just law, code is also life.

'Free Money'

In Bitcoin circles, the grudge against taxes is clear ('imposition is thievery'), but also against fees and commissions that banks levy on all possible transactions, and which, due to ultra-low interest rates, appear to have become their main source of income, in the payment system at least. A result of this sentiment is the invisibility of the Bitcoin system's own intermediates, such as mining operations and exchanges that operate in the background. This is a general weakness of cyberculture that tends to black out its own infrastructure and takes it for granted as a 'second nature'. Bitcoiners believe their currency is the unique answer to the current global finance mess, especially at the level of micro-payments. This is true in a technical sense – all virtual currencies have the potential to enable friction- and fee-free transactions – but the volatility of Bitcoin makes this assumption problematic, especially for micro-payments.

In keeping with its supposedly 'friction-less' status, Bitcoin is hailed as a uniquely community-managed adventure, based on the DIY activity of its members. This apparent Do-It-Yourself aspect of Bitcoin must be seen in the tradition of neoliberal free labour. This time, free only means 'free of fees' (i.e. 'free for me'). Given the increasingly complex aspect of Bitcoin's principal occupation, mining, now restricted to a limited number of (terabyte-) powerful entities, it is unclear what this activity of the many is precisely made of (unless one considers hoarding as work). In consonance with the nature of anarcho-capitalism, very little is known of the community itself and, also, of whom it consists – except that it is a closed circle of geeky white guys.

Insofar as DIY is made equivalent to free labour, it is hard to fathom how exactly this works in a set-up that is so specifically geared towards (economic) transactions on one side and over-concerned with value and possession on the other. Given Bitcoiners' absolute detestation of fees and other transaction costs charged by 'the system', it is interesting to note that Bitcoin, which is supposed to do away with these institutional charges and banking fees, actually does provide for them on (very) small transactions (but not on large ones, itself a non-too-egalitarian feature). Further, its theoreticians assert that when mining terminates (in 2040, when the 21 million Bitcoins are all in circulation), the system will maintain itself ... through fees.

Bifurcations of Possible Futures

In 2014–15, Bitcoin reached a cruising speed (however bumpy the ride). That this is not only in the minds of its believers is attested by the fact that new problems are popping up in its relationship with 'the real world'. The powers that be – and more specifically their financial/monetary arms – want to regulate the new kid on the block. Meanwhile, part of the Bitcoin 'community' has decided it wants this too, spurred partly by a desire for wider recognition and acceptance, but also because Bitcoin's reputation, already shaky at best, has been further tarnished by a number of high-exposure scandals, such as the mysterious disappearance in February 2014 of Mt Gox, the Japanese Bitcoin exchange site (along with 850,000 Bitcoins amounting to $450 million in value), and the conviction of the owner of the drugs trading platform Silk Road. Regulation under a central, external authority is, of course, entirely at variance with Bitcoin's central tenets. Besides exemplifying the 'open contradiction' that is Bitcoin, such moves have now split the community and the Bitcoin Foundation. It is easy to argue that regulating Bitcoin degrades it as nothing more than yet another flashy financial vehicle. This is, in any case, how it is looked at by the 'financial sector'.

Rather than a mainstream, regulated Bitcoin, it is more likely that any future currencies will remain split between morally bankrupted official kinds and informal (local) kinds. The need for P2P payments will only increase. The banking system as we know it has become largely dysfunctional for ordinary monetary transactions between small and medium-size economic actors. Low interest rates and other factors 'force' banks to levy hefty fees and commissions, while, on the other hand, ubiquitous electronic networks hold out the promise of next-to-cost-free transactions and transfers of money (and more). It is unavoidable that ordinary payments will drop out of the cumbersome and expensive banking system and that various other platforms will fill this space (based on the blockchain technology). The evolution has already started on the mobile phone front, as I discuss in the next chapter. P2P transactions, whereby the exchange is entirely in the hands of participants, with no middle management in between, is the realization of this trend.

Bitcoin's pretensions to being the ultimate solution within this fast-paced transformation of the monetary sphere are questionable on many practical and social grounds. The forces of contradiction at work raise the possibility of forking: Bitcoins after Bitcoin. The other direction would be to go 'meta' and create a meta exchange for all the different crypto-currencies (see Ethereum[7]). Whatever directions are taken, they must always return to the nature of trust, and especially practical, design-based attention to the difference between contract and distributed trust, on a 'working scale'.

Bitcoin after Bitcoin

The future of Bitcoin is bright, but it will come after Bitcoin. Farewell, Winkelvoss Bros. The advance of small-scale digital (crypto-)currencies that operate within a specific social setting (be it local or translocal), labelled either alternative or complementary, is unstoppable. The trickiest part, in terms of adoption and economic effectiveness, is always going to be their relation with the 'real existing' money (€, £, $, whatever ...). On this point, complementary currencies are much more flexible than alternative ones. Still, these are technological advances that the current banking system is ill prepared for, especially at the 'retail' level (never mind the not-improbable collapse of the financial/monetary system as we know it). For retail, probably non-banking, and possibly non-centrally regulated, electronic payment systems will win the day, especially in the realm of transactions by or between individuals. Banks already want to get rid of individual customers; they are a nuisance, with their puppet house payments and their expensive customer service requirements. Minimizing the branches did not scare them off; neither did high fees. The fact remains that their profit margins remain too low despite all efforts to get rid of the Johnsons. When and how this will all 'flip' remains a matter of speculation and depends on a lot of factors, including political ones.

What is less speculative, however, is that the currencies that will emerge will not be denominated 'Bitcoin', at least not in its current representation. Bitcoin has massively accelerated thinking about this evolution, spawned a multitude of parallel experiments and partial solutions, and has – both on the social as well as on the technical plane, by trial and error – cleared a lot of ground for others in this process. This is the currency's greatest, and most undeniable, merit.

While all kinds of new, mostly net-born formats will continue to arise, large-scale use of mobile money in parts of Africa also provides an interesting *Lehrstück*, one that is not easily transferable to other parts of the world where the existing banking system still has a tight grip on the economy. What mobile money does have in common with Bitcoin is the larger techno-historical movement from banks to telcos. As Bitcoin is 100 per cent internet-based from day one, it does not see itself explicitly as built on top of the telecom infrastructure. Internet and smart phones are the unconscious *a priori* here.

If Bitcoin did not assemble from the beginning such contradictory ambitions, or was 'merely' planned to be a (built-in) payment protocol – for instance, inside HTML – it would be a genuinely bold undertaking. It would be an interesting experiment to strip off its libertarian mining ritual and blockchain religion to see what's left. Right now, crypto currencies are the avant-garde movements of our age. In line with the Zeitgeist, this avant-garde is neither progressive nor artistic (no aesthetics please, we're strictly geeks). But if everything fails, it can always retroactively enter history as an artwork, a true (anti-)social sculpture (so less Duchamp, or Beuys, than neo-Futurism). Indeed, Bitcoin turns out to be 100 per cent technical and entrepreneurial, fuelling growing social inequality – willingly or not. As Nathaniel Popper concluded in his Bitcoin account *Digital Gold*: 'Bitcoin had promised that it would spread its benefits to all its users, but by 2014 large chunks of the Bitcoin economy were owned by a few people who had been wealthy enough before Bitcoin came along to invest in this new system. Most of the new coins being released each day were collected by a few large mining syndicates.'[8] Limited social sculpting indeed.

The Possibility of a Currency Island

There are a host of alternative currency models beyond Bitcoin presently in operation. All depart from the current monetary and financial system in anticipation of fearful futures (from endless stagnation to total collapse). As most desires do when they embrace the Open and start to mobilize social forces, they tend to overlook disturbing realities, while focusing on low-hanging fruits. This usually goes with a longing to withdraw from the political realm, resulting in schemes that irremediably condemn themselves to be either localized or gated. In other words, they cannot scale up to the requirements of large and complex societies. As economist and ex-Greek minister of finance Yanis Varoufakis rightly noted: 'There can be no de-politicised currency capable of "powering" an advanced, industrial society.'[9] It does not make sense to counter this argument with the 'small is beautiful' phrase – unless, of course, one calls for a total overhaul of (or withdrawal from) the current social order, a movement 'back to the land' and generalization of 'de-growth'.

On the other hand, given advances in technology, it seems safe to assume that future money and payment systems will be largely, if not exclusively, digital. This is in fact already the case, but not in the way being envisaged by current proponents of alternative models (who want to keep things in their own hands), nor by the 'big ticket' banks and institutions (that remain wary of such an evolution). For both, Bitcoin and other current (crypto-)currency models are just daring frontrunners; the tech will mature, new brands will emerge – in money as in many other domains – but it is assumed the networked immateriality of finance will universally prevail. Whether gambling with or reluctant to participate in such developments, the predominant worry of the banks is only about not missing the boat. Because the banks share – with considerably less enthusiasm

– the same expectations about 'the future of money' as the libertarian crowd, we can ignore them for now. If one follows through the hi-octane techno-optimism of the *digerati* – the assumption that we will soon be able to make swift and next-to-cost-free payments on the global level, even if not tomorrow – we confront a more tricky, even embarrassing assortment of instruments, with ranges of associated risks, which throws the techno-libertarian consensus into crisis.

The transition from a hybrid, if largely digital, payment system to one that is completely and exclusively digital is not at all an unproblematic idea. On the technical side, there exist a wide range of IT-related issues and potential glitches, which remain unacknowledged (exposed by various mishaps, only to be trivialized, or simply ignored). Even more importantly, such a transition has consequences going far beyond money and finance, concerning our whole social order. Advocates and supporters of digital solutions are unable, or unwilling, to discuss these, since the evolution towards totally networked, 'virtual' systems appears to them so natural, evident, even inexorable. Such an approach is remarkably disingenuous. Libertarians are loath to admit that this 'liberation' into digitality, and of money from the State, already happened when the financial system was, for all practical purposes, privatized in the 1970s. A complete digitalization of currency is merely a technical continuation of this trend. Libertarian gripe is mostly about not being first in line to benefit, before banks and other corporations.

Let's always be clear in correcting the widespread misunderstanding, recently pinpointed again by Saskia Sassen, that 'Finance is not about money.'[10] The financial system has now delinked itself completely from money as it was generally understood and used in day-to-day life by the general public, while at the same time maintaining a one-sided, predatory relationship with it, which forms the basis of its undeserved – and by now, shaky – legitimacy.

Thus, feeling that money has been taken hostage by finance, and fearing a Great Dispossession,[11] as the various brands of believers in crypto-currencies interpret the way the financial system has evolved over the past thirty years, carry the risk of entertaining the idea of a very large-scale confiscation of monetary assets. Such a consensus might even have this as its purpose. According to crypto-currencies' advocates and developers, this threat can be countered with their distributed, algorithmic models that provide fool-proof security against external interference and seizure. This line of reasoning may be technically credible (it might not even be that, but let's leave this discussion to geeks), but it is, in any case, politically, socially and economically very naïve.

The current financial system is in a zombie stage that was entered into many years ago, and this will only become more manifest in the near future. I have argued that a complete overhaul of the monetary system is at hand and that it will not assume the shape of a reform but will be a brutal shake-up that will include a wide range of emergency measures, perhaps including the return of high interest rates, closure of ATMs, disappearance of cash and confiscation of savings. These developments are already underway, in (still) tiny bits and pieces – just ask the Greek Cypriots, or consider what the Argentines experienced before and after them. For many, 'done deals' money is relatively irrelevant and may represent no net worth – as is the case of so-called 'demurrage' currencies. Let us truly open the discussion on whether alternative currencies might be considered parallel resolution instruments rather than tokens of – well, value.

Bitcoiners initially appeared to call not for the internet of the military, telecommunications giants and associated centralized logistics, but for a peer-to-peer assemblage of users who arrange their own monetary rewards: 'No more data centres; welcome back to the Interzone'. That is still its mythology. It is true that the currency realized a tech-solution whereby transactions between individual persons are unhampered by despicable middle entities, such as banks, governments and government regulations, including taxes. But Bitcoiners are clearly not part of the multitudes – and most probably do not want to be associated with them. Their currency is complementary rather than being alternative, while also leaving off political aims to foster local economies or produce values that extend beyond centrally managed capitalist utility (think fair trade, eco-friendly, small-scale, not-for-profit, etc.). For all practical purposes, Bitcoin so far serves the anarcho-capitalist agenda of individual achievement and wealth accumulation in a 'rugged individualist', competitive environment. It offers a partial and temporary future, a complementary and not an alternative currency, after all. Its valuation remains its most baffling issue.

Any Bitcoin 2.0 should be anti-speculative in nature and have built-in mechanisms that prevent extraordinary value swings (both up and down). This will make the currency more user-friendly and prevent not only hoarding but also investors and speculators from entering the field. Bitcoin 1.0 is a speculative currency whose value almost completely hinges on its exchange rates with established, existing currencies, mostly the US dollar. Given Bitcoin's rather remarkable volatility, both short- and long-term, value arbitrage appears a distinctly hopeless proposition, especially for those accepting Bitcoins as payment for real goods or services. In the end, why should 1 BTC, stable in 2009–10 around US$1–5, suddenly be worth 100 times its value? The currency's virtually absent demand certainly does not explain such a rise – only excessive mining for hoarding purposes explains it.

From the perspective of social movements that fight for global justice, solidarity and the redistribution of wealth, the currency's hoarding principle is simply unacceptable. The 'mining' mode of Bitcoin's value accumulation, with its 'first mover' privileges, will have to be replaced by an independent body that issues the coins and sets exchange value in comparison to neighbouring currencies. This doesn't necessarily have to be done by a nation state or even an established international governing body. The critique I'm outlining here is not about redirecting Bitcoin *vis-à-vis* some 'reformist' policy that stamps out the anarchist roots of the project. We do have to make clear, however, that there is simply no way to legitimize this specific alternative finance system's rather sick start-up logic. The logic solely benefits founders and early investors, while leaving ordinary users, and all those who continue to build up the venture, relatively empty-handed, just because they came in a little later. Bitcoin (and offspring like it) needs to go back to the drawing board and come up with genuinely alternative principles of operation that differ from the value-mining principle (and use less electricity).

If you remove mining from Bitcoin, as I would propose, the problem then is always going to be trust. Trust is the major weakness in the Bitcoin model, since it assumes the permanency of powerful, always-online computers / server farms / cloud services that supposedly no one pays for, and does not technically factor in the complex and fragile infrastructure that sustains them. Next-generation crypto-currencies may well do away with the blockchain as the implementer of 'designed trust'.[12] The problem then will be how *else* to position trust – the imperative constituent of any monetary system. At this point, we arrive back at the scalability issue, which basically says that, as the number of participants in a system grows, the need for an impartial, 'enforced authority' (which only needs to be voluntarily accepted) increases, to the point of becoming mandatory. What happens to Bitcoin once we decline its parasitic relationship to infrastructure?

Sooner, rather than later, an unemployed algo army of fin tech programmers, presently on the move because of the hedge fund failures, will invade the digital currency field. We will observe the launch of more and more Morozov-defined 'solutions in search of a problem' – non-working technical fixes for systems that are not *technically* broken. A battle for supremacy between proof-based crypto currencies and trust-based digital currencies, a.k.a. (digital) fiat money, will most likely take place. And this will occur in parallel with experimentations with alternative and complementary money models. In this future 'competitive market of ideas', the algo army will no doubt make the loudest claims that their technically proven model is the only valid approach. But a truly alternative economy requires a different kind of trust. And that trust will mostly be socially distributed and local. It is, therefore, questionable whether a truly alternative (cyber) economy can ever really scale.

— 8 —

NETCORE IN UGANDA: THE I-NETWORK COMMUNITY

Seeking Knowledge to Serve.
Slogan on statue in front of Makerere University, Kampala, Uganda

Normcore[1] has been described as a 'unisex fashion trend character-ised by unpretentious, average-looking clothing', and its wearers as 'people who do not wish to distinguish themselves from others'. Given normcore, what is netcore? Here I define it as the vitalist everyday of network logic, expressed, for example, in incessant, profane dialogue. Trolls might be considered netcore, but it is spam that is its pure sign. What happens when networks become hardcore, catering to this sphere of supra-normality, not just extreme culture. What's the core of a network? Can we note this core form in action? I'm talking here about how net culture works in down-to-earth networks, involving dedicated communities with a clear eye on self-interest, mixed with mutual aid, and kept alive by invisible mecha-nisms in a socio-technological condition we no longer even register in the West as foundational.[2]

African mobile phone culture is netcore. It has been around for a long time, and devices are so widely spread that they've been fully integrated into the busy, and often harsh everyday life of the conti-nent. The progress-oriented 'high-tech' vs 'low-tech' distinctions don't get you far here; dialectics at play between old and new often even surprise the insiders. In this chapter, I am interested in netcore as a style of practice and critique in the Ugandan context in relation to a local ICT community called i-network, a classic email mailing list dedicated to 'knowledge sharing, advocacy and expertise in ICT4D [ICT for development]'. The list is run by a small NGO with the same name, based in Kampala. In my mail program, I have a folder with over 30,000 mails posted to i-network in the period of February 2010 – August 2015 (which comes down to an average of 15 postings a day). The list gives a unique inside view of the everyday troubles of a medium-sized – in terms of IT-industry and internet use – African country (with South Africa, Egypt, Kenya and Nigeria being the largest). The i-network list has over 1,700 subscribers, a dedicated and lively community that discusses general ICT and internet issues in a convivial mood. Flame wars are rare. The atmosphere on the list is surprisingly informal, direct and to the point ('your website is a total mess', 'stop being overly dramatic', 'what is unethical about publishing the truth?', 'how can someone post a message that simply goes ... 'Hahahahahahahaha ...', seriously?'). Most members seem to know each other from start-up firms and ICT-related events in Kampala and are keen to give each other technical advice. In other countries and contexts, this information would be shared through informal chat channels, but in this case email works very well and enables outsiders like me to read and enjoy the Ugandan ICT dialogues.

The i-network list operates as an interface to academics, journalists, policy makers, network operators, freelance programmers, web designers and telecom regulators, all firing questions, comments and URLs at each other. In most cases, the short exchanges deal with the technical specs of software, mobile phones and web procedures such as electronic payments. Some of the list members work at the Makerere Faculty of Computing, or the Parliamentary Sessional Committee on ICT that discusses the Cyber Bills, or the Africa Leadership Institute. Others work as correspondents at the *East African*, researchers at Uganda Christian University, companies like Techsys, SecondLife Uganda Ltd (specializing in the sale of refurbished branded computers), E-Tech, Appfrica Labs, Elmot Ltd, Best Grade (a free school management program designed for use by schools in sub-Saharan Africa and pioneered in Senegal), Eight Technologies, Owino Solutions and non-profits like the Community Open Software Solutions Network. A considerable portion of i-network members work overseas in tech firms in the UK, South Africa, the Netherlands and the US.

The list's high-frequency discourse is denser than life itself. The most discussed topics are mobile phone rates and related issues of coverage, mergers and regulation in the industry, formal and informal ('the company website was registered in March 2015. In 3 weeks they have put a website and advertised 1,000 jobs. You can develop a website in 4 hours. I smell something fishy').[3] What is phenomenal, though, is the range: the first Apps Circus on 21 November 2011; reports from the Digital Africa Summit and the African Network Operators' Group; mobile money scams; medical data delivery by SMS; Internet Explorer exploits; fraudulent SIMBOXs; the growing challenge of e-waste; the value of professional web design; a workshop on Business Process Outsourcing (BPO) Enterprise; laptops being stolen at Ntinda Fuel Station; the Swedish ambassador officially launching Makerere University's wireless hot spots; reasons to promote Linux; Cisco vs Huawei routers; repeated calls for local content; meetings of the Google Technology User Group Kampala; Mobile Monday Kampala; the beginnings of the Mozilla community in Uganda; messages from the Women of Uganda Network; MIT open courseware usage; CEO salaries; the Uganda Linux User Group hosting a party at Guzzlers Pub in Bugolobi to celebrate the launch of Ubuntu 10.04; the first free webmail service ugamail.co.ug; critiques of the PR launch of YouTube Uganda; .ug management issues; the use of PayPal for online checkout; GSM signal jammers; online district maps; the deplorable state of the Uganda ICT Excellence Awards website; how ICT can help reduce AIDS infections; deconstructions of company data promises ('we can't have high-speed, unlimited *and* cheap plans' – Reinier Battenberg); content sharing of the new *PC Tech Magazine* 'distributed in high impact retail outlets, newsstands, airport, gift shops and bookstores Uganda, Kenya, Rwanda, Ghana, and Nigeria' but '72 megs, can you please compress it or host it on a local mirror? It's going to take me about 45 minutes to get it'; mapping landslides; summaries of the Fifth eLearning Africa conference; the Conference on M4D (Mobile Communication Technology for Development); news from the African Network Operators' Group; the 2004 Electronic Signatures Act; frequent job announcements – 'the company Nodesix looks to hire some young talent'. As ICT starts to impact all aspects of life and organization, a list member remarks: 'I've seen stuff on i-network, but this must be the first time I am seeing a wedding budget. There really is a first time for everything!', followed by 'I am looking for power adapters for Cisco IP phones 7900 series for online purchasing.'

I-network was built on the so-called 'development through dialogue' D-group software, developed by the (now defunct) Dutch ICT4D agency IICD in The Hague, in a co-organization with the Uganda Communication Committee designed to promote 'knowledge sharing' in the lead-up to the 2003 and 2005 World Summits on the Information Society. From such origins, i-netter activity appears most netcore when negotiating so-called 'research agendas' and memes within political, infrastructural and technical frameworks of the real-time Ugandan everyday. In December 2012 I paid a visit to the i-network office in Kampala where I was received by its 'content manager' Margaret Sevume and other staff. The trip had been arranged by a former student of mine at the University of Amsterdam, Ali Balunywa, an experienced journalist turned ICT consultant for the media and NGO sector. Ali is my age. Sevume explained how i-network's primary focus was to advocate for ICT use and policies at a time when ICT as an agenda was still new in the country. Later on, i-network also started to carry out consultancy and implementation of ICT projects. In order to consolidate, i-network set up nodes on networked education, health, agriculture and livelihood, youth and journalism. Initially, these nodes had separate lists but what eventually proved the strength of i-network was to bring them together. Sevume:

> Because ICT cut across all sectors, it was easy to bring players from various fields on board. All sectors do benefit from ICTs' ability to increase efficiency and effectiveness. At times, the mailing list is used for people with complaints against ICT service providers because complaints are expeditiously addressed when shared through this list. All ICT service providers have a presence on the list so that they can pick up issues and attend to them.[4]

I-netters, as the list members call themselves, also distribute addresses of fibre cable suppliers and attend meetings on internet freedom in East Africa. Someone remarks, 'I sent a student to buy me air time'; someone else, that BarefootLaw has won the Facebook Page of the Year award. Others discuss tips on how to track a conman, prepaid roaming charges in Burundi, a report from the Ugandan Communications Commission on tackling unwanted SMSs, and whose site had just been hacked by a group called Indonesian Cyber Freedom. They comment in group form on a draft Data Protection and Privacy Bill, make calls to share individual and company experiences with vendors, and want to know how to unlock a DVD player, or express their feeling about failed services: 'I am depressed by Umeme Ltd [an electricity supply company] the way they conduct their duties towards our Community in Kasambya.' Another member asks: 'There are many case of malaria here of which I need to map using GIS system. Where can I get such application, and how much does it cost?' In late 2014, WhatsApp was discussed as an additional i-network channel but was kindly rejected by the office: 'We appreciate the swift responses associated with WhatsApp but feel that it is not quite suitable for serious knowledge sharing issues.'[5] WhatsApp groups are currently limited to 100 members and lack subject lines, which makes them notoriously messy. Not much later, the list moderator warns: 'And next time you have a function that needs fundraising such as your child's baptism, please do not do it here.'[6] On WhatsApp (owned by Facebook) entering the local market, Edgar Mutebi remarks: 'Telecoms in developing nations have invested heavily, often at great risk, in GSM network that will soon become redundant. I personally feel WhatsApp should compensate our telecoms since they are benefitting from their (telecom) investment.' This prompts Jude Mukundane: 'The world is moving towards smarter systems – that means less people, smaller computers, less physical space so inevitably companies have to downsize.'[7]

The i-network is a 'digital natives' community in which sharing knowledge, rather than affect, coolness or resentment, is the central fulfilled need. Printer parts are more important than emoticons. One member, Green Mugerwa, reminds the list of the value of their participation: 'We applaud your efforts to ensure that ICTs positively impact on our lives.'[8] Its younger members are mostly IT and NGO professionals, not teenagers or college students.[9] The tech news that is regularly shared is primarily US-focused. At some point, Daniel Okalany asks: 'Can someone please tell me where piracy laws are in this country? I don't seem to have heard of anyone being arrested for illegal software/music/movies. Are they existent?' The list moderator responds that 'Microsoft goons fly in occasionally and help the cops kick down a few doors. Other than that, I don't think there's any enforcement.' Statistics say that 83 per cent of software in East Africa is pirated. The country's (relative) absence of help desks and other customer services is clearly related to this, as is the need for i-network in their absence.

Another issue frequently raised is the value and use of recycled computers. While Uganda is planning to reverse its ban on imports of used computers, Kenya is joining Zambia in prohibiting what authorities allege are old PCs being dumped on their markets by developed countries. Semakula Abdul: 'I think for starters like Uganda, banning used computers will stall the development of the ICT sector. Our society is so in love with cheap items.' Also discussed is medical equipment and related software for hospitals, such as the Navivision / ClinicMaster debate. Kyle Spencer:

Microsoft charges us $706 per seat for the legacy NaviVision system. This is a bargained down price from a standard fee of ~$1000. Furthermore, they want us to buy in blocks of 15. To illustrate just how much money this is, we recently opened a new clinic in Kololo, which required us to put ~10 computers on NaviVision. The NaviVision license fees accounted for 10% of the entire budget for building and opening the clinic.

Debates and discussions on i-network directly prompt action by policy makers, who are usually 'silent listeners'. Eunice Namirembe, the Monitoring and Evaluation Coordinator at i-network, the ICT4D coordination network behind the list, says about thirty people join the platform every month for various reasons, especially when there is a 'hot' topic under discussion. Interestingly, about 40 per cent of the membership are women, reflecting the trend for so many now to be involved with advocacy issues. Meanwhile, advocates and activists re-entering university to pursue further studies use the D-group for research.[10] One silent listener is Hon. Nathan Igeme Nabeta, the (former) Chairperson of the Parliamentary Committee on ICTs, who follows debates on his BlackBerry. 'It is always important to keep abreast of what is happening in the sector, and i-network has provided this platform for us', he says. It is the same for Eunice Namirembe, who moderates the list mostly through unseen direct exchanges off-list, sending out a public warning every now and then concerning off-list topics and excessive debating. Sometimes, subscribers themselves express their concern that the list is being turned into an advertising forum. Whether or not overall list anxiety will grow in accordance with the ICT business expansion in Uganda remains to be seen.

The only fibre which is worth its salt in Uganda is the Banana Fibre. The disadvantages of Uganda as a landlocked country without direct access to sea cables are obvious. Needless to say, the politics of bandwidth is the number one topic on i-network. We get factual data about ISP pricing, hear about the landing of the third cable in Mombasa (http://twitpic.com/1a69bb) and read discussions on how difficult it is 'building tech companies in the land of dialup'. Back in 2010, it was revealed that Uganda was laying the wrong fibre-optic cable, spending $30,000 per kilometer and $61.6m to cover 2,100 km, with Chinese firms handling the contract. Rwanda, by comparison, purchased cabling according to internally researched specifications and now has a higher bandwidth capacity.

The i-network list also shares information on repeater stations without generators, and shallow trenches used for cabling, which were not sufficient to avoid interruptions by even minor excavations:

> The recommended depth is at least 1.2 meters and within the designated road reserves along highways etc this will typically protect the fiber from culverts and other minor excavations due to road works, where major road works are ongoing it's safer to go deeper as the cost benefit analysis of the Cost of the interruptions vs. the Cost of trenching deeper come to play.'

Raymond Kukundakwe responds: 'You may argue that the cost is exorbitant, but you can't say you are being "cheated" – that's like holding a demonstration outside Spear House (Mercedes Benz Agent) complaining about the high cost of Mercedes Benzes.' Mayengo Thomas Kizito adds: 'People watching Chelsea vs. Arsenal in rainy areas of the country can bear me witness. We all understand that the weather affects digital signals but not for two hours and most importantly during a crucial game like that one.'

Corruption, real vs perceived, seems to dog IT projects in the region. Paul Asimwe: 'The republic is a grand casino ... I am not so afraid to say Ugandans are not interested in Uganda.' If we take productivity losses (because of persistent electricity load shedding) also into account, it's actually very difficult to have a strong ethical and political economic grasp of the overall picture. Or consider this news report:

> Controversy has arisen over a $3.9m contract awarded to M/S Cyber School Technology solutions by the ministry of education. This comes two days after donors cut support to the sector over alleged corruption and mismanagement in the sector. The proprietor of the company, Mr. Keneth Lubega is the chairman of National Information Technology Authority-Uganda, and MPs on the ICT committee allege that Mr. Lubega could have used his influence to win the contract.[11]

The connectivity outages dealt with on i-network are rarely so mysterious, and can be easily traced back to the precise source of trouble. While solutions are each time eventually found to be satisfactory, the frustration remains. See here the bandwidth dialectics, Ugandan style: 'Two years ago, we were used to slow internet, we never complained. Now that we expect better, it seems that it has become slower' (Joshua Twinamasiko). The submarine cable company SEACOM[12]

> still does not give any ISP a service level agreement and because of that what we have recently witnessed, it is clear why they don't. They had promised redundancy on the fiber cable that runs to Mombasa for quite some time now and the time to deliver has moved to the end of the week. This having been said, they have been plagued with vandalism on their fiber, equipment failure and yesterday a routing problem.
>
> (Letter to Datanet.com customers, 16 March 2010)

'It almost feels faster to walk to pick up a page than to get the bytes delivered to me by my ISP' (Stephen). A little while later, SEACOM is down for five days because of a broken cable somewhere around the Seychelles. Members express the fear of overemphasizing these stressors on-list: 'the network is losing its sense of existence if all we do is point fingers at which ISP is at fault'. Joshua Twinamasiko puts the anxiety in perspective: 'Internet may be a basic of life (1M link is a human right in Finland where over 95% of the population have internet access), and important in efforts to overcome poverty, corruption and potholes, but it's not yet a reality in Uganda. First give people food, shelter, electricity, then you can talk about internet being basic.'[13]

Related to access is the debate over the status of content, and where it ends. Whereas for some this might be a chicken 'n' egg question that, at least in the West, is assumed to have been 'dealt with' (especially in the late nineties), the list captures rich philosophical and everyday business-level discussion. One i-netter writes: 'Providers such as MTN, Warid, Zain, UTL and Orange all bring connectivity to parts of the country. Not content (they don't do content, they don't know how, it's not their strength). Voice is not considered content the way we understand content today. SMS is not considered content the way we understand content today.' Others contradict this: 'Voice is content, SMS is content, electrical current passing over a wire is content. All give connectivity and, by extension, infrastructure providers a purpose' (Kyle Spencer). Reinier Battenberg responds by saying:

> Voice is not considered content so far, as it's vaporous. It disappears right after it happened. It also tends to be 1–1. The web on the other hand is 1–many and 'content' is stored. It's a whole 'new' (mark

where have you been) paradigm. Storing & sharing content allows content to be transformed into 'information'. Information creates (or even is) economic value.

If the network is down, nothing happens anyway: 'I have over 200 staff members on Airtel CUG but for now a week we cannot communicate and work in Mbarara town. The network is too pathetic' (Thomas Kizito).

The question often discussed is how to kickstart a rich, local internet culture. Do you have to wait for higher bandwidth to reach a critical mass? Do you set up a geekish/engineering-driven start-up scene first, which can provide the emerging users with basic code? Or would you rather emphasise the development of content first? Local apps first? And then the nationwide 4G network? Or? Reinier Battenberg asserts:

> Local content has to be started and then we can track progress. We are the campaign. Every single one of us. If you don't know where to start: create a Wikipedia page about your cultural heritage. Tip: there is no page for *Kwanjula* [local engagement ceremony] yet. Map your neighbourhood. Go to www.openstreetmap.org create an account and off you go. www.walking-papers.org has helped me greatly mapping mine. Create a Facebook page about a subject that is close to you and find others that think alike.

Local apps play an interesting role in this context as accelerators of local content production, and, even while – strictly speaking – about content, perhaps they are a promising way ahead.

My engagement with Uganda dates back to November 2008 when five Dutch new media students at the University of Amsterdam first came together and decided to conduct their MA research in Uganda and write their thesis about it.[14] The students were enrolled in the one-year master's course 'New Media & Digital Culture', which was part of the media studies track inside the humanities faculty at the University of Amsterdam. The program granted neither a business nor technical degree, nor did it lead to international relations or development studies qualifications. Instead, what the emerging discipline of new media was capable of researching – and which the students knew about already – was the cultural and critical dimensions of internet and mobile phones. Their research priorities and methods were assuredly distant from the fashionable 'lead' theory topics in Europe at the time (e.g. 'object oriented ontologies', 'next natures', 'New Aesthetics'). The field trip that the students undertook in April–June 2009 was designed overall to forge beyond the usual (suspect) development rhetorics, to explore instead what Uganda's actual practices looked like, outside of market hype, NGO discourse, government reporting and so-called 'digital divide' data.

After the students' thesis research was completed in early 2010, we reassembled as a group and started organizing the idea and framework of a publication. The Institute of Network Cultures had just started the Theory on Demand series. Publishing the outcomes in Kampala had already proved difficult to arrange from Amsterdam, so we decided to shorten, edit and collect together the individual projects, along with a general overview chapter. In this, rather than synthesizing the five papers, I emphasized my own motivation and our emerging framework for conducting 'post ICT for development' research. Independent 'ICT4D' critique was the topic of the first-ever course I gave at the University of Amsterdam back in 2004/5, during the UN World Summit on the Information Society in Geneva and Tunis. At that time, I took part in a collective intervention into this field with the Incommunicado network, one of the first INC research networks. Incommunicado ran parallel to my involvement in the Sarai new media centre in Delhi. Since then, I have stimulated more students to do their MA research overseas. Following the five members of the New Media Research in Uganda group, Rikus Wegman studied the use of ICT in Zambian high schools, Pieter-Paul Walraven investigated the Chinese internet industry, Ellen de Vries and Fei-An Tjan worked with media activists in Brazil and Colombia, and Jidi Guo witnessed the arrival of 3G smart phones in urban China.

It was in late 2005, during the second meeting in Tunis of the World Summit on the Information Society, that I was exposed to issues in Uganda via that country's delegation, who were kind enough to adopt me as a fellow traveller for a couple of days. I was not only impressed with the self-confidence of the group as engaged civil society agents (a few had become official members of the delegation) but also interested in the large role that government agencies were playing in the country in the roll-out of ICTs on top of a rapidly emerging telecom sector. Despite Africa having the lowest overall ICT penetration compared to the rest of the world (11 per cent), Uganda is in the African Connectivity Top Ten and enjoys impressive growth rates.[15] What struck me also about the Uganda delegation was the warmth and informal character and the open communication between the different 'stakeholders' such as government bodies, companies and NGOs. In most countries, this 'multistakeholderism' is mere ideology. As I was rather sceptical about the 'corporatist' nature of such 'social-governance' constructions (society as an organic body has such a fascist history), I thought it was an odd coincidence that I could see such coalitions in action. Was I perhaps tricked or enamoured by cultural differences that I was unfamiliar with?

The contradiction of 'development aid' has been a research interest of mine since my very first political activities in the mid-seventies.[16] For me, the 'ICT4D' rhetoric most often works as a mirror, a detour operation through which it is possible to investigate the essence of unevenly distributed technology in a present where functionality and vital access to information via new media have become more and more overshadowed by marketing, celebrity and corporate dictatorship. Ever since 2005, media studies has followed the same shift away from general claims and demands voiced in policy reports, towards the actual expansion of telecommunication infrastructures and the creation of new media markets on a truly global scale. The Solaris and Incommunicado networks in which I was involved (2002–10) criticized the roll-out of telecom infrastructure from a deconstructivist post-colonial policy perspective.[17] This took in the ideology critique of the 'good intentions' of Western NGOs, followed the companies involved in the wiring of the 'rest' of the world to e-waste dumping, and outlined cognitive justice and the already mentioned 'multistakeholderism'.[18] The projects with Sarai, and even more so the Wikipedia research project Critical Point of View at INC, together with the Centre for Internet and Society in Bangalore, were all collaborations – collective efforts to go beyond the rhetoric and methods of development (aid).

Since 2005, the critique of development – already well established decades ago from Fanon on, and through later scholars such as Arturo Escobar – has reached the mainstream. Titles from the most recent generation of development critique include *The White Man's Burden* by William Easterly (2006) and Dambisa Moyo's *Dead Aid: Why Aid is not Working and How There is Another Way for Africa* (2009). My own formative content cloud would include Linda Polman's investigative journalism into the role of the UN and emergency aid, including *We Did Nothing* (2003) and *The Crisis Caravan* (2010), and Renzo Martens' video artwork *Enjoy Poverty* from 2009 (and related projects in Congo). Widely screened at festivals, in museums and on TV, *Enjoy Poverty* was an artwork in the form of a video documentary calling for Africans to take media representation into their own hands, and to sell their suffering directly by leaving out the NGO middle man, thus taking over the production means of aid income. It is no coincidence that this 'critique of development' has all but disappeared in the wake of the global financial crisis and the rise of the BRIC countries.[19] Since 11 September 2001, development budgets have been handed over to private players such as the Gates Foundation and large multinational NGOs acting as government contractors, which have more similarities to global logistics companies than to grassroots social movements.

In the first decade of the 2000s, an already justified critique of the development and emergency aid industries started to coincide with the militarization of aid after 9/11. At the same time, rising of right-wing populist demands to radically cut back spending of development aid by Western countries became mainstream policy in the West, while countries such as India refused to receive development aid, and China became a major player in the development game itself. Meanwhile, the scholarly-activist work around ICT for development made some progress – for example, Richard Heeks' 'development informatics' methods.[20] The bytesforall email list and related efforts that came together at the 2010 London and 2012 Atlanta conferences on ICT technology and the internet in the development context (www.ictd2010.org and www.ictd2012.org) remain active. I wonder how many of us still follow the progress reports on Nicolas Negroponte's 'One Laptop per Child' project? As is often the case in the period of implementation, the fanfare around good intentions tends to disappear from the headlines, not even showing up on Facebook timelines or Twitter feeds. More recently, public attention once given to 'ICT and development' has shifted to the rise of Chinese infrastructure projects in Africa, the Ebola issue, and the ever-growing presence of Islamist Jihad groups such as Boko Haram, which grew off the newly established telecom infrastructure.

Mobile phones are the social tool of the 'post-colony'. This sticky term introduced by Achille Mbembe has stayed with me ever since I read his book *On the Postcolony*. In an unpublished transcript of the interview Bregtje van der Haak made for Dutch television broadcaster VPRO and Tegenlicht in Johannesburg on 22 February 2015, Mbembe described the internet in Africa as a 'total social phenomenon', penetrating well beyond the rising middle classes: 'They understand themselves as part of a broader world. Africans are aware of what is going on elsewhere in the rest of the world.'[21] For Mbembe, the internet has a cosmopolitical impact: 'The function of religion is to preach salvation. This function is now played by technological forces.' The companies that are dominant in this field are no longer imperial but hegemonic, and operate out of enclaves, the offshore, the zone, which Mbembe elaborates as a segmented, zebra-like globe. Mobile technologies are not at all alien to African cosmologies, 'in which a human being was always a bit more than a human person and could metamorphose into something else. He or she could become a lion and then a horse or a tree. The philosophy of the new digital technologies is more or less exactly the same as ancient African philosophies.' Mbembe references here the novel *My Life in the Bush of Ghosts* (1954) by Amos Tutuola, an account of someone who keeps changing from one form into another: 'The internet responds directly to that drive. If you want to have any idea of the world that is coming, look at Africa!' Africa is here a laboratory of institutions and practices where, according to Mbembe, virtual movements were entangled with the real well before the digital moment: 'African societies constituted themselves through circulation and mobility, through movement. Migration occupies a central role in all African myths of origin. There is not one single ethnic group in Africa that can seriously claim to have never moved.'[22]

Instead of applying yet another ICT4D critique, in the African context I try to listen to what is actually out there in an attempt to do post-colonial research that is not (again) only focusing on plugging the latest concepts and products from the West. I was very curious to listen, read and form new questions from what's going on in Uganda, the Commonwealth neighbour of Kenya, where technology trends follow the nearby and internationally more visible hub of Nairobi. Call it the 'ethnographic turn' but what fascinates me are places where technology uptake has a sovereign element and takes off in its own direction. In other words, mobile phone and internet users in Africa are not just consumers. It is a cynical approach to see only either market opportunities or policy victims in the history and culture of an ICT install. Increasingly, people start to take matters into their own hands and develop their own websites, software, apps, and this led in Africa to the phenomenon of (among other things) mobile money. Not only can African netcore cultures speak for themselves here, and already do so without representations (like this one) that return to, or began in, the West. It's also important to emphasize

121

their fun and drama working with tech – that this net core, like any-where else, can be as annoyed as anyone else about software mishaps, failing connectivity and corporate lock-ins. Finally, we've left the cliched 'you can't eat phones' attitude of paranoid and benevolent Western media theory 'spokespeople' behind.

The rate of the 'mobile' roll-out is mind-blowing. Africa as the 'last frontier' is said to be the fastest-growing mobile phone market in the world – the biggest one after Asia. The number of subscribers on the continent has grown almost 20 per cent each year. Former Nokia researcher Jan Chipchase: 'In parts of Africa they're talking about a 4G rollout next year. The speed at which that just becomes part of the landscape still manages to surprise. It's progress. Whether it's good or bad, it's progress. It just is.'[23] Chipchase observes that a lower-middle-class, 21-year-old woman in Nigeria now has a Black-Berry as her first phone: 'What used to be strictly the domain of the "Wall Street Warrior" is now an accessible accessory.' The trend to emphasize real-existing new media practices, instead of time-and-again repeating digital divide statistics, can also be found in the study by the Centre for Internet & Society (Bangalore) and Hivos (The Hague) entitled *Digital AlterNatives with a Cause?*[24] The main finding here was that ICT is not merely a fashion amongst youngsters, even though young people are indeed the main drivers of market expansion, and experiment most when it comes to social media deployment in political protests. The term 'digital natives' is both a reference to a particular generation (born in the 1980s and later) and a positive-productive attitude towards technology, media and social networking by both young and old.

Becoming familiar with the i-network community over the past years has made me wonder at what point the compacted ICT-telco-NGO-government network culture in Uganda might erode – if ever. The separation of powers and spheres might be a Western fiction anyway. Will local academic media and communication studies even-tually also step in and present their research outcomes in such a forum? Academia has so far been surprisingly silent in this context. The same can be said about design, nor does there seem to be much local conversation around screen aesthetics. Web designers are out there, but when will their own handiwork, in terms of aesthetic interfaces, become visible and publicly an issue? Or will the global tech aesthetics remain a given, lacking any African layers? What about the Voice of the People? Needless to say, for now, i-network is most focused on infrastructure, regulation and the business side of new media in Uganda.

Meanwhile on i-network we read that Mobofree.com, an African social marketplace, has announced that the number of registered users in Uganda has increased by more than 1,555 per cent.[25] The post that follows reads: 'I would like to set up a VPN for about 70 health facilities within Uganda. If you can supply the service, inbox me.' Then it is raised whether all members of parliament need iPads. Someone asks who is tracking stolen cell phones. A novum: there is an app that 'keeps you up to date with fuel prices in your area'. The list also debates the building of a 30-storey hotel in China in 15 days, and the required communication level of English for IT engineers there. Besides complaint posts, there are also reports like this: 'I watch streaming TV (Netflix, Hulu, etc) in Gulu using internet from Zoom Wireless. Their quality is great and with prices starting at UGX 110,000 for unlimited, uncapped service it is definitely within reach. Their speeds are amazing as they connect directly from Gulu to Mombasa via submarine fiber from NITA Uganda's national backbone and tier one carriers' (Brian Longwe, 2 May 2015).

While visiting Uganda, I was keen to observe the mobile money system as up-close as possible. Ali took me to the headquarters of telecom providers that offered mobile money services, such as Airtel ('Helps your Money do More'), where we managed to talk with in-house researchers. They confirmed that they closely monitored developments in neighbouring Kenya, where M-Pesa originates from.[26] Kenya is not only the most mature market in terms of uptake. It is also advanced in terms of additional services, such as 'pay your utility bill on the go' savings accounts, which attach to your phone and include the possibility of transmitting money overseas via Western Union. Speculating about mergers is one thing, and in Uganda there is plenty of reason to do this … but most impressive for me was a visit to an actual MTN Mobile Money booth located somewhere in a slum. There it was possible to watch actual transactions happening in front of your eyes. While I stood below a billboard advertising 'Orange: Best Network – No Congestion', the simple ASCII green interface of the mobile phones indicated to buyer and seller how much credit was registering. Young kids dropped in daily with cash to be wired into their friend's phone. The number and nickname of the local official agent was on display next to the toothpaste and cold drinks. The woman who ran this shop got out a tablet for me and showed the account overviews of all the money that had moved in and out of the booth that day. She ran three booths, across Kampala, and travelled between them, while keeping an eye on the transfers in the other two, on the same tablet, in real-time.

Besides this, visiting one of Kampala's very few dark and dusty bookstores turned into an interesting experience, when I found the small corner on 'Development', with titles such as *The Aid Trap*, *Foreign Aid after the Cold War*, *Ending Aid Dependence*, *The Trouble with Aid*, *How to Manage an Aid Exit Strategy*, featuring most prominently Lee Kuan Yew's *From Third World to First: Singapore and the Asian Economic Boom*. Tellingly, the internet section only carried marketing titles such as *Social Boom!*, *Social Networking for Business*, *Brilliant Online Marketing*, *Guerilla Social Marketing*, *The 22 Immutable Laws of Marketing*, *No Bullshit Social Media* and *The Advertised Mind*.

Ali also took me to see his brother, the Principal of the Makerere University Business School. I shied away from an invitation to give a course to MBA students ... this wasn't really my prerogative. We then went to the library in the main building to see the computer labs, reading rooms and the bookbinding department. Makerere is in the top ten of African universities, and students from all over the continent go there to study and do research. We dropped into Media & Communications and found out they indeed offered some courses on internet research. In a surprising ceremony the next day, I handed over the Alexandria Project offline library to the chief librarian of Makerere, a project developed by Toronto-based scholar and musician Henry Warwick, who developed the concept of the offline library as part of his Ph.D. at the European Graduate School – the first Ph.D. I ever supervised.[27]

In the Western development context, mobile money runs under the rubric of 'financial inclusion'. It remains a question, however, whether and in what contexts access to financial services such as savings, credit and insurance could be called a human right. What is the relationship of the monetization of the billions to the Decline of the Rest? Expulsion, as Saskia Sassen calls it, is a managerial strategy to withdraw services from common people, who have been written off as customers and are considered ballast which 'smart and lean' companies should get rid of. It is one thing to say that the poor are excluded from the global economy. On the other hand, the global financial sector has such a bad karma that it's a strange proposition to demand 'full' participation in it. While Kofi Annan has prioritized attention to 'the constraints that exclude people from full participation in the financial sector', we still need to be wary about what this entails.

What does 'financial inclusion' look like in the context of decades of mergers, branch closures and job losses?

If we discuss mobile money, it is a straightforward observation that the telecom sector has jumped into this hole with a service that has considerably brought down transaction costs. While rhetoric can easily lead us to portray the thriving mobile money sector as a technology-driven autonomous one, the dirty reality behind the scenes is different from this. Mobile money is not just a do-good proposition. It is a fast-moving industry that provides services to hundreds of millions in Africa and Asia. In terms of its omnipresence, it is not comparable at all to micro-credit initiatives, whose user communities are quite small in comparison.

Someone on the i-network list noticed that, during a Kampala conference, the vast majority of content accessed by local users was hosted overseas.[28] The high dependency on content and services from elsewhere is reflected in the danger of local content providers dropping off altogether from global web rankings – such as Alexa. The same can happen to mobile money. What some see as successful local solutions can make foreign online services invisible – a.k.a. non-existent – for outsiders. Also a severe problem is the hot, and often humid, climate that affects IT equipment and infrastructure. Africa will have to look for 'local solutions in order to ensure data sovereignty and efficient network performance. Reduce cooling needs. Using free cool air at night to pass through the conditioning systems; or exploiting ground-source cooling are both mechanisms that can make a significant difference to the electricity that is needed to cool a data centre.'[29] The African ICT infrastructure will also need to take into consideration 'earthquakes, tsunamis, volcanoes, heavy rain, high temperatures, fires, epidemics and floods'.

In the words of an i-netter, 'For every challenge a digital solution can be found. But is then the problem approached at its root?' The critique of development rhetoric has always been one that was sceptical of messianic solutions. Moving beyond the provision of anomic technical solutions is a widely shared desire in Africa, and proof that Evgeny Morozov is both right and wrong: on this continent, his critique of 'solutionism' had already been voiced decades ago. On the ground at the Community Computer Centre in Kasambya Sub-County, Mubende District,[30] the work of Morozov most relevant in Silicon Valley and Europe seems to be somehow common knowledge. This makes it a much more convivial effort to work on 'net criticism' in Africa. Referring to the digital divide – though this is alive in many places – is no longer a potent strategy. The situation is no longer captured by access vs. no access analyses. It is speed that is decisive – and how much one is willing to pay for it. If technology never quite works the way it was intended, the role of criticism is going to be a different one from the start. The hard work of deconstructing the tech agenda can easily be skipped through, and we move in a much more socially attuned sphere of mutual aid, as the netcore attitude of the i-netters so successfully proves.

— 9 —

JONATHAN FRANZEN AS SYMPTOM: INTERNET RESENTMENT

We were complicated enough to build machines and too primitive to make them serve us.

Karl Kraus

Wer denkt, ist nicht wütend.

Theodor Adorno

The American writer Jonathan Franzen is known for 'grumpily critiquing everything from the looks of classic female authors to the Internet at large'.[1] In his translations of Karl Kraus for contemporary readers, this 21st-century Spengler dares to compare the vicissitudes of Windows Vista to Vienna before the First World War: the Decline of Empire is at hand. *The Kraus Project*, from 2013, consists of three major essays by the Austrian playwright, poet, social commentator and 'satirical genius', translated by Franzen and supplemented with annotations by him and two other literary critics. Fascinatingly, the PR for this book gave no indication that the majority of the novelist's footnotes upon Kraus' texts would consist of an eccentric, 21st-century media critique. The novelist ventriloquizes sections of the text, to pose whole other statements about what Kraus' (or Franzen's) opinion might be on, for example, Macs and PCs, Twitter's contentious political value in the Arab Spring, and the impact of media power on Western democracies.

The muteness of net critique in global culture and mainstream art is the argument running through most of this chapter. The Kraus book is not Franzen's first – or even most famous – effort at media critical commentary. Distaste for media tech runs throughout his *oeuvre*. He once wrote on cell phones, sentiment and the decline of public space for *MIT Technology Review*.[2] He momentously fumbled his way, in a series of interviews, out of an invitation to Oprah's televized Book Club – a media event in itself that enabled him to speak as an anti-corporate rebel against a range of contemporary things, excepting his own sections of the book industry.[3] In early 2012, Franzen made headlines again by attacking e-books and Amazon, essentially updating his prior anxiety about corporate tele-vized book culture to include more recent media changes. He said: 'the difference between Shakespeare on a BlackBerry phone and Shakespeare in the Arden Edition is like the difference between vows taken in a shoe store and vows taken in a cathedral'. Arguing that e-books were damaging society, he stated:

> Am I fetishising ink and paper? Sure, and I'm fetishising truth and integrity too. I think, for serious readers, a sense of permanence has always been part of the experience. Everything else in your life is fluid, but here is this text that doesn't change ... *The Great Gatsby* was last updated in 1924. You don't need it to be refreshed, do you? It's like making believe there's another kind of sex. There isn't another kind of sex. There isn't another kind of book! A book is a book is a book.[4]

Giving his rants an explicitly anti-capitalist twist, he confessed: 'The technology I like is the paperback. I can spill water on it and it would still work! So it's pretty good technology. And what's more, it will work great 10 years from now. So no wonder the capitalists hate it. It's a bad business model.'

Franzen repeatedly talks about the internet as a pernicious organi-zation of stupidity. These warnings against online culture, of course, enrage swarms of tweeting hipsters. For the more mature baby-boomer media columnists – salaried spokespeople with supposedly anti-elitist sense – this infamous social media absentee is an easy target, an unappreciative smart guy who got stuck in modern old times they personally overcame. Who does he think he is, taking up so much opinion space on something he hates? The novelist fulmi-nates against the latest digital gadgets and aims hard at the big tech monopolies. He's particularly concerned about the internet being dangerous for the people who write serious fiction – its producers – which is a valid practical Sloterdijkian worry: 'I know writers who use computer software that denies them access to the internet during working hours. I use noise-cancelling headphones when it's loud at my office, and, for me, email and digital voice mail are vital tools in restricting and managing the flood of communication that modern technology has unleashed.'[5] Clearly, he is no Luddite. However, unable to switch off computers, tablets and phones, he dramatizes his angst most clearly when he lunges for (contradictory) autonomy and moral high ground: 'I am enchanted with everything about my new Lenovo Ultrabook computer except its name. Working on something called an IdeaPad tempts me to refuse to have ideas. I don't mind technology as my servant; I mind it only as my master.'[6] He also speaks actively against his dismissal as a Luddite: 'when I was intemperate enough to call Twitter "dumb" in public, the response of Twitter addicts was to call me a Luddite. Nyah, nyah, nyah. It was as if I'd said it was "dumb" to smoke cigarettes, except that in this case I had no medical evidence to back me up.'[7]

Franzen is assuredly not a net critic. But right now he is one of the few people saying anything in the popular international Anglo press about the internet who are getting mass-circulated. Almost all of the philosophers remain silent; there are very few who step up to take an interest in, let alone a position on, debates about its present governance, operations and futures. The ones who do write with any sophistication about its impact on culture are mostly European, and quite marginal also in Europe. In Franzen's head, in Continental Europe, writers still have a hold on the public intellectual consciousness of a culture – this is what he assumes, while the crisis of finance capital is also unfolding on the Continent, impacting worshipped civilizational 'centres'. But intellectual authority has never really been technologized – not anywhere.

The internet is just not a Big Topic of this age, not even indirectly. I am focused on this, and I am no literary critic by any means. Kraus, whom Franzen uses to write his anti-net critiques, is also not one of my preferred twentieth-century authors. He never wrote about technology or the media of his time at the level that Benjamin did, for instance. What I am interested in is how something resembling criticism blurs with media tech awareness in this writer's grasping at a (however outdated) authoritative critique of the fully technologized twenty-first century. My curiosity was piqued further to go through his *oeuvre* and the related chatter online, when, after reading his writing on net culture, I found out that he was less than two weeks older than me. As both members of the in-between, post-punk generation, defined by stagnation and depression, neither hippies nor yuppies, I recognized a certain will of a shared generation – to find one's own way, desiring autonomy, in a way that borders on the crankiness of the loner. Having grown up with a typewriter, the personal computer appeared in Franzen's and my early twenties – while we embraced it carefully, we both remain ever ready to confront any inner bad intentions of the Machine. So what that he is sometimes misguided or plain wrong with his highly consumed (and just as often rejected) analyses? It is easy, and irrelevant for me, to fact-check him. The geeks have already done this; you can find all that online. Nor am I critiquing or appreciating his novels. Whether or not a next apparent Great American novel can be written about the internet for these times to come is also not really my concern. Nor is the question of whether the internet industry lacks common interests with the publishing elite. I am interested mostly in why and how his cultural productionist rage against the internet machine stands out, with a specific inbuilt cultural logic. In this, Franzen is just one figure through which to think the otherwise ongoing rejection and disappearance of net culture and criticism from our mediated everyday life.

What stands out most, from my view as a net critic working in the time of Franzen's mass circulation, is the always 'secondary' nature of his internet complaints. Twitter or Amazon has never been the central topic of any of his essays. The clear taboo in our media culture (and education) against addressing the internet topic in a direct fashion started to fascinate me with regard to his work. One can make indirect remarks about the internet, but one has to stay away, as much as possible, from the 'internet writer' label (or internet artist, theorist, critic, etc.). Franzen's remarks on media tech are often implicit, which is a too-obvious sign of a repressed resentment of the digital. Would it hurt his literary career if he was a more forthright critic of new media tech? He's a great white American Novelist, really an endangered and much-loved species. So no, not at all! It is precisely this confused modality of 'net resentment' (c.f. net critique) – on the one hand, a legitimate registration of negative affect about the current state of the internet's economy, and, on the other, a libidinal economy of indirect affect notorious *across* net culture for never taking up its issues with the right objects – that Franzen traffics in. Amidst the continued uptake of his media-critical novels, with net resentment having become so ordinary, this is what I find so important to deal with in his commentary.

To be even more explicit, let me say that, twenty years after Pit Schultz and I launched the Nettime initiative in 1995, I wonder whether we can say that much progress has been made with regard to 'net criticism'.[8] I make this comment not without reservations – bearing in mind, for example, that it took two decades after the birth of early cinema for film criticism to start to take shape as an emerging field (around 1912). In the founding years of that new medium, it was virtually absent. Pioneering years are always exciting, but always insignificant for outsiders; this is still the case. Where are the great critical works on internet culture? Since 2008, dissenting voices have mainly spoken out from the industry itself; critique remains not so strong from academia, nor from the literary field. Of course, I would love for a next epic novel that changes our attitude towards social media. And wouldn't it be significant if a writer like Franzen had something important to say about American internet culture?

Franzen is most sincere and convincing when he talks about relationships. Along the lines of Sherry Turkle's *Alone Together*,[9] his *oeuvre* laments, in particular, our intimate relationship with smart phone gadgets as they replace direct engagements with others. All electronic devices – so says Franzen – are designed to be 'immensely likable', in contrast to the product that is simply itself: 'The ultimate goal of technology is to replace a natural world that's indifferent to our wishes – a world of hurricanes and hardships and breakable hearts; a world of resistance – with a world so responsive to our wishes as to be, effectively, a mere extension of the self.' According to the logic of techno-consumerism, Franzen says, 'our technology has become extremely adept at creating products that correspond to our fantasy ideal of an erotic relationship, in which the beloved object asks for nothing and gives everything, instantly, and makes us feel all-powerful, and doesn't throw terrible scenes when it's replaced by an even sexier object and is consigned to a drawer'.[10]

Following Andrew Keen's social media analysis in *Digital Vertigo*,[11] Franzen points out the narcissistic tendencies of social media:

> Our lives look a lot more interesting when they're filtered through the sexy Facebook interface. We star in our own movies, we photograph ourselves incessantly, we click the mouse, and a machine confirms our sense of mastery. And since our technology is really just an extension of ourselves, we don't have contempt for its manipulability, the way we might with actual people. To friend a person is merely to include the person in our private hall of flattering mirrors.[12]

And then there is the significant problem, infinitely repeated in Franzen, of actual love:

> Suddenly there is a real choice to be made, not a fake consumer choice between a BlackBerry and an iPhone, but a question: Do I love this person? And, for the other person: Does this person love me? This is why a world of liking is ultimately a lie. There is such a thing as a

person whose real self you love every particle of. And this is why love is such an existential threat to the techno-consumerist order: it exposes the lie.'

Franzen is fascinated by the hazards of relationships, noting that, 'Even Facebook, whose users collectively spend billions of hours renovating their self-regarding projections, contains an ontological exit door, the Relationship Status menu, among whose options is the phrase "It's complicated." This may be a euphemism for "on my way out", but it's also a description of all those other options. As long as we have such complications, how dare we be bored?'[13]

While he is anxious about the narcissistic mis-connect of youth in public media space, Franzen's critique of participatory net culture stands out for being adamantly non-participatory. Like a streaker in a square – and, indeed, any novelist – he tends to dump his material and run away back to the security of his one-way regime. During one of these media-dump-and-run controversies (regarding Twitter of all things), Maria Bustillos appealed to Franzen that he 'really ought to come online and talk with everybody. Come on in, Mr. Franzen! The water's fine.' But, so far, such calls have been in vain. Franzen has been accused of being a hypocrite who prefers only the in-crowd, a writer who shows off his superiority in the old media towers. Regardless, Bustillos writes (with an appreciation for media affects that Franzen never shows): 'He may be a dork but he's our dork.' Indeed, when Franzen is convincing, it is because he can still hit the cool hipsters in a tender spot, pointing out the intellectual and spiritual poverty of creatives 'who buy what they're told rather than rage against the machine, who are too infatuated with their wonderful little toys to look up from them while the world burns'.[14] Still, another internet commentator remarks: 'The web is to him what a lamp post is to a dog: something to spray with his urine while sniffing contemptuously at the scent left by others.'[15] The scent may be remembered, but it remains an act without consequences. Is this fair? I'm not sure. The greater question is whether it is interesting, or critical.

Can this ageing 'media-sensitive', known for his novels *The Corrections* and *Freedom*, make claims of being a 'net critic'? No – but, as I said, that is not the point. He is also not the Thomas Pynchon of this hipster age, nor its in-depth techno critic *à la* Nicolas Carr. What stands out again and again is the very strain of his agitation: 'If you choose to spend an hour every day tinkering with your Facebook profile, or if you don't see any difference between reading Jane

Austin on a Kindle and reading her on a printed page, or if you think Grand Theft Auto VI is the greatest *Gesamtkunstwerk* since Wagner, I'm very happy for you, as long as you keep it to yourself.'[16]Again the implicit references to our technological condition, hanging upon a neo-Kantian backdrop. Why can't such a repressed revolt against digital trash be played out in the open, and discussed in-depth? Is the network architecture of Google, Twitter and Facebook not important enough, or is there actual public anxiety now about hitting this power too directly? Or is it presumed so technical that our writers can't deal with it? Or is it just the old high (literary criticism) versus low (social media) division playing out as usual?

If, in Continental Europe, the writer still has a grasp on the public intellectual consciousness of a culture – which is debatable (but true if compared to the US) – then, having grown up in St Louis, this responsibility may be Franzen's craving. Being aware of his early provincial position, the writer-turned-celebrity certainly does play a particular role in the US tabloid press – which is where aggro most often heads home to roost. But Franzen is not exactly known for tackling the Biggest Topics of our time. Instead, he's got more the image of a 'happy hater'.

There are so many reasons that both net culture and net critique are not valued in contemporary media spaces and art industries. Through platforms, the net has been naturalized and obfuscated as a foundation of our digitized being, while the continued disconnect of tech from (academic and other) political economy thinking leaves the commentariat to debate nineteenth-century moralities across increasingly virtual opinion pages and networks. In Europe at least, the art scene, however infrequently, will discuss this fact of the weird absence of net knowledge and critique. In the gap left by the absent facts, I contribute to provocatively framed booklets and essay collections, such as *The Internet Does Not Exist*, edited by the e-flux contemporary arts gang.[17] In my work as a net critic, these never-internet positions of our contemporary culture both are essential to focus on, and have become increasingly weird for all of us to navigate. Franzen captures the conundrum even when – or perhaps especially when – he is slightly off the mark.

To look into Franzen's world is to journey into the ordinary lives of America's stagnating middle classes.[18] His fiction lacks the hyped-up superficiality of the slightly younger Doug Coupland, who describes media-saturated environments in existential McLuhanite slogans. Franzen refrains from advertisement babble entirely. To use a term by Leon Wieseltier, when we're reading Franzen, we are 'among the disrupted'.[19] The disrupted are the late adopters who neither supported nor objected to Silicon Valley and willingly take up digital products and services once the hype is over. Technology reaches disrupted users via a predetermined course of events. 'Check out the Web site. I'll give you the address. "The implications are disturbing, but there's no stopping this powerful new technology. " That could be the motto for our age, don't you think?', the main character Greg in *The Corrections* is told. We read a similar sense of technological destiny in the following passage, also from *The Corrections*:

> Among her favourite books was *The Technological Imagination: What Today's Children Have to Teach Their Parents*, in which Nancy Claymore, Ph.D., contrasting the 'tired paradigm' of Gifted Child as Socially Isolated Genius with the 'wired paradigm' of Gifted Child as Creatively Connected Consumer, argued that electronic toys would soon be so cheap and widespread that a child's imagination would no longer be exercised in crayon drawings and made-up stories but in the synthesis and exploitation of existing technologies – an idea that Gary found both persuasive and depressing.[20]

Successful in post-9/11 culture (*The Corrections* was launched six days prior) but set in the 1980s and after, Franzen's 'slow novels' are written in a Balzac-style: his 'multigenerational American epics' are filled with the streams of consciousness of worrisome characters that are lively yet unstable, in which not all that much happens. If anything, most events occur in the past. From a media perspective, the virtual absence of modern communication is notable. The protagonists do not have their televisions on (as in most households), phones do not ring, there are no faxes or computers, nor even the occasional skimming of newspaper headlines. Needless to say, our heroes do not receive text messages either, let alone check Facebook on their smart phones in the elevator. What sounds unusual – if not liberating – at first starts to become somewhat unrealistic, if not old-fashioned, when we progress further into the story each time. The fact that the writer doesn't want to be disturbed[21] doesn't mean his characters should be demi-gods that have mastered all the contemporary temptations (let alone that the reader should be assumed to be part of this Sloterdijkian normal). There is an element of nostalgic tourism in this style: the novel takes you away – it feels no urge to represent.[22]

In *The Corrections*, we still find an author registering postmodernism's doubts regarding the usefulness of criticism, its possible genres and too-familiar privileges:

Criticising a sick culture, even if the criticism accomplished nothing, had always felt like useful work. But what if the supposed sickness wasn't a sickness at all – if the great Materialist Order of technology and consumer appetite and medical science really was improving the lives of the oppressed; if it was only straight white males like Chip who had a problem with this order – then there was no longer even the most abstract utility to his criticism.[23]

The question at stake here – also for Franzen – is whether American Negation tends to manifest itself as a Culture of Complaint. Rants that deserve the label 'critique', voiced in mainstream media outlets, by default play out in the US like a scandal of sorts. The act of speaking up alone can be shocking and seem too deeply personal: 'There must be something wrong with this guy. What's he raving on about?' But it is important to read criticism also from a media affects perspective, and appreciate Franzen's presence as a kernel of anarchic affect shared much more broadly, against the internet's current operations and workings.

I prefer to measure Franzen's sentiments against Peter Sloterdijk's considerations in his 2006 book *Zorn und Zeit* (*Rage and Time: A Psychopolitical Investigation*). In his philosophical reading of these concepts together, Sloterdijk states that in Europe literally everything of any philosophical, cultural importance began with anger.[24] The tract contributes much to contemporary debates about the role of (histories of) affects in politics. These days, anger is no longer a divine capacity, exclusively possessed by heroes and rulers such as the Greek figure of Thymos. The all-too-human desire for recognition is now expressed by the online billions – and properly stored in databases, to be read by Google bots and other software, intelligence agencies and other authorities.

Is there still a place for the authentic outcry? How can we distinguish genuine uproar from the cult of resentment[25] witnessed in today's internet forums? Is Franzen's critique of internet monopolies neutralized by being labelled as fury so that, in the end, ordinary users will remain unruffled by valid criticism – so they can continue to click and like? The military–entertainment complex frequently delivers us spirited, 'engaged' celebrities who accompany us only ever momentarily to sites of injustice. Far less often do fiction writers act as if they are wrathful gods. Is Franzen's anger a call for revenge? Do we know any more how to hate with dignity? Or, to put it a different way: how can we grasp for any authority on what matters, in a world with a multitude of channels and opinions?

Rage is a modality of energetic force; Nietzsche called it the Will to Power. Is this how we should think with Franzen? Or should we rather, with Sloterdijk, see Franzen's desperate attempt as part of a movement of dispersion? 'The rage, so it seems, no longer wants to learn.'[26] I argue that resentment in the age of the internet – already a complex affect – should additionally be thought of in technical terms. Most events these days are social media events, recorded and transmitted by smart phones. *Kultur* is now techno-culture. However, few are prepared to make such an analysis. This even includes scholars growing up in the digital age, who continue to reduce the world of ideas to a tree-like structure of hermeneutics in which one book author refers to another. It is much easier to trace a conceptual history back to Nietzsche and the old Greeks than it is to understand the content fallout of interactive applications and their networked implications.

These days, technology facilitates individual wellbeing and wealth creation but no longer provides society with public infrastructure that everyone can use. In *The Corrections*, we read the following: 'Things cellular were killing public phones. But unlike Denise, who considered cell phones the vulgar accessories of vulgar people, and unlike Gary, who not only didn't hate them but had bought one for each of his three sons, Chip hated cell phones mainly because he didn't have one.'[27] In turn, this loss (or never-arrival) of privileges is what creates Franzen's characters' resentment, their constant looking for a way out. Emerging in the absence of a clear enemy, resentment grows out of a diffuse feeling of discontent that can be neither forgotten nor properly processed. Uneasy memories replay and get stuck in a loop. The compulsive repetition of motives[28] is a necessary precondition for resentment to build up: 'We love the internet, but it's stupid.' This vengefulness is not the kind that seeks revenge. Rather, we are talking about a drawn-out state that only in the last instance can fully express its discontent. In the case of social media, there is often not even a clear object of disgust. Rage as an affective disposition can only express itself within a (fake) nihilistic framework. We might see Franzen's characters not just as angry mini-Franzens but as the author's tracking of a very real problem of unprocessed impasses in our affective relationship to a hard-core digital ordinary. A next step would be to decouple the 'thymotic' (meaning 'spirited' in Greek) instincts as they are expressed online from the (today mostly dominant) legal discourse of 'freedom of speech'. The current internet discourse can only pose the tensions of spirit and representation in one-dimensional binary terms: either you're allowed to express

136

whatever you say, or your contributions need to be regulated and ultimately forbidden. This legalistic over-determination of media culture reflects the skewed power position of lawyers and consultants in Western business culture. Is it possible to oppose this legal dead-end street with a 'spirited' techno-philosophy? According to Jeffery Bernstein, Sloterdijk's work on rage runs the risk of having devised 'an empty concept without an object'. In my view, this is because Sloterdijk, as with so many of his generation, remains detached from, for example, Twitter's 'shit storms'[29] (Google explains: 'a situation marked by violent controversy'[30]) and other ugly battles of today's comment space. The ideological clashes in the blogosphere and on internet forums are heavily male-centred and focused on religion and celebrities (Franzen being one of them).[31]

Goldberg characterized Twitter as 'a machine that runs on rage':[32] 'You see something that disgusts or infuriates you. Tweeting about it provides momentary relief, followed by the brief validation of the retweet. As you scan your feed, you take in other little microbursts of nastiness. So you get angry all over again and respond, perpetuating the cycle.' Goldberg refers to a study of Weibo (the Chinese Twitter) which found that angry messages spread faster than any other kind. Goldberg noticed that she preferred reading despicable news in easily digestible ways: 'The easiest way to write for the internet is to take offence. Twitter rewards ideological policing.' Franzen's anger, on the other hand, remains diffuse. He's frustrated, like so many of his generation, about missed opportunities ('another internet is/was possible'), without being able to zoom in on specific issues or solutions beyond his own profession. With Michelle Goldberg, I'd say that Franzen lacks a sense of bad online affects, such as that a Twitter shit storm can be objectively horrible and destructive, but can be a true experience, especially for an historicist.

In an interview with Manjula Martin, the real issue for Franzen was not the internet as such but its addictive nature – as he phrases it: 'the tipping point you reach where you can't get away from the electronic community, where you become almost physically dependent on it'.[33] In the same interview, Franzen asks why Apple shareholders should be getting rich while working journalists are getting fired. Much unlike the techno-libertarians, he proposes the internet should be regulated:

the way the airwaves used to be. If an entire region of the country has its main industry suddenly lose 90% of its paying jobs because of the predatory practices of a different region's industry, you might, if you were the government, step in and say: 'We can't actually let the entire region starve. We're going to subsidise prices, we're going to redistribute some income.'

The revolt against the unholy alliance of hippies and yuppies to screw up the world on display here does not take into effect the disappearance of the Keynesian model of the interventionist state now replaced by neoliberal policies. But what appears as a justified critique should transcend sentiment and become an informed statement. Concerning internet criticism, we could say that Franzen needs to match a technical understanding of software and interfaces with insights about the political economy of IT, telecoms and the state of the art of capitalism itself.

The political alignment and analysis at play in Franzen's 'buried' internet rage have come out most clearly in his 2013 multi-layered translation project called *The Kraus Project*. Since his early twenties, Franzen has had a fascination with the early twentieth-century Viennese critic and *Die Fackel* editor. The book is divided into three parts, with the original German text of Karl Kraus' essays on the versos, Franzen's translation on the rectos, and a good half of the text below a dividing line reserved for his raving footnotes on the state of US internet culture. This footnote engagement mirrors the secondary, informal treatment of social media in Western culture, which are not considered primary forms of expression by the official culture industries.

In an article in the *Guardian*, Franzen explains the background to his interest in the work of the Viennese satirist, tracing it back to the time he studied in West Germany. He talks about a certain kind of world anger that seems without a primordial or historical source, and far from punk. The anecdote he uses to explain the link between his 22-year-old self, Karl Kraus, and his aspirations as a critic, is both weirdly upfront and completely oblique. On one particular afternoon in April 1982:

> I was angry at the world in a way I'd never been before. The proximate cause of my anger was my failure to have sex with an unbelievably pretty girl in Munich, except that it hadn't actually been a failure, it had been a decision on my part. A few hours later, on a platform in Hannover, I marked my entry into the life that came after that decision by throwing away my coins. Then I boarded a train and went back to Berlin and enrolled in a class on Karl Kraus.[34]

The footnotes go back farther than this to include memories of Franzen's early computer use in the 1970s and early 1980s. Somehow Kraus helped with that too:

> Immersing myself in Kraus in my twenties helped inoculate me against technology envy. I internalized his distrust, even though, in the early 1980s, technology to me meant little more than TV, airliners, nuclear weaponry, and the minibus-size computer at the seismology lab where I worked part-time. Because I'd used computers in high school and college and was an early adopter of computerized word processing, I've persisted in the quaint conviction that technology is a tool, not a way of life. The metastatic and culturally transformative technological advances of the last two decades have struck me as vindications of Kraus's warnings. In 1910 he was already not impressed; and his work showed me the way to not being impressed myself. But even I am not immune to feelings of dread and, yes, envy when I see books being routed by electronics in the sexiness contest.[35]

It is hard to tell where the actual objects of net critique and the rationalization of the critical disposition in general begin and end.

Through a fairly straightforward Decline of Civilization trope, Franzen compares the United States after 9/11, its consecutive failed wars in the Middle East and the 2008 financial crisis to the Austro-Hungarian Monarchy under which Kraus lived: 'Vienna in 1910 was a special case. And yet you could argue that America in 2013 is a similarly special case: another weakened empire telling itself stories of its exceptionalism while it drifts toward apocalypse of some sort.'[36] There is both a spatial and temporal displacement, and formalization of negative, impassive affects here. Franzen likes German culture because it is uncool. He prefers German solidity and intensity over any new-wave romantic frivolity. Kraus is a role model, but not because he didn't care about hipness: 'He was a sophisticate, and this is one reason *Die Fackel* has a bloglike feel.' Retro-activating Kraus as a blogger does not prohibit Franzen from saying more:

> The tyranny of niceness in contemporary fiction is enforced by terror of the internet and its ninth-grade social dynamics. Writers afraid of running afoul of the bloggers and tweeters, of becoming universally 'known' as not a nice person, can defend themselves with laudable sentiments: literacy and self-expression are good, bigotry is bad, working people are the salt of the earth, love is more important than money, technology is fun, gentrification is a serious issue, animals have feelings, children are less corrupt than adults, and so on.[37]

Real artists have a character and personality, but this quality is no longer recognized in society: 'A lot of good writers have lately been fretting, mostly in private, about what it means that they can't interest themselves in Facebook and Twitter. I think it means that they have personalities. This feels like strangely meagre consolation, though, when you see the rest of the world giving itself heedlessly to the new technologies.'[38]

No one in the serious European intelligentsia or commentariat would come out flagrantly to say that the internet is so irrelevant or superfluous. They wouldn't, because they are too cautious to make a *historical* mistake. The German and French elite, it is true – more so than others – are more ready to think about the net or net culture as something that comes and goes like a fashion. But there is no one who actually writes publicly about the net as a fashion. This is also the curious difference with Franzen. For the European intellectual, the best thing is always to ignore the net, and that is indeed what most of them do – rather than get something wrong from their positions of respected hermeneutic expertise 'otherwise' (or right for that matter, I have no historical investment in proving myself right 'over' the non-media intellectuals – I wish, on the contrary, that this were not an issue). Franzen is interesting therefore also because, in his cravings to 'be European', he really tries to say something about contemporary (net) culture that a European would not say, and in ways that they would not engage with.

Franzen asserts: 'Kraus spent a lot of time reading stuff he hated, so as to be able to hate it with authority.'[39] This is likely how Franzen wants himself to be perceived, as a contemporary literary authority in a blog-proliferated world: 'By most accounts Kraus was a tender and generous man in his private life, with many loyal friends. But once he starts winding the stem of his polemical rhetoric, it carries him into extremely harsh registers.'[40] But what is Franzen's more specific purchase on media tech and net critique here? Theatre critics need to be passionate about plays and actors, and they need to know its history. Is this also the case with Franzen and the internet? Does he really care about the medium at issue? Is he, for instance, ready to dig deeply into 'platform capitalism' as a redistribution of work and a destruction of skills, resulting in monopolistic tendencies?

According to Franzen, the substance of our lives is total electronic distraction. As a result:

> we can't face the real problems. ... What we can all agree to do instead
> is to deliver ourselves to the cool new media and technologies, to Steve

Jobs, Mark Zuckerberg and Jeff Bezos, and to let them profit at our expense. Our situation looks quite a bit like Vienna's in 1910, except that newspaper technology (telephone, telegraph, the high-speed printing press) has been replaced by digital technology and Viennese charm by American coolness.[41]

And who has time to read literature 'when there are so many blogs to keep up with, so many food fights to follow on Twitter'?[42] Complaining about Salman Rushdie, who 'succumbs to Twitter', Franzen also rightly attacks the magazine n+1 'that neglects to consider the Internet's accelerating pauperization of freelance writers and lashes on lefty professors who call the internet "revolutionary" and happily embrace Apple computers and persist in their virtues'.[43] These are the contradictions we want to know more about. How can we make these convulsions more productive and liberating, without creating a personalized culture of guilt? Step one is always to see that you're not alone; step two is to know that there are alternatives. Maybe it's not the task of public writers to walk us through these steps?

Franzen raises the real question of why net culture itself has techno-culturally reached this 'resentment moment' – in the way it is talked about so 'secondarily' in public media. From this unfocused, displaced and secondary position, popular net critique has become somehow dangerous, contagious, while being 'potentially' transformative of nothing. Why, indeed, are people consuming Franzen when he is sometimes wrong or contradictory in processing complex fin- and political tech? I am not interested in proving him wrong, but in trying to understand this phenomenon – the way American culture, as global mainstream culture, mostly refuses to deal with the internet, while it is at the same time the obsession of the majority of its subjects. How do we work through this resentment politico-philosophically, and specifically with regard to the objects of net critique?

A central analytical theme here is the under-acknowledged history and theory of tech in the long-term withdrawal of culture as the central meaning-provider in society: 'Around 1908 Kraus came to believe that our technological capabilities and our imaginative faculties were going in opposite directions – the former going up and, as a result, the latter down – and this thought really scared him.'[44] Culture is replaced by technologies. Says Franzen, echoing Morozov's critique of solutionism:

Techno-visionaries of the 1990s promised that the internet would usher in a new world of peace, love and understanding, and Twitter executives are still banging the utopianist drum, claiming foundational credit for the Arab Spring. To listen to them, you'd think it was inconceivable that Eastern Europe could liberate itself from the Soviets without the benefit of cell phones, or that a bunch of Americans revolted against the British and produced the U.S. Constitution without 4G capability.[45]

It has taken decades, centuries, for the Western bourgeois class to build up a sophisticated self-understanding of its own culture. Such a differentiated language, however, is still lacking when we're challenged to engage critically with the 'temples' of engineering culture, which, so far, have only been dealt with in straightforward technical-business terms.

Franzen redacts Kraus in stating that the invention and implementation of technology has become an automated process that lacks key conscious elements of decision-making: 'Nowadays, the refrain is that "there's no stopping our powerful new technologies". Grassroots resistance to these technologies is almost entirely confined to health and safety issues, and meanwhile most of our waking hours [we are] texting and e-mailing and tweeting and posting on colour-screen gadgets because Moore's law said we could.' Franzen links this to harsh neoliberal policies:

We're told that, to remain competitive economically, we need to forget about the humanities and teach our children 'passion' (to use Thomas Friedman's word in a 2013 Times column) for digital technology and prepare them to spend their entire lives incessantly re-educating themselves to keep up with it. The logic says that if we want things like Zappos.com or home DVR capacity – and who wouldn't want them? – we need to say goodbye to job stability and hello to a life-time of anxiety. We need to become as restless as capitalism itself.[46]

Franzen makes an important link here between the world of commodities and the jobs we end up doing. There are no gadgets without consequences. Our devices provoke a lifestyle and are not simply the result of personal choice. We do not buy these products as a reward but equip ourselves with them first, and then enter the world – and afterwards read it in a different way.

In the fragment that follows, Franzen finally formulates his own thesis:

For Kraus, the infernal thing about newspapers was their fraudulent coupling of Enlightenment ideas with a relentless and ingenious pursuit

142

of profit and power. With techno-consumerism, a humanist rhetoric of 'empowerment' and 'creativity' and 'freedom' and 'connection' and 'democracy' abets the frank monopolism of the techno-titans; the new infernal machine seems increasingly to obey nothing but its own developmental logic, and it's far more enslavingly addictive, and far more pandering to people's worst impulses, than newspapers ever were.[47]

Everything digital comes from within, and this embeddedness inside the neoliberal subject makes it that much harder to investigate what the nature of this new power is all about. This quality is why McLuhan's metaphor no longer applies to us – media are no longer extensions, we've incorporated them. The techno devices have become so small, so familiar, so intimate, that we can no longer distance ourselves from them and hence have so much difficulty critically reflecting on their influence.

Franzen writes:

> The sea of trivial or false or empty data is thousands of times larger now. Kraus was merely prognosticating when he envisioned a day when people had forgotten how to add and subtract; now it's hard to get through a meal with friends without somebody reaching for an iPhone to retrieve the kind of fact it used to be the brain's responsibility to remember. The techno-boosters, of course, see nothing wrong here. They point out that human beings have always outsourced memory – to bards, historians, spouses, and books. But I'm enough of a child of the sixties to see a difference between letting your spouse remember your nieces' birthdays and handing over basic memory function to a global corporate system of control.[48]

What's memorized is no longer information but bodily repetitions and gestures. These are the most difficult 'addictions' to combat – such as checking your smart phone in the elevator.

Karl Kraus then is not just a historical escapade. Still, Franzen's use of him becomes more contentious in the historical analogies that it does produce. Franzen writes about how reading the *Boston Globe* back in the 1980s was self-inflicted punishment and training for him in reaching Krausian levels of responsive commentary.[49] He aimed already back then to 'make a larger apocalyptic argument about the logic of the machine, which in Kraus's day was still localized in Europe and America but has now gone global and is accelerating the denaturisation of the planet and the sterilization of the oceans'.[50] In linking Vienna 1910 to America a century later, Franzen is claiming that both are moments of negative immanence, situations in which,

143

according to Ezra Pound, a culture is being the antenna of human-kind's civilizational regress, and all signals say the Empire is going to fall. But, importantly for us, these are only cultural signals of collapse – they are on the level of affect, there is no proof, and much performativity. To state the obvious, Kraus actually witnessed Empire's decline and fall, with all its consequences (Hitler, etc.). Neither Franzen, you nor I will witness the fall of the US empire in our lifetimes. The US empire and its installed regimes is still strong and very much in charge. But even if it is not literally falling, it is falling apart because of internal contradictions (not because of opposition, or because its rulers are tired). Franzen appears in this sense an artistic antenna and committed performer of symptoms, expressing a reactivity that I think is widely shared. Kraus is a means to this goal, as Franzen is mine.

As I outlined in chapter 6, America is going through its Picketty moment. This is acknowledged by the most conservative pundits: the middle class is shrinking, and the polarity between rich and poor is increasing. Assuredly, ten years ago, this level of consensus would have been not only impossible but also completely taboo as public opinion. Now, because of the overwhelming evidence, even conservatives warn that the dream is over. But the thing is, the system hasn't fallen apart. Franzen is trying to capture this; however, this new ordinary is not so continuous with the eighties aesthetic of decline, when the industrial music in the rust belt corroded away the early sheen of the young decade. In a way, we've already moved well beyond the affects associated with industrial decline, about which, not coincidentally, Franzen wrote so beautifully in his first bestselling book, getting inside the head of the soft old patriarch of the modern US railway system. Now, the might of China is a fact; the reality that all industries have left the US is a sad truth. This is not nostalgia anymore, so even the affect logics of Franzen's early work have melted into air.

In one of his signature warnings of dramatic decline, Franzen sidesteps realities of networked political economy to fix his view upon the world of book publishing. 'Apocalypse, after seeming to recede, is still in the picture', Franzen remarks:

> In my own little corner of the world, which is to say American fiction, Jeff Bezos of Amazon may not be the Antichrist, but he surely looks like one of the Four Horsemen. Amazon wants a world in which books are either self-published or published by Amazon itself, with readers dependent on Amazon reviewers in choosing books, and with authors responsible for their own promotion. The work of yackers

and tweeters and braggers, and of people with the money to pay somebody to churn out hundreds of five-star reviews for them, will flourish in that world.[51]

But defending the borders of professions is going to be a matter of collective struggle, Jonathan. Writers should write, and marketers do their PR thing. Agreed. If writers start to tweet, they undermine the division of labour? Instead of defending work relations of the past, we should get actively involved in defining new skills and professions, and refuse attempts to delegate all work to the individual creator.

So what does it really mean to hate today's internet, when you are not talking about its past and present of being *produced*? Franzen's anger is not about a world that we inherited together. It is about a lost opportunity, a slowly growing realization that suddenly hits the surface: we fucked it up. We were not in charge, but are still responsible. What Franzen expresses is guilt about the lost opportunity of building a more intelligent network culture ('Wir haben es nicht gebaut'). We demanded, and practised, media diversity, multiple sources, a new scene devoid of the authoritarian voices of the same old journalist, critic, host, the predictable opinions of monopoly channels – and all we got is Google, Facebook and Twitter. We could no longer tolerate the reasonable, cold reporting of the same old. Franzen mentions that his regular reading of the *Boston Globe* was in preparation for the setbacks of the neoliberal age, in which technical opportunities precisely did not materialize in a more democratic and open 'network society'.

The question of how to estimate the impact of Franzen's arguments is a political-strategic one. His media tactics so far have been entirely old school (appearing on a popular TV show, contracts with a traditional publisher, writing for the *Guardian*, etc.). He tries to influence public debate and, through this, to limit public valorization and usage of social media such as Facebook and Twitter. Franzen even shies away from valuing blogs. In the end, he is satisfied with literary formats such as his much-loved nineteenth-century novel format (his *Kulturideal*), complemented by occasional essays for a magazine or newspaper. This retro perspective weakens his position. Regardless of the direction in which we look – backwards, forward, to the side or downward at the gutter – Franzen's advice goes along with Konrad Adenauer's: no experiments. We even skip twentieth-century literary experiments, as if they never happened.

Franzen once remarked that 'Reactionary theory and revolutionary practice didn't just coexist in Kraus's work: they fed off each other.'[52]

We will search in vain for a similarly productive clash in Franzen's own work: though there are moments of such promise and even some felicity, he has hidden himself too much in the almost invisible everyday dramas of his characters to dig much into today's larger techno-cultural contradictions, between a united world-view and the fragmented overkill of impressions. Big Literature is not a solution for the interactive real-time networked age, no matter how much we love to be entertained by a Netflix TV series and the classic 90-minute blockbusters. Extended experiences do not replace, let alone alter, the real, existing fragmentation of parallel data streams that demand our constant attention. It is not enough to observe that the 'internet and social media are so seductive, so immediately gratifying that you can get carried away from yourself rather easily'.[53] 'We have a responsibility to remain ourselves', Franzen stresses. But what is this self, outside of the big issues of our time? We can hide behind the motifs of the humanistic nineteenth century, but the twentieth century's experimentation in literature, film and visual culture happened for a reason. The famous Self has since been analysed, medicalized, fragmented, deconstructed, amplified, mirrored and regained.[54] It's one thing to identify the undesirable aspects of technological development and say 'no' to them. It is another to take up the aesthetic task of narrating the present – no matter how scattered.

— 10 —

URBANIZING AS A VERB:
THE MAP IS NOT THE TECH

Human movement equals informatics.[1] This is assumed in our digital mobility. Not only are our movements caught by traffic cameras, we constantly provide 'the system' with our location and inform our networks of our 'mobility affects' through social media like Twitter, Facebook, Ping and SMS. We're tracked, we track ourselves, and we keep the data in motion. There is hardly time for data to 'mature'. This is the crisis of the archive as theory and metaphor. In this chapter, I examine the changes underlying mobility concepts from the critical perspective of new media networks and media aesthetics. The work presented here builds from an earlier project done under the 'distributed aesthetics' umbrella.[2] This time my focus is not so much on the object that dissolves through virtualization and digitization, but on movement within dense (urban) networks. The key challenge is to think through the relationship between mobility and IT beyond predictable rhetorics of 'traceability' and 'control'.[3] If the Smart City can now potentially know everything that we do, doesn't this fundamentally alter our ideas of the Smart City? Before we start to design even more 'smart citizen' systems (and related 'ethics') and develop art projects whose ideas will inevitably prototype new shoes, bags, phones and, of course, bikes, cars, trains and planes that track our every movement, it seems necessary to map out some of the critical issues. It is no longer sufficient to complain about visual quality being dissolved through speed. What roles do these (new) aesthetics play?

Defining Urbanizing Technology

How do we understand the notion of 'urbanizing' in relation to technological development,[4] once we take into account that every technology has its boom-and-bust cycle? The city as a metropolis is busy and cool in the model of the city inherited from the nineteenth century (Paris, London, etc.), without networks being talked about at all, necessarily. I would define the current 'urbanizing' meme as a 'second stage' phenomenon after the boom-and-bust cycle of the first 'digital cities' stage has passed. Urban information systems have, of course, existed throughout the twentieth century. The 'virtual cities' wave reached its height around 1995–7, when the implications of the introduction of the internet were discussed – and tested – on the municipal level (without them being implemented because broadband hadn't spread sufficiently).[5] We are nearing the end of this latest top-down 'smart cities' hype. Still, layering technology onto a nineteenth-century nostalgic version of the city of the twenty-first century, many still frame networks as sociological instances, cold tools, infrastructure. Networks are intuitively understood as a scientific meta category, made by and for technocrats to run the world, while presented to laymen as abstract and mathematical shapes. The untimely result is a rational, outdated twentieth-century engineered city concept – ultimately boring, as well as irrelevant. The worldwide nature of the internet is installed in the smart city as a given now. But still, the specific possible relationships of cities to network infrastructures remains ever beyond imagination's scope. What is fascinating, and remains mysterious, is precisely the impact of the network on cities at the local level. The city is a dense ground and readable territory – and it is precisely its boundaries, even without traditional city walls, that make it so attractive as a metaphor to work with.

My question concerning a 'new aesthetic' in relation to today's urban tech is this: is it possible to shift the emphasis of the discussion between artists and scholars of 'the City' from the avant-garde notion of speculative design in the social use of ICT (by early adopters) towards interventions in the political economy of mass use? What happens once information technologies grow beyond their critical mass and become ubiquitous? Traditionally, electronic arts avoided this question in order to focus on the next new things – the Internet of Things, DIY sensors, drones, and so on. Complex info visualizations have been developed, but which of these have been put to any radical grounded use?

There is a dialectic turn once fibre-optic cables have been laid, and wireless signals cover a territory. After digital technologies achieve 'saturation', they no longer retain the same significance. Scale Questions edged long ago towards Global Consciousness models. But can we, ultimately, comprehend what it means that there are 7 billion mobile phone subscriptions worldwide? John Perry Barlow's global connecting tissue from synapse to synapse is becoming a reality – however, this is not properly understood by most. What type of visualization would help us in this? This is the moment where system obesity flips into entropy. What does it mean when availability and access become meaningless omnipresent global concepts? What happens when we make the jump beyond sheer quantity, beyond ubiquitous saturation and reach an as yet unknown synthesis? Time and time again, we have watched the perfect overview lead to indifference, doomed to reappear in the sphere of the collective unconscious. Is the next phase the 'revenge of the object', as Jean Baudrillard speculated (dead batteries, lost connection, a broken cable)? Or will other versions of the social be realized?

Having passed the moment when the smart city moved on from ideology to a functioning machine, 'urbanizing' as a metaphor can be read in a number of ways.[6] We can emphasize the density of its sensors and information points. But we can also read this as a 'civilizing process', comparable – or not – to Norbert Elias' sociology[7] in which social use produces sophisticated rules, gestures, habits and manners, thus overcoming the infrastructural emphasis of economists and techno-determinists. This 'civilizing turn' takes us beyond bare functionality (i.e. the density challenge) and points us towards sophisticated aesthetics and odd everyday uses that do not necessarily break from or question existing protocols (think of the Proustian 'datadandy' app sophistication in the age of the smart phone). Which figures are the 21st-century equivalent of Walter Benjamin's nineteenth-century Parisian *flâneur*? In the late 1980s, we would have suggested the *gestalt* of cyberpunk, but that's too sub-cultural these days. The nineties equivalent would be the nerd, but that is still too marginal, too specifically bound to the emotional economy of the young geek white Western male. What about the busy yet introverted hipster, staring at his or her smart phone? Technology *per se* is no longer an identity provider – it's all about brands. The idea of urbanizing IT needs time in order to mainstream, but will there be enough time? People move on, and so do cities. There is no time for 'locative media' to reach critical mass. Design concepts no longer predate the present, they are made for it if we are lucky, and this condition challenges the already marginal position of theory. Indeed, no matter how fast technologies scale up, everyday rituals need time to establish themselves. This process of tech 'becoming culture' furnishes the opportunity for utilities to take root in society by ignoring over-reported hype cycles – of chic, über-designed, quickly obsolete gadgets produced by the darlings of contemporary techno-capitalism.

Becoming Public (in the End)

Let us put aside the Big Data wave that is part of the 'smart cities' policies, currently (still) in vogue. Instead, I am interested in 'fast data' at the level of users and internet / mobile phone applications, and how this manifests in 'locative media' and the RFID tagged Internet of Things. These are examples of technologies of digital mobility that are passing from the stage of fashionable experimentation to the ubiquitous mundane. Is the omnipresence of GPS devices a sign of total discursive and surveillance power over civilians? When is the moment this technology turns to move into its perverse and pornographic phase? Consider the shift from Google Maps to Google Earth to Google Street View as an example. Which one is the 'innovative moment'? This should be redefined. While focus on economic growth and profit has glorified the genius, tenacity and openness of venture capitalists and 'early adopters', the second moment of innovation happens at the end of the adoption cycle, when technology is ritually integrated into society. What happens when we move *as media*, at this point where the confluence of mobility and communication becomes ritualized? Technology use can turn into a habit remarkably fast. When that occurs, the actuality of tech is pushed into the background and remains undiscussed, even amongst scholars (ignoring knowledge production's dependence on the internet itself). The time this move takes is relative. The typewriter took a long time to 'become habit', the mobile phone less so. There is a speeding up of technological development. The moment when technology use enters its stage of 'collective unconscious' is ironically also the time when techno-architectures like GPS or RFID start to produce their own forms of awareness of 'publicness'.[8] That is the time when people express the need either to design new public spaces or to occupy existing ones. The design and governance of digital spaces of mobility thus comes at the very end of a process of social and technological change. This makes for odd historical coincidences: the moment the PR policies around 'smart cities' begin, we see the emergence of the 'movement of squares' from Cairo and Madrid to Gezi Park and Maidan by civilians, formerly known as users. I deal with the latter in more depth in chapter 12.

150

The Role of Concepts

To make a difference in this domain of techno-politics, it is important to understand the interplay between discontent, creativity, subversion and desire. The venture capital-dominated start-up may be the model of agency that is most commonly promoted, but there are numerous others that are either more cultural in nature, political-sub-cultural, or state and academic research-driven. The gestation period also counts. Where do ideas originate? How do vague notions turn into workable concepts? And how do such concepts become accepted as 'cool' ideas and turned into executable entities? Artists and scholars of the meme claim to investigate this field, but so far this notion of a spontaneous species-evolutionary agency that 'catches on', made famous by Richard Dawkins, has had few serious followers since *The Selfish Gene* came out in 1976. Ars Electronica's 1996 'Memesis' online debate on this issue of mobile concepts did not further the use of the concept much. With perhaps the exception of the 4chan message board, 'memes' remain reduced to those minor bits of vernacular online culture that are born every few minutes, spread across the network, and quickly die.[9] Instead of the biological model of the 'cultural gene', more complex social explanations of general intellect, network pressures and opinion-sharing have needed to emerge to deal with how ideas spread online.[10]

It is important that concepts are scalable – basic and easy to understand but also abstract and general, able to contain complex issues. Examples of concepts that grew out of my own theory–practice are 'tactical media', 'datadandyism', 'net criticism' and 'organized networks'. The concepts that remain, for now, influential in the tech world of networks include 'open', 'free', 'decentralized', 'distributed'. A recent and key concept from the field of politics and design is 'Occupy', developed by the Vancouver-based design magazine *Adbusters* to be coupled with Wall Street first, and then scaled to a universal, connecting an emergent politics with literally everything (from 'Occupy Wallstreet' to 'Occupy the Economy/ Education / the Museum/ Everything').[11] As is the case with any good concept that turns into a name and then a brand, 'Occupy' was already self-explanatory. To return to the issue of digital mobility: how do concepts such as 'urbanizing technologies' play a role in the understanding of our mobility complex, and what do we expect these concepts to do? Should they mobilize the imagination? Drive the development of code? Form the basis of an innovative business plan, or become the corner stone of a new organizational structure?

Critique of Mapping

The most common 'first-response' of the media-savvy to the proliferation of (spatial) information around digital mobility is to create maps and start to navigate the surface. If we view and navigate through the same data visualization more critically, however, the result is often disappointing. Are maps generating (counter-)knowledge?[12] Don't we merely display what we already know: the status quo, in content, software architecture, worldview and aesthetics? To understand digital mobility in the networked age, we need to go further than this, and leave behind the 1990s obsession with flows (the 'eye candy' of visual culture), to revisit fundamental concepts of design and related ethics. Mapping enables the visualization of ideas-in-action, from people who come up with alternatives that supersede the speed of technology. Such approaches can overcome the blind spots of the understandably powerful yet inadequate 'open data' movement. Mapping should be about potentialities and not be reduced to cartographies of the status quo. Maps are never any solution either. As an insular act, open data is insufficient to the task. We need at the very least to question the fetishistic character of the current data visualization craze. What is necessary, in my view, is a new integrated mapping modesty. Societal analysis only ends up with a map – it doesn't start there.

We have to think from within the realm of (sensual) experience – the 'aesthesia' of networked events. How do we, as developers and critics, relate to the experience of the waves of blog postings, podcasts, tweets and Facebook or Instagram updates? Is it sufficient to be able to search them? Have we switched to the 'like economy' ourselves? What if we were to push collectively for a 'wisdom economy' instead? Would it then be possible to become 'information agnostic' and less dependent on the recommendation principle? Can we move away from Google's agenda (manipulating the ranking of search outcomes to the point of uselessness) and work towards integrated 'knowledge engines'? Will it ever become possible to introduce critical insight inside of information systems? Networks cannot be fully studied if seen only as mere tools with schematizations and diagrams. They need to be apprehended as complex environments that are contextualized within the networked ecologies in which they

152

are forming. We are moving from living, analysing and imaging contemporary culture as an information society that is technically underwritten by the computer, to inhabiting and imagining relays of entwined and fragmented techno-social networks (as digital mobility shows). The contemporary popularity of digital forms of distribution is just one indication that new media require a thorough rethinking of aesthetics. Involved in this too would be a decoupling of the twinned concepts of form and medium that have continued to shape the analysis of the social long after their used-by date.

In *Zero Comments* (2007), I summarized the debates on mapping and visualization that occurred under the label of 'distributed aesthetics', through a project that I ran with Australian media theorist Anna Munster. One of our premises was that the slow disappearance of the visual element of networks was underway (in a time of its absolute power and overall presence). Apart from the structural problem of analysing network flows from singular image or data captures, we registered a growing discontent over the 'eye candy' of network visualizations, in which supposedly neutral but wholly useful representations of so-called 'complex data sets' were being produced. Was the disgruntlement that we registered at that moment coming from our own lack of 'visual literacy', or the impossibility of making sense of so much data? The fact that we can, so easily, produce maps of our data is not a sufficient reason to continue this practice. We are not working in some Big Brother war room where all the information from experts is flowing together, being processed to await its destiny inside of a more Major Decision by the Leader, aka the Project Team. Or are we? Have we seen too many bad sci-fi films? Who needs these overviews anyway? What is the future knowledge that we are looking for? Is it hidden in the Big Data Pile, as many digital humanities advocates suggest? Theory has lost a lot of its hegemony and in this temporary lapse of presence, a new movement of data positivism has risen, ready to fill the gap in the name of everything digital. On top of this, there is the more fundamental question of how we should deal with the aesthetics of the invisible in the first place. Making Things Visible may not always be the right strategy if we want to get a deeper understanding of how things work.

Often, info-visualizations are produced without a clear idea of the questions they need to address. How practitioners visualize things (rather than why) and the fascination for the generated object's beauty take over.[13] But how do we deal with the level of complexity that the issue requires? The art of network visualization deals with several limitations: those of the screen, algorithms and the boundaries of

153

human perception. We can read, and understand, only so many linked elements. In order to understand and appreciate network maps, we have to familiarize ourselves with 'cloud thinking' in which we zoom in and out between the relational levels of links, between virtual objects and the 'bigger picture'. This requires the negotiation of pleasurable yet disorientating feelings of being inside the cloud.

Mapping: from Ushahidi to AADHAAR

Let us retain the idea of mapping as a broad gesture, so we can focus on map making in the narrower sense – as the work of producing a (limited) object. Apart from the French initiative Bureau d'Etude (invested in conspiracies, mapping the world of secrets)[14] and the collaborative Wikipedia-type OpenSteetMap, the Kenya-based Ushahidi is perhaps the most well-known contemporary NGO in the area of mapping unfolding crises. Ushahidi is a 'non-profit software company that develops free and open source software for information collection, visualization and interactive mapping'.[15] Any critical investigation of digital mobility as a variable is almost impossible without considering projects like Ushahidi and similar types of civil society initiatives. This is because what Ushahidi investigates is precisely the shady terrain of the informal. It would be interesting to see whether their agenda might be stretched, and also questioned.

Ushahidi is described in more detail as:

> a platform for crowd-sourcing information. Members of the public submit reports that are geo-located and then put on a map. The platform is used in disaster relief, election monitoring and just about any other situation where people need to learn things from one another quickly and concisely. Out of the box, Ushahidi allows people to submit reports via the web, mobile applications, Twitter, Facebook with support for a few SMS APIs as well.[16]

Crowdmap is one of its applications, 'a simple map-making tool, built on an open API, that allows you and the world to collaboratively map your world'. One of the questions that the work of Ushahidi raises is the ethics of mapping itself: whether research can be conducted through observations done by outsiders, or whether the act of observation is itself an intervention into distributed agencies. This question has particular significance for the study of informal urban initiatives and cultures.[17]

A similar discussion, but on a much larger scale, played out in India when some official civil society players and media outlets such as *The Economist* were backing the roll-out of the national ID system, which also integrated fingerprint data (AADHAAR). Smaller initiatives and cyber activists continue to warn against such top-down surveillance systems that are an assault on the privacy and basic rights of individuals.[18] AADHAAR is rapidly becoming the largest biometric experiment in the world.

The strategic questions here are numerous. Do the global poor have to be pushed into official numerical and legal structures in order to create the formal structures for, for example, poverty alleviation? Is the formalization of the informal as a bottom-up strategy even the way to go? And what does it mean if 'the informal' (which has traditionally been seen as equivalent to the offline) is itself already deeply digital and connected? What is the price of the gained visibility of the informal players – for example, in the experience of slum dwellers? Needless to say that Ushahidi, like others, is not keen to discuss these sensitive, strategic issues with strangers. The resistance against AADHAAR in India is pretty straight-forward, and to a large degree based on Western notions of individual privacy. There is an element of NGO 'political correctness' in Ushahidi's official statements, which assumes that (self-generated) maps will automatically empower the user-'victims' and underprivileged. One of the most sensitive issues mapped is real estate property in settlements. Their examples and representations can be moved and used within broader contexts such as data journalism, open data movements, hackathons, etc. How can radical players in this field distinguish themselves from the more interpassive pseudo-activism that never breaks into real space? Ushahidi is bottom-up, whereas AADHAAR utilizes an extreme top-down model. Despite their other differences, what they have in common is the way both initiatives close in on 'the informal'. Here the digital maps, and, while it maps, it notates and becomes a record, and, sooner rather than later, the same digital file has the potential to be a legal document.

More on the Mystery of the Invisible

The opposite of mobility is not immobility or inertia but acceleration. Contradictions and dialectics are no longer the driving forces here. Rather, we need to think in the direction of alternative and changing forms of access and speed. The point is not to disconnect from 'the flow'. Let's see what happens when we remain tuned in and don't log out. What if we start to make unexpected side-connections? We can learn as much from Chatroulette as from the mobilization techniques of Anonymous: in this world of seamless and homogeneous connectivity, the unexpected and unwanted become subversive. Just think of the never properly understood bluedating technology as an example.[19] Bluefriending is interesting because it is voluntary. The defining element of bluedating is the proximity itself. Participants do not depend on the random logic of the dating algorithms that present themselves as rational: 'Here is your perfect match.' Possible social and political versions of 'near sensing' (as metaphor and practice) have hardly been explored by artists and activists, and could radically alter today's atomized mass experiences, perhaps finally catalysing sudden transformations of the 'lonely crowd' into something else. Proximity, in an urban context, can indeed be used for political purposes, as the Hong Kong case of the 'off the grid' (non-encrypted) wireless mobile FireChat app showed during the 2014 Umbrella Revolution.[20]

Can one-off affinity swarms arise out of the blue in order to commit random acts of sense-filled beauty? The smart mobs craze of the early 2000s was cute but hardly spontaneous. We all know that the desire for collective insurgency runs high in the post-democracy spaces with its full trains, traffic jams, filled sport stadiums, and concert halls – random acts of senseless beauty. We sense the energy can go either way: destructive anger or collective creativity. Can we organize discontent in such a situation? How do we connect to the 'sweet stranger'? And how can the social be extended organizationally beyond the known echo chamber of social media based as it is on 'befriending'?

Speeding up social exchanges outside of centralized corporate platforms such as Facebook and Twitter – online or offline – is going to be the technological challenge for years to come. We have to understand the attractive side of short messages in this context – SMS, chat, tweets, status updates, short URLs, pictures on cell phones – without resorting to the paradigm that they are simply 'content' (or 'noise'), but rather to consider them as phatic expressions in the way Bronisław Malinowski once described: a speech act whose only function is to perform a social task, as opposed to conveying information.[21]

Many artists already address the transformative quality of location and geography in a time of heightened mobility where subjects are no longer bound to one place. Transitory existences increasingly constitute and transform the spaces that they cross or temporarily

occupy, due to migration or new working conditions. Human trajectories, and also the traffic of signs, goods and visual information,
form particular cultural, social and virtual landscapes that inscribe
themselves materially in the terrain.

In a directly geographical sense, 'critical mobility' artists and theorists, such as Ursula Biemann, Brian Holmes, Anna Munster and
many more, address the logic of human economic circuits within a
changed world order. In their work, we see the feminized tele-service
industry in India, illegal refugee boats crossing the Mediterranean, or
smuggling routes over the Spanish–Moroccan border. On a different
plane, geography plays the role of a thought model in their work
that allows for complex, spatial reflections upon societal transformations, and changes also to concepts – of borders, connectivity and
transgression.

'(Im)Mobility: Exploring the Limits of Hypermobility'

This is the title of a special issue of the Dutch bi-lingual Magazine
Open!, edited by media theorist Eric Kluitenberg.[22] The context of
its production was a festival Kluitenberg organized in 2010 called
ElectroSmog, which had the explicit aim that all the speakers and
presenters would stay home, use Skype, telephone or chat software
and be financially rewarded for *not* travelling to participate.
The *Open!* issue collates an interesting mix of critical mobility
discourse: the role design plays in ecology and sustainability (by
John Thackara); the 'polar inertia' theories of Paul Virilio (the faster
we go the more we stay put); David Harvey on the 'special effects
of capital accumulation'; mobility within the issue of border politics
and refugees' relation to migration (Florian Schneider); and last but
not least the political meaning of the word 'mobilization', explained
using the cases of the Arab Spring protests in Tunisia and Egypt, in
early 2011.

Different uses of the 'mobility' concept ultimately come together
in the term 'hyper-mobility'. All subjects, objects, processes and procedures in society can – and will – be put into motion. Nothing can
remain the same and stay in its current position. Stability is entropy.
Written a number of years before the birth of the 'accelerationist'
meme,[23] this insight leads Kluitenberg to the conclusion that our
boundless longing for freedom of movement, operative in parallel to
extreme development, may be intensifying to the point of a 'fatal
worldwide standstill'. The real existing growth of traffic, coupled

with immobile bodies, stuck in front of the screen, summarizes the plights of knowledge production in contradiction, and the need for other visions of what critical theory (and practice) might do and be able to articulate. The ElectroSmog festival wasn't a big success in terms of audience, neither online nor in-real-life. Perhaps the event was too conceptual and lacked focus – or maybe it happened, as is often the case, a few years or decades too early. We have belatedly developed an awareness of how much electricity computers and data centres, in particular, consume to go with this. Funnily enough, the use of the ElectroSmog web archive has been significant in the event's aftermath. Elsewhere, we do see a substantial growth of Skype presentations during public debates now that overall bandwidth and speed across the fibres are increasing. Still, the visible, public use of (real-time) video tools such as Google Hangout and periscope.tv somehow remains limited.

Deep Politics of Locative Media and RFID Protocols

Artists, activists and programmers creatively intervene in future techno-politics using 'locative media', and a cloud of diverse technologies and devices, varying from geo-tags for smart phones to Internet of Things a.k.a. the internal architecture of RFID chips. So far, most concerns have focused on the politics of the digital 'traces' of data that travelling objects are causing. Canadian scholar and media artist Marc Tuters narrates the move beyond mere possibilities towards the artistic (mis)uses of tracing technologies.[24] Initially, locative media were defined as solely GPS-based, playfully re-imaging the city with a more or less openly Situationist agenda. Projects like this later absorbed WiFi and then apps for smart phones. Tuters reads the notion of traceability literally: what if commodities could speak about the conditions of labour behind them? Tuters' aim is to radicalize the agenda of the 'collaborative consumption' movement (championed by Clay Shirky and others). No doubt the 'cloud' of new media arts projects that Tuters is part of, theorizes, and reflects upon is part of a 'spatial' turn in media studies, in which the urban environment is becoming 'electronically aware' and is more than just a raw, nostalgic, rusty, post-industrial backdrop for the cinema and digital gaming industries.

In contrast to the rather experimental and open, quasi-subversive agenda of the 'locative' media and its artists, RFID has had a negative Big Brother image from the start. Secretive tiny chips sending unknown messages using proprietary code and closed hardware requires quite some imagination to radicalize. The RFID discourse has emphasized the non-human 'object' dimension *à la* Bruno Latour, to follow automated flows of goods, steered within complex supply chain software. One of the best-informed researchers and activists in this field is Rob van Kranenburg (based in Ghent, Belgium). In 2008, our Institute of Network Cultures published his report on the Internet of Things (IoT).[25] Since then, van Kranenburg has made inroads into the vast EU bureaucracy concerning industry policies and standards. One of the outcomes of his efforts has been the IoT Council, 'a think tank, consultancy, accelerator and forecasting group'. The IoT initiative describes itself as a 'loose group of professionals with different ideas and opinions on Internet of Things'. A virtual entity between a network and a think tank, it could instead be described as a typical example of an organized network. A lot of the work that these changing coalitions of experts, bureaucrats, politicians and tinkerers do is 'protocological' (as described by Alexander Galloway in his book *Protocol*[26]). Ultimately, this kind of attention must be directed to the development of open hardware and open source products. This is where the real desire and motivation amongst activist-programmers lies.

Internet of Things (as a generic term used for RFID tags) is becoming part of a wider tendency of radically integrating material and virtual aspects (think of 3D printers or Hollywood films such as *The Adventures of Tintin*). Lessons are being learned the hard way here by mobile phone hackers and activists – to address the politics of mobile and smart phones you cannot merely invoke (and realize) open standards, it is also necessary to apply this at the hardware level as well. It has proven insufficient to be 'allowed' to develop an 'app' that must first be approved by either Apple (i-phone/i-pad), Microsoft (Windows Phone) or Google (Android). All three use remarkably restrictive criteria. The first free software / open source phone has yet to be developed. Will this first free and open phone also have a crypto layer?[27] And what happens when tinkering inside the Bricolab network is taken one step further and assembles with open source drones, meant for citizen use?[28]

We can distinguish two main blocks of thought on the Internet of Things. The first is a reactive framework of ideas and knowledge, which sees IoT as a layer of digital connectivity on top of existing infrastructure and things. IoT is thus envisioned as a manageable set of convergent developments on infrastructure, services, applications and governance tools. As in the transition from the giant IBM mainframes to the desktop PC-based internet, it is assumed that some businesses will fail, and new ones will emerge. This will happen within and across current governance, currency and business models. Much like other governance examples, this 'reactive' model is working along the lines of a World Summit on the Information Society and ICANN-like 'multi-stakeholder' approach, with three groups of actors: (1) citizens and end users; (2) industry and small–medium-size businesses; and (3) the legal layer of governance.

The second framework is a proactive assemblage of ideas and possible models that sees the Internet of Things as a severely disruptive convergence that will only be manageable with new tools. It wants to change operative definitions of data and noise, from the supply chain level onwards, to enable the sharing of mission-critical services like energy through social networks. In this vision, the data flow of IoT will engender new entities consisting of different qualities taken from all three groups of actors outlined above. There will thus be no more 'users' who need to secure 'privacy' as their sole concern because the concept of privacy is itself distributed through new industry tools. To state this plainly, in this conceptual space, the 'reactive' interests of all three groups are deliberately mixed. Notions of privacy, security, assets, risks and threats are thus culminating in a predominantly 'ethics' model of compulsory relational behaviour. What does privacy look like once privacies and securities are inseparable?

Internet of Things will facilitate the sharing of mission-critical services to bring massive datasets to individuals and groups through open hardware sensors, along the way messing up notions of the 'object' at the level of the supply chain. Here, new objects become involved in dynamic relations that cannot yet be foreseen. But we can distinguish a few levels: Body Area Networks (glasses, hearing aids); Local Area Networks (the digital home with the 'smart meter', the all-in-one IoT gateway a.k.a. data collection point);[29] Wide Area Networks (the car); Very Wide Area Networks (the 'smart city').[30] Whoever connects these gateways in a seamless way will rule the network, while new laws and new mobilities will effortlessly become part of the 'services' rhetoric. The Matrix will undoubtedly be a constant. What affordances we'll have has yet to be designed, and decided, but the choice is becoming clear. The field will be defined by either the old-school CISCO/IBM/Microsoft gated community, or a distributed coalition of open software, open hardware, open data initiatives that collaboratively define the protocols. The nineties dream of a 'governance' coalition between the two forces is still circulating, but not the likely (dirty) reality.

160

To discuss media aesthetics in the digital realm, we cannot merely point at the possibilities (and dangers) of technologies. We need to understand that the general tendency towards localization will always be in vogue, in particular now when desktop PCs are disappearing, hardware is shrinking and invisible networks, hidden in WiFi and walled gardens like Facebook and Twitter, are gaining importance. Our task is not only to explore and engage with the flux of experiments: there are clear choices to be made. It is not enough, either, to reduce our critique to the level of the interface. Media aesthetics covers the entire spectrum of networked ecologies. The problem is that today's technologies are becoming concrete, wearable, intimate, abstract and invisible all at the same time. It is pointless to bend this reality back in the direction and level of the image, only to read and judge it (fantastically) away. Networked aesthetics are distributed for a reason, and we need to leave the multitude of threats intact. For they are there. This is the politics of a complex techno-materialism, in contrast to simple reductions to any ontological essence.

Is space still the number one identity provider? While there is a rich history to this discourse, there are some serious issues and dominant modes of nostalgia surrounding it. We should be duly afraid of locative retromania, much like the retroactivity there is in pop culture (adequately theorized by Simon Reynolds[31])? Do trans-media and other foci such as embodiment and new materialism express a similar retro aspect, back to network theory's 'roots'? From early on, it was all about the triangulated dialectics of space – media – events. In the 1980s, this version of the political materialized in squats, alternative media and riots. These days, (real-estate) space is more costly due to gentrification, whereas the price of media (and data storage in particular) has dwindled. The rise of cheap digital technologies has resulted in a fragmentation of earlier struggles, while activistic media practices and analyses think well beyond ideology critiques of centralized news and broadcasting media. But what has remained as mysterious as ever are the complex conditions under which the Event occurs.

Under the current conditions of the Former-West, urban space has been colonized by capital. It is still contested, but in different ways from 30–40 years ago, when, during the post-industrial era, middle-class families, factories and offices moved out of town. The new frontier is now empty office spaces and decaying postwar suburbs, no longer factories and lofts. No matter how attractive, we should be wary of withdrawing to focus too much on the politics of space alone, giving a false notion of 'reality'.

Take David Harvey:

> The new technologies are a double-edged sword. On the one hand they can function as 'weapons of mass distraction' and divert people to believing politics is possible solely in some virtual world. Or, they can be used to inspire and coordinate political action on the streets, in the neighbourhoods and throughout the city. There is no substitute for bodies on the street for political action as we have seen in Cairo, Istanbul, Athens, São Paulo, etc. Working together with active street politics, the new technologies can be a fabulous resource.[32]

But, as Eric Kluitenberg has proven, today's social movements are already hybrid, with or without bodies.[33] The real–virtual opposition is old hat. The so-called 'real' experiences on the streets and squares of Sofia, Tel Aviv and New York are intensely mediated and discussed across the globe, in real-time, as they unfold. Instead of playing them out against each other, we need to find a vocabulary that expresses the way in which locations, networks and events mingle, in real-time.

A key aspect of the struggle will (always) be the (temporary) occupation of space. It is nonsense to say that today's battles have moved on to cyberspace. Material resources will remain essential. The virtual is material. But how do (occupied) spaces communicate with the larger context in which they operate? The issue is that the material sphere has been deeply inundated with signals, data. We're not floating off in some abstract parallel metaphysical realm. Quite the contrary, we're facing an invasion of metaphysics into the smallest veins of our bodies, our systems. What we need to do is 'make visible' – in order to confront – what's running in the background, behind our backs, under our very eyes.

11

EXPANDED UPDATES:
FRAGMENTS OF NET CRITICISM

MyResources: 'Power is invisible, until you provoke it.' (GFK) – Unlikely futures: jobs at the Centre for Emerging Cultures – They only read low-impact journals. – 'In einem Land leben, wo alle Namen unbekannt sind.' (Elias Canetti) – 'We pay the debts of the last generation by issuing bonds payable by the next generation.' (Lawrence J. Peter) – Big data is like drugs money, it should be considered dirty data. – iPlasticity and the singular selfie: I'm not like you. – 'progress means that bad things happen faster.' (email sig file) – 'Soon after, the Military Council took over Facebook and reported full control over all profiles.' – 'Provincialising the Net' (conference in Bad Blankenburg) – 'A name is like a numbing blow from which you never recover.' (Marshall McLuhan) – Mind shaping moguls saturating my brain – Unmeasuring the World – A century later, the abstract is the scandal, again. – 'Perilous idiots + good intentions + funding + tech skills = lethal' (Evgeny Morozov) – 'A muscular subject who willfully overcomes the bankruptcy of the world might have been a radical subject position at some point in the past. But today the most radical gesture is to withhold the sufficiency of power.' (Alex Galloway) – 'Amid the bacchanal of disruption, let us pause to honor the disrupted. The streets of American cities are haunted by the ghosts of bookstores and record stores, which have been destroyed by the greatest thugs in the history of the culture industries.' (Leon Wieseltier)

Retro-critique of the Link

'I am not responsible for your website.' I can spend days contemplating this sentence, which streams into consciousness each time I read the statement 'This link is not an endorsement.' It is. A link confirms the existence of the other document. The sovereign strategy in this instance is the unquantifiable act of negation: link denial. This is how superior power operates. I know these data bits exist but I won't make the relation between me and this piece of information public. Linking makes things complicit. We cannot blame machines for making links (because they don't); we are the ones who are guilty of tasting strange fruits. In the golden days of the autopoietic hypertexts, the hyperlink was defined as 'a reference in a document to an external piece of information' (Wikipedia).[1] What is absent in this definition is the element of agency. Back in the 1980s, the link was thought of as both a polite library science technology and a hippie statement, an invitation to broaden one's mind, to open those doors of perception and enter new worlds. The link was part of an expedition that navigated through unknown territory: we want to know, tell me more, explain. Knowledge was not seen as instrumental but as an artistic act, achieved, in the best cases, through serendipity. Jumping away from the main text was not perceived as escapist. Why downgrade the link as an invitation to leave the party? No way, surfing IS the party! Whereas the aim of each site or service these days is now to keep you where you are, the main problem for the user is in fact not surfing itself but multitasking between applications, leaving the browser or app altogether.

On the web there is no such thing as an ignorant link. Once, US judge Richard Posner proposed the barring of linking to newspaper articles or any copyrighted material without the copyright holder's consent. According to Posner, we had to ask permission to link to a newspaper article online:

> Expanding copyright law to bar online access to copyrighted materials without the copyright holder's consent, or to bar linking to or paraphrasing copyrighted materials without the copyright holder's consent, might be necessary to keep free riding on content financed by online newspapers from so impairing the incentive to create costly newsgathering operations that news services like Reuters and the Associated Press would become the only professional, nongovernmental sources of news and opinion.[2]

The Valley news site TechCrunch responded:

> Blogs and other sites just take content from newspapers, Posner asserts, but they share none of the costs of news gathering. Of course, that blanket assertion is simply not true. A growing number of blogs,

164

including TechCrunch, do their own newsgathering and send writers to cover events at their own cost. But even if we limit the discussion to cut-and-paste sites, the free rider argument still doesn't hold much water. You can't be a free rider if you are giving something back of value. A link on its own is valuable. ... Where does Judge Posner think all of these newspaper sites get their readers? It is mostly through links, not direct traffic. Removing the links would obliterate the majority of the online readership for many newspapers.[3]

See here the ideology of the free at full force.

Another example comes from one of NASA's websites. It's cold, technical and to the point:

DASHlink links to websites created and maintained by other public and/or private organizations. These links may be provided by a community member or the NASA DASHlink Team; however, the presence of a link is not an endorsement of the site by us or NASA. When users follow an external link, they are leaving DASHlink and are subject to the privacy and security policies of the owners/sponsors of the outside website(s). NASA and DASHlink are not responsible for the information collection practices of external sites.[4]

Decades into the internet game, the link still exists, but, as many have already indicated, is currently being overtaken by the 'like'.[5] The link was too ambivalent and not enough of a positive endorsement. The like is part of an integrated recommendation system in which the mini appraisals are first acknowledged, then collected, before they are monetized later on in the process, well outside of the view of the user. Whereas linking is a tedious, technical procedure (copy pasting, moving to another window, checking to see if it works and how it looks), liking occurs in a matter of milliseconds and thus belongs to the realm of the cyber subconscious. We still click on links but ordinary customers are not supposed to put links in their social media feeds anymore – that's all automated and done for them. You might manually upload a picture every now and again, if your phone isn't doing that already automatically, but that's it. In response to this, the Google search algorithm has already moved on and is no longer solely dependent on automatically ranking link popularity. Due to the slow demise of links, search engines will become known for what they always were: corrupted, all-too-human 'databases', igniting a wave of nostalgia about 'pure' machine logics from the age before advertising and the related politics of filtering.[6]

The Internet Is Not an Archive

The internet is always ready to disappoint when it comes to its functions as a public memory device.[7] It serves the purpose of what Wolfgang Ernst calls 'temporary storage'.[8] Despite a range of popular myths, scholarly references and journalistic presumptions, there is no evidence that computer networks should be considered archival. Due to state and corporate interests, the 'network of networks' is simply too dynamic and too unstable to be useful for the long-term preservation of cultural artifacts. When bills go unpaid, sysadmins move on, retire or die, operating system versions are not upgraded, companies go bankrupt, and telco policies change; then hard disks crash and become inaccessible, connectivity breaks down or simply shuts off, server racks are forgotten, disconnected and then sold off for scrap and recycled, and domain names expire or are not renewed. It is this dynamic vitality of the internet that runs counter to the implied stasis of the archive.

If the idea of the 'archive' is too formal, too institutional compared to the technical reality of the internet, perhaps it is better thought of as a momentary pseudo-archive of the present? A meta 'anarchive' (Siegfried Zielinski) that offers up 'alternative activity to the archive'.[9] This is a market anarchy with military origins and specifications, filled with incomplete indexes, dead or corrupted links in half-finished digitization projects, and outdated information in forgotten databases. In short, an open collection of collections and half-baked or forgotten assemblages, or 'wild archaeologies' (Knut Ebeling), driven by the 'logic of multiplicity and wealth of variety' and limited by a fixed design. The contrast Zielinski paints between institutional archives that 'collect, select and preserve from the perspective of an (apparatus-related) whole' and the 'autarkic, resistant, easily perishable, autonomous anarchive' may be a false one. The previous complementary blocs of state-run institutions and large corporations working against alternative subcultures – a condition that culminated in the 1960s – has been superseded by the Big Data paradigm, a coalition of innocent entrepreneurial IT monopolies and equally large security agencies in which the ignorant user is more than willing to comply and collaborate.

Computers were developed to excel at one very specific thing: number crunching. This is what they begin to do from the moment they are switched on. There is no such thing (yet) as an idle computer. Only after being switched off can it rest and be silent. Computers lack the primal capacity to be passive. They are manic machines. In contrast to this conception and use, when it was launched in the sixties the internet was understood by its expanding user base to be a medium of lively electronic exchanges, connected machines that communicate, just for the sake of it, with or without the human presence of administration, a.k.a. the user. Be it through streaming data or the transfer of fixed files, it was clear that what happens in a network is communication between nodes. The internet consists of endless cycles of servers contacting other servers, copying this, storing that, time and again.

Fifty years after its inception, this 'vitalist' aspect of the internet is only understood by network administrators. General knowledge about the built-in back-and-forth has gradually been pushed to the background. How many ordinary users are still using Unix commands such as telnet, ping and traceroute? Only the machines themselves, or specialized users like sysadmins, do. The techno-vitalism of the internet is one of the main obstacles to us being able to treat or use the internet as an archive. If only we could let devices 'sleep' and wake them up remotely in order to restore the connectivity ... without versioning problems. Inadequate or broken backwards compatibility is a plague of the computer age – and future generations will despise us for it. This is not simply a user interface or a computer language problem. Those can all be learned. It's the jumbled mass of incompatible and disused data formats, file extensions and network protocols that make any potential archive inaccessible and impossible.

Taken off the network, a server is merely a collection of digital data, not much more than a storage device. As we all know, the storage capacity of computers continues to grow exponentially, and the cost per byte is going down at the same rate. But the problem we're fighting with here is the static worldview of a computer terminal (smartphone, tablet, notebook, etc.) that requests access to a database elsewhere in order to transfer requested files. Archives, on the other hand, don't usually work like that. Traditionally, archives were (and still often are) protected against instant access. Bureaucratic, and often economic, rituals pre- and proscribed who had access to which data. This was even the case with public records. The cool rationality of instantaneous access to any possible data is a utopia of a frictionless, automated rationality that fully understands, and incorporates, the need to store all information and make it universally available.

The archive, with its claims on value in the *longue durée*, on the other hand, has to be protected against the present. It is a conspiracy

167

against time. Digitization has made 'time capsule' procedures a thing of the past and shifted this work to an endless ritual of neo-medieval copying (and upgrading) of digital material, and endless translations from substrate to substrate and file format to file format. This is in order to prevent hackers from deleting material, to compensate for hardware that is prone to failure, and to prevent files becoming unreadable through the demise of formats and standards.

Needless to say, analogue paper archives of the past did not have an eternal life either. All objects, digital or not, dissolve into entropy. Thus, a primary concern and purpose of an archive is to safeguard a given set of materials until the world is ready to process it. In some cases, this can be months or a few years; in others, a century or even more.

Therefore, the future of the archive remains resolutely offline. Online material is the exception. Digitization and 'open access' are the demands of a civic democratization movement and the culturally specific procedures of (Western) network societies. This is how neo-liberal late-capitalist society reproduces its legitimacy. Even future assemblages of computer hardware, software and connectivity will be far too fragile and unstable to last very long untouched. Dependency on the undisrupted flow of electricity alone makes computer networks profoundly unreliable, which explains why so many digital companies locate themselves near uninterruptible power supplies, like hydroelectric dams in the case of Google, or geothermal power in the case of IBM.

Computer networks can only thrive with the massive 24/7 attention paid by millions of users, workers and volunteers who maintain the vital elements and systems of their existence. This is the true rationality of techno-vitality. The internet cannot be stashed away and re-accessed a few decades or centuries later. It only exists as a dynamic entity whose sustainable operation depends on the permanent involvement of a multitude of highly trained players: server software programmers, network managers and analysts, sysadmins, local and global telcos and fibre-optics companies (and their shareholders), satellite programs, as well as national regulatory and global governance organizations such as the Internet Assigned Numbers Authority (IANA), Internet Corporation for Assigned Names and Numbers (ICANN) and Internet Engineering Task Force (IETF).

A special place in the current delicate internet ecology is held by the rapidly growing number of large-size data centres. At first glance, their remoteness and futuristic techno-look suggest that these data storage locations are here to stay – and could even be considered the internet archives we are looking for. But nothing could be further from the truth. Sudden and simple changes in geopolitics, electricity pricing, land and real-estate costs (and, not to forget, the rapid aging of electronics), along with the profitability of rentable rack space can all cause an overnight closure of such facilities. Services can be banned by national policies, hosting companies can go bankrupt, and the taste of the online multitudes for apps and content can suddenly shift.

All archives require curation. This is why there are, strictly speaking, no Big Data archives. The unsorted, raw data collections can – and will be – stored for the next generations to investigate them. However, it remains an open question as to whether or not thousands of servers holding Big Data will hold any cultural value, let alone whether anyone will take a look at them. Given enough time, all rubbish turns into gold, but is this also the case for Big Data? Google's Artificial Intelligence I project, under the guidance of mad scientist and member of the US corporate royalty Ray Kurzweil, is presently digitizing and storing edited, curated and reviewed material, guided by the parasitic Google mantra 'let others do the work first that we won't pay for. You write the book, we scan it and put our ads next to it.' Condensed, high-value information is the kind of heritage you want to feed your AI with.[10] This elitist approach, however, presumes that Big Data will have to be heavily filtered and interpreted (by humans) as the data might otherwise 'pollute' the AI. It is up to simple machines to do the slave work of collecting and processing Big Data. The same could be said of the many heroic attempts to archive the internet. The best parts of Brewster Kahle's Internet Archive are the curated sections. Random parts of the Internet Archive's Wayback Machine are plagued by technical issues, such as outdated plug-ins and missing pages. Humankind can be similarly relieved that Google is not able to archive Facebook and similar social media services, as their AI would soon become worthless because of the overwhelming amount of junk data.

A similar problem already exists in the context of search engines. At a certain point, adding extra information flips the data set into a state of entropy. One cannot endlessly refine the search query. Showing the latest information is not a solution. This might also be the reason why the deep web remains hidden and why we should be happy to access 'merely' 30 per cent of the Net. Must the data generated by common household appliances and remotely controlled by mobile apps be fully searchable? The multi-million results from ordinary search terms no longer bothers us. We've become inured and complacent to the malignant growth in data and the resources it requires. Perhaps this should concern us?

In *Radical Tactics of the Offline Library*, Henry Warwick reflects on the rise of personal portable libraries. Because of the dramatic drop in prices of consumer data storage devices, we can now store 10,000 books on a USB flash drive purchased for 30 euro, or pass around 120-euro hard drives containing 800 feature films. Entire university libraries can fit onto a 3-terabyte drive. Because of draconian copyright regimes that were devised prior to and as a reaction against the ubiquity provided by the digital, the online world has become a precarious trap. Henry Warwick concludes:

> Resisting the precarities of the online and the encroachments of the security state, in a reversalism of older practices based in the replication of knowledge substrates, the Personal Portable Library propels us into a future beyond the sociopathic greed of Proprietarian regimes. Owning and managing a Personal Portable Library is more than just good research practice – it's a radical tactic of resistance against informational feudalism, a strategy of dismantling Proprietarian theory, and an ennobling act of sharing the fruits of culture with all, for the good of all.[11]

The term 'library' may be preferable after all to the over-theorized notion of the archive, which, until recently, was primarily associated with the file-controlling (nation) state. At a time when storage size (now measured in terabytes) and access no longer matter, all that users care about is the social setting. Soon, indexed digital libraries attached to offline Wi-Fi networks or meshnets will be social centres where members consult for their informational needs, combined with the irresistible plus of humans meeting other humans through reading clubs, orgnets, meet-ups, LAN parties, cafés, student lounges and other hybrid forums. When multiple lifetimes-worth of media, books and information can be easily stored and shared on cheap consumer technology, how will the politics and poetics of our digital libraries play out when we design the next generation of public libraries?

On Trolling

The problem of trolling can easily be isolated to individual cases. Trolls are figures of exception. Editors, programmers and, eventually,

170

the Law will deal with the unstoppable deviant Other. Filters are installed to provide protection from annoying information, and bots roam in cyberspace 24/7 to delete undesired provocations. The way a society deals with those who cross invisible lines tells us a lot about the limits of the rhetoric of tolerance, openness and freedom. The troll as outlaw is a trope that can be entertaining, guaranteeing high-quality narratives, human drama and an insight into the stakes of different players and the roles they play. But what if trolling becomes the norm, expanding out of youth culture?

We still live under the spell of Robert Hughes' *Culture of Complaint*. Meanwhile, we are dreaming of a task-related, community-focused, consensus-driven online reality, which may never have existed, and might never arrive in the future. It was during the early 1990s that Hughes described this ongoing situation of a 'polity obsessed with therapies and filled with distrust of formal politics; sceptical of authority and prey to superstition; its political language is corroded by fake pity and euphemism'.[12] Complaining about the vulgarity of confessional culture, Hughes notices that the idea of distinction has long gone. He targets the rock-bottom cheapness of American TV shows. But one big difference between Hughes-type criticism and its application to today's social media dazzle is the indifference of the current elites towards internet comment culture amongst adults (policing teenagers is another matter). Cultural scholars will not step in to rescue this part of popular culture. The troll is a lone wolf, who, unlike the Islamic terrorist, can easily be identified and isolated, filtered, and neutralized with therapies. There is no cultural ideal here, just resentment. There is no historical task for the rambling machine called the internet to be elevating. In the old cybernetic command-and-control style, the computer network was responsible for processing data. These days, it calculates measurable ideology by blocking sites, setting time limits and app restrictions, monitoring chat rooms, filtering search results, setting up email alerts and checking audio and webcams. This is the faith of the troll: expect legal techno-medical responses.

Unlike the politically correct puritanism that Hughes attacked, populist online comment culture, two decades later, is much more roguish and mean. The architectures set up to capture discourse are not so sophisticated at making room for 'difference'. Instead, users are enticed to uncover a hidden truth that can be provoked into being; the rude and the radical are experienced as undesired side-effects, even though they are a direct product of social media design that emphasizes 'news', updates, and fast, short replies while sidelining

171

background stories and lengthy debate. Truth in society is not a collaborative effort, composed in an assemblage of 1,000 puzzle pieces but revealed under the pure pressure of (discursive) violence. The operative 'ideal' is that the one user who pushes hardest will burst the PR bubble that exists around any and every single activity, product and policy. But comments are not just complaints. In today's world of social media, users are precisely not discontent outsiders, venting their anger in some input device. The difference between a genuine debate and trolling is entirely subjective. There is no longer participation, despite all the efforts of Henry Jenkins and his followers to emphasize the 'positive' side of 'user generated content'. In this age, when internet culture has reduced participation to the use of a handful of platforms, every response can and will potentially qualify as trolling.

New Media as a Profession

The term 'new media' has quietly disappeared by now. The reason for this isn't the lack of new technologies entering the market. Just think of 3D printing, RFID, the quantified self, Oculus Rift, Bitcoin and its related blockchain technology, reading tablets, self-driving cars and other gadgets of the day, such as Google Glass and the iWatch. They are all, more or less, having an impact on society. So it is not the case that new media is turning 'old'. All technologies age and disappear at some stage. Computer technology is now seventy years old, but the problem is not exactly the *Antiquiertheit des Digitalen*,[13] no matter how much we speculate about the 'post-digital'. 'New media' as a label disappeared more because the utopia of its promoters did not materialize. Digitization is taking command in an era of growing social inequality and overall cultural stagnation in (Western) society. It is tempting to conclude that 'new media' have become part of the problem. Promises have worn out. Big Data turns out to be a top-down tool to control the population. Despite the worthy efforts of 'citizen data scientists', data are associated with secrecy, privacy breaches and surveillance. The cool factor that comes with newness is no longer going to cut it. What remains is the permanent, and still growing, pressure on the workforce to update and master the latest waves of apps, programming languages and hybrid solutions that connect one system to the other. 'New media studies', as some academic programmes are still called, is caught in a difficult situation of having to fence off its own autonomy in order to create a legitimate position of expertise in society, while also passing on its expertise to existing professions, such as nursing and farming, that were traditionally light years away from the world of information technology.

Our understanding of the stagnation of 'new media' needs to be connected to the critical makers' movements and related discourse in Richard Sennett's *The Craftsman*, the debates around precarity, and propositions to organize guilds and unions for new media and design workers. In the age of Uber, in what direction could the further professionalization of 'new media' be pushed? There are no institutions left to march through. Now that new media studies has shaken off its film and television studies appendages, is it doomed to return to its roots of information studies a.k.a. library science, and become an archive itself? The dream of a separate discipline is over, the conservative forces won. The internet is not perceived as a medium after all, and is not perceived as needing the special attention that literature and film deserve. The real reason for this is the deeply unstable technical nature of the apparatus, which does not allow for its culture to emerge in the foreground for any sustainable amount of time. The internet proves to be the medium of disappearance *par excellence*. The next thing to vanish might be the term 'internet' itself.

Responses to Photography's Omnipresence

The true mystery of the world is the visible, not the invisible.

Oscar Wilde

In his notes on the photo-sharing social network Instagram, Vincent Larach observes 'the photograph has become an integral part of our lives. It is so deeply embedded in the way we capture moments in time and share information that we barely notice the medium that we employ to do so much.' We barely notice: welcome to the 'techno-subconscious', a rapidly growing realm, facilitated by the ever-growing amount of gadgets and recording devices that surround us. The part of the mind below the level of conscious perception is constantly steered by the feedback loops of the machines. At first we are fascinated and sense the 'disruption', but, soon after, the app or feature dissolves into the background and becomes part of everyday life. Image production and consumption have become an integral part of the 'not wholly conscious' sphere, resulting in the victory of the public gaze over privacy – in every possible circumstance.

173

In today's ever-changing media environment, it is an ongoing effort to build up – and maintain – a critical understanding of all the hidden ideologies inside the software, interfaces and platforms that directly feed the techno-subconscious. This is also the case for artists and activists who, for aesthetic and socio-political reasons, intensively explore the possibilities of new technologies. Artists, Ezra Pound once declared, 'are the antennae of the race'. A century ago, they were supposed to be the first to sense the dramatic changes to come. However, these days our avant-garde consists of geeks and venture capitalists. It is the virtual class that defines the user framework of new products and services. Artists and activists, once outsiders and radicals, are today's 'users', early adopters, like you and me.

What happens when miniaturization takes command and the camera becomes omnipresent, given we no longer notice? Jean Baudrillard, a passionate photographer himself, would say: the images have lost their 'scene'. There is no longer an act of 'taking a picture' (a gesture the producer of the selfie adores and repeats in public, time and again). Whereas artistic strategies try to 'restore' the artificiality of the photographic act, activists get caught up in the 'reality' genre, submitting to the socio-technical rules that underlie billions of pictures taken on a daily basis. It's time for an update of John Berger's *Ways of Seeing*. How do we depict images in the age of Tumblr, Instagram and Pinterest? Let's face it: Vilem Flusser's definition of images as 'significant surfaces' has become out-dated. Situated inside the image stream, there is no time left for meaning to solidify. Only the next one is significant.

Massive storage and automated analyses of digital images have taken over from a previous paradigm defined by selection. A photo is no longer perceived by humans as a symbol or summary of an event but has become a part of a post-industrial process, driven by search and identification procedures. The image is always part of a flow. Photographs are no longer illustrating a story, nor do they function as decoration. Because of real-time image transmission and the omnipresence of the camera, the image-as-evidence has gained further importance. The rough quality of 'reality reporting' has become a special effect and can be studied, and exhibited, in the same way as we explore the 'glitch' aesthetics of digital imagery.

In response to these technical and economic conditions, artistic and activist strategies have been diverging: whereas artists were forced to 'beautify' their images in order to maintain their already precarious position in the art market, activists have been pushed in the opposite direction. They take up the iconoclast position of the 'maker' who takes the 'post-digital condition' a bit too literally, and return to the artisan life of unmediated experiences while the rest of society submits themselves to the stacks. However, most of us work within the framework of contemporary image production and its corporate logic of linking, liking, recommendation, commenting, meta-tagging, etc. Subjected to the logic of algorithmic culture, the majority of activists do not study the political economy of social media and quickly run into the traps of these platforms.

Besides the well-known limitations of corporate ownership, the reality of state censorship and other, more sophisticated forms of filtering, the short-term nature of social media attention is a significant problem. The main limitation of today's social movements lies in the non-sustainable form of organization that comes with ubiquitous social media dependency. Across the globe we see a similar pattern: protest movements consume their own imagery and disappear even before 'the social' can come into being. Even though visual material often plays a positive role in their initial mobilization, the image of the street protests in itself no longer has a lasting, symbolic value. Revolts quickly are given a code name (suitable for meta-tagging and Twitter hashtags) and can thus travel at the speed of light through the electronic networks, but quick social interactions do not consolidate into long-lasting social action (such as community memberships, specific task groups through email lists, forums or similar groupware).

Before we start to judge images, we need to explore our collective *a-priori*, our Empire of Image, whose subjects we are. To get an understanding of the political economy of our visual culture is one thing – but before we get there, we need to broaden our desires. Photography can function as a temporary shelter. Stop swiping the pics and start questioning. How would a call for awakening the creative imaginary (in the tradition of Castoriadis) relate to the current mass production of digital images? That's when we start to deal with our unknown knowns, also called fantasy. How can we break through the complex networks of implicit rules and expectations that surround us? Can we reprogram our techno-subconcious? And what's the role of the image sphere in this possible escape route?

The Eternal Return of Real-time

As painters understand abstract space, I understand abstract time.
Nam June Paik

175

We need artworks that slow down and speed up real-time. In the age of Web 2.0 and social media, we have, once again, experienced a set-back in global real-time culture. The underlying concepts of Facebook and Twitter are not at all real-time – quite the opposite. These platforms synthesize all the different times on the globe and present a quasi-new experience of historical time: one that unfolds when accessing our timeline. Streaming media, in contrast, have the ability to be live in the way radio is, but it is more often than not a file that is being pulled off a database. Being part of a live event is an exciting experience, in particular when it is combined with chats and online calling services such as Skype. Reporting live through Twitter can be a border case, as it is obviously delayed and highly personal. If there is one aspect that the current start-up culture is ignoring, it's the further exploration of peer-to-peer real-time (one of the reasons for this might be the low speed of the overall internet connectivity throughout the USA, which hampers mass uptake of new real-time networking tools). Sensing remote presence can have a subversive potential that has yet to be explored. So far, the true innovators in this context remain local/free/pirate radio initiatives across the globe. Brecht and Guattari, we're still on the case!

A Micro-Sociology of the Tech Elite

As Corey Robin writes, 'conservatives have asked us not to obey them, but to feel sorry for them – or to obey them because we feel sorry for them. Conservatives are not content with illumination. They want restoration, an opportunity presented by the new forces of revolution and counterrevolution.'[14] Neo-cons, as Robin described them, viewed the world as their stage, unlike their corporate counterparts. Neo-cons traded in ideas and saw the world as a landscape of intellectual projection. Cybercons, those who rule Silicon Valley, clearly have another mind-set. Why bother with an invasion in Iraq if you can build up a Facebook empire in the meantime? Silicon Valley may be the new upper class, but they have outsourced the role of being a 'governing class' to a secondary elite that administrates the remainders of the state on their behalf.

The thesis here is radically different from the distinction C. Wright Mills made in *The Power Elite* (1956), between celebrities, who mostly bedazzle the populace, and those in power. Already in 1969, from Santa Cruz, G. William Domhoff noticed the flaw in this analysis. Domhoff is concerned with social mobility, the role of women, intermarriages and the role of the 'jet set' as part of the spectacle. Why did Domhoff, writing in the year of the American moon landing and the invention of the internet, go wrong on computer engineers, coding like mad under his very eyes? The role of engineers in society was studied at the time; however, political theory concentrated primarily on their subordinate position in totalitarian regimes. 'Who's running the show?' is an altogether misguided question these days, now that media professionals struggle to maintain their economic position in the lower ranges of the middle class. Today, we live in the era of the Piketty consensus. The question is no longer whether or not 'the power elite' dominates the political process, but which interests steer that very same power elite. The administration of the population was a Cold War issue for the welfare state. In this neoliberal age of the new networks, population management is back to square one: it is ultimately handed over to private surveillance firms, police and the army, while the elite is busy with its own affairs.

For the rising Silicon Valley tech elite there is no harmony in the world, only disruption (of others). In this world, there are no fundamental conflicts (except for markets vs the state). Disruption is a natural, historical process. It's time for the state to leave the stage, so please pack your bag and leave the table. The choice is no longer between reactive and ad hoc (the Clintons and Obama) and the proactive, forceful approach of the Bush clan. That's why some inside the Valley have been developing their own US foreign policy, outside the logic of hawks vs doves.[15]

In contrast to the crowd logic, the Valley lacks the imagination, and the will power, to oppose the masses. 'Unique leadership is a human thing, and is not going to be produced by a mass social community', Kissinger once said. Imagine if you ignore this rule and start to set your own policy goals (such as Elon Musk's aim to visit Mars)? What happens when an elite goes on strike? The Silicon Valley tech elite refuses to govern. They are reluctant to participate in any 'global governance' game with 'reasonable' players such as NGOs, state agencies, international bodies and old-school global corporations. Libertarian nerds also refuse to play the celebrity game, and do not show much interest in the media cults of self-representation. Why bother? Why compromise? Say it in code. Opinion is ... so twentieth century. The libertarian consensus of the start-up scene assumes the state should no longer be taken over and reformed, but forced to reduce its size – and inevitably crumble. Public programmes should have supposedly been privatized decades ago. The best way to achieve this is to ignore the very existence of politics. The Californian doctrine of rule has already been deconstructed as a contemporary adaptation of Ayn Rand. But where is superman? Where is our Howard Roark? What is a critique of altruism without the heroic figure expressing it?

Cyber-libertarians love to ignore the state. Most geeks are sympathetic to this idea but lack the abolitionist's impulse and rather go for a softer indifferent approach that does not provoke confrontations with authorities. In the end, geeks will work for anyone. Whoever rules, they will, ultimately, hire the programmers, as nothing can run without them. In the start-up scene, the cynical 'disruption' model has replaced the Cyber-utopian visions of the 1990s. The impetus is no longer to build a parallel world but to move quickly into an existing market and change the rules of the game. The idea of constructing a better world in all its virtuality has passed. While Enlightenment notions about the power of ideas and the need to spread them remain, they no longer provide alternative blueprints of society. Instead, IT parasitically extracts existing value flows and captures large economic procedures, from 'smart cities' to food logistics. This numerical minority, brilliantly described by Kroker and Weinstein in 1994 as the harvesting 'virtual class', is not about to take command.[16] Not even conspiracy theories accurately describe their rise. What does this ruling class do when it rules? It relaxes, submerged in its own autism. Banality's refusal to command. Clearly, we need a new political theory here, and first of all to dig into our own disappointment at such an answer. ('This can't be true!', etc.) Welcome to the universe of Michel Houellebecq. Neither Hegel nor Freud can adequately explain these provisional states of implosion and boredom that encapsulate us. Let's look away and not deal with it – maybe the computer was only a fad, after all. That would be the Continental European response: at some point, ICT was revolutionary, like the steam engine – however, we've passed that moment, like horses in the street that were once necessary for mass transportation but are now a hobby item of the rich.

Jaron Lanier's description of the Valley is one of a village-type atmosphere, in which quitting your job and starting to work for the competitor is not seen as betrayal. What counts is the general interest of the overall network. The Californian tech elite celebrates the post-apocalyptic cyberpunk condition and withdraws into a self-built 'island in the net'. This long-term escapist strategy has a much deeper impact than the sadistic neoliberal agenda that intends to remove all redistribution functions of the post-war welfare state. While Thatcher said there was no society, parts still remain to be bulldozed. Due to their engagement to eradicate the (socialist) past, neoliberals are stuck in revenge mode and cannot escape the (mental) state of permanent demolition, budget cuts, austerity, privatization and foreclosures. Greed and resentment are two sides of the same dire coin. Restructuring and precarious labour conditions lead to depression. Stuck in this never-ending downward spiral, neoliberals ironically need a strong state to execute their repressive agenda of violence, surveillance and control. However, techno-libertarians have moved to a post-crisis stage and presume they possess the technological solutions for all social, political and ecological problems (Morozov's 'solutionism'). The presumed 'complexity' of problems is just another smoke screen: the solutions are already there, we just need to scale them.

The extraction of surplus value by the New Intermediaries such as Google, Facebook and Amazon has to be done invisibly, *sub rosa*. Any critical attention to the way these corporations operate, as in the revelations of whistleblower Edward Snowden, is seen as profoundly undesirable. We're not supposed to understand how the algorithm economy operates. In our network society, masses have become individual users of social media platforms, like multi-player online games. To study the values of the tech elite, just install the video game *Elite: Dangerous* and start the battle. At first sight, 'the Federation society appears to be based on democratic principles with leaders being voted to power'. However, 'in reality, corporate loyalty oils the machine, and Federation space is a battleground of commerce. Commercial organizations compete as aggressively as the law will allow for the time and attention of the Federal citizen, who goes through life bombarded by advertising.' The game manual continues: 'culturally the Federation is tolerant of some things (like religions) but utterly intolerant of drug-taking, political activism, and certain cultures. A great many things are illegal, like slavery, cloning and certain narcotics.' Does this sound familiar?

The distinction that the Italian political scientist Gaetano Mosca once made, between a class that rules and a class that is ruled, has itself been overruled.[17] In the twenty-first century, it is an honour, a privilege, to gain the status of subject (a.k.a. user). The greatest danger for the global workforce is to be left to its own devices. Millions fight for the right to be exploited. The upper stratum no longer needs armies of slaves to maintain its hegemony and can outsource production to such an extent that all dependencies become blurred, and invisible. For digital solidarity, it will be vital to 'make visible' the global infrastructures and to give a face and voice to the multitudes of anonymous workers (who all have smart phones, a presence in social media, etc.) that keep our fragile world afloat. We haven't even started to design a collective imagination for how such a planetary reachability could be used and shaped.

At best, the tech elites are early adopters of their own gadgets. Becoming 'upper class' is merely a matter of style, not a *Kulturideal* shared amongst hipsters. Their permanent state of withdrawal does not mean that the programmers have raised themselves above society – quite the opposite. Deeply marinated in pop culture, the hoodies cabal does not pretend to be any better than the rest. Today's higher circles are high – on drugs. Is this our nobility? There is no hidden *Übermensch* syndrome here – zero charisma, not even that of the engineer. The excellence is hidden in code and should not be searched for elsewhere. The aqueducts of our time can be admired inside Github. Take it or leave it, that's where we ought to allocate our Leonardo da Vinci. The defining art of our age won't be Bruce Nauman. Instead, we're condemned to hover around the heights of mediocre, templated virtual environments.

The bible for those interested in the interface between geek culture and the humanities is (still) Alan Liu's *Laws of Cool*. Please reread this classic. There is no trace of an avant-garde, not even a single historical reference. Unlike for traditional ruling classes, for the Valley tech elite, art is not seen as the highest value in life. Cars might be? The art market has not yet dealt with this emerging reality, and neither has charity. Free of guilt, the tech elite sees no need to 'pay back to society', let alone adopt a living artist – the poor suckers. Instead, it invests in even more tech (this can even be said of the worthy Gates Foundation). The exception here was financier George Soros (alas, an East Coast Wall Street guy), with his Open Society Foundation, who abandoned his network of contemporary arts centres, which he ran in Eastern Europe, after a decade, when it was decided that the European Union and individual nation states had to invest in a contemporary arts infrastructure (which, of course, they didn't).

Inside tech circles, the critique of parliamentary democracy has become a given. Their notion of post-democracy is not a concern or treat but a half-baked reality that is hard to escape. Corruption is seen as a symptom of a lack of transparency, and presented as a by-product of the cult of deliberation in the former-West. The computer logic is a preferred given that doesn't need debate. Political chattering only steals valuable time we could have used to implement techno-governance solutions for global warming, Ebola, efficient food distribution and other noble causes. Google's massive political lobbying efforts in Washington DC and Brussels should be read in this light. Its aim is to achieve the right for corporations to be left alone to pursue their own interests.

12

OCCUPY AND THE POLITICS OF ORGANIZED NETWORKS

'I forgot my network externalities.' – 'We walk slowly since we are going far.' (Zappatista saying) – 'Finding the meaning of life individually is an anthropological illusion.' (D'Alisa, Kallis and Demaria) – 'We need help, and it needs to come from people who wear suits, studied hard, talk the talk and are willing to die for their cause.' (Jonathan Brun in Adbusters) – 'The soul sees nothing that does not distress it on reflection.' (Pascal) – 'I feel protected by unpublished Suite A algorithms.' (J. Sjerpstra) – 'I am on an angry squirrel's shitlist.' – Join the Object Oriented People – 'When philosophy sucks – but you don't.' – 'See you in the Sinkhole of Stupid, at 5 pm.' – 'I got my dating site profile rewritten by a ghost writer.' – 'Meet the co-editor of the Idiocracy Constitution' – The Military–Entrepreneurial Complex: 'They are bad enough to do it, but are they mad enough?' – 'There really should be something like Anti-Kickstarter for the things you'd be willing to pay to have not happen.' (Gerry Canavan) – 'Waning of the Social Media: Ruin Aesthetics in Peer-to-Peer Enterprises' (dissertation) – 'Forget the Data Scientist, I need a Data Janitor.'

Net.activism has grown up and is huge, comparable to race and gender struggles and the climate change issue.[1] This is the age of Wikileaks, Anomymous, denial-of-service attacks on vital infrastructure and NSA-whistleblower Edward Snowden, all capturing the global imagination. It is a world which, already for decades, has remained *terra incognita* to institutions. Here, communication is no longer a luxury and flips into a much larger issue that leaves behind tactics once designed for the ghetto. But how do we measure size? We no longer have to look at social media analytics tools to convince ourselves of the scope of the phenomenon. Today's net activism links interaction with action and puts the Organization Question on the table. How do we design the art of collective coordination? How do we move on beyond liking and stage actual events that intervene? Is there a place for technology in the decision-making process? And how do these social media-driven movements compare with traditional institutional forms of politics such as the NGO and the political party? Will they ever become a sustainable form of self-organization?

We are all still struggling to make sense of what happened during 2011, the 'belated' Year of Protest that started off with the Arab Spring and culminated in the Occupy movement, so neatly summarized by Slavoj Žižek in his 2012 book *The Year of Dreaming Dangerously*. Why did it take 3–4 years from the 2008 Global Financial Crisis for these movements to unfold – and why have we already been interpreting these chains of global events for an equal number of years? Did people need a break during 2012 ('Pause for the People'?), before the next wave of protests occurred in Bulgaria, Sweden, Turkey, Brazil and the Ukraine?[2] Why didn't 2011 produce a larger political momentum? How is it that the mass mobilization of political passion is neutralized and absorbed so quickly into the prevailing status quo? Is the energy of activism really so incapable of building political-technological infrastructures that survive beyond the spectacle of the event? Are we optimally making use of our slowness-by-design to rethink movement tactics? And why is it so hard for movements to regroup and return to the stage?

David DeGraw commented: 'Through Anonymous, Occupy and the 99% Movement, we collectively proved that decentralised self-organizing networks of like-minded people rallying together can set the world on fire. However, we lacked an exit strategy and the resources required to build a self-sustaining movement that can truly achieve the change and evolution of society that we all know we need.'[3] This discussion is by no means limited to the (overrated) role of social media and mobile phones in these mass mobilizations. We have to ask ourselves: what does this hermeneutic delay mean in an age of real-time digital networks where events travel with the speed of light? According to Michael Levitin:

> Occupy was, at its core, a movement constrained by its own contradictions: filled with leaders who declared themselves leaderless, governed by a consensus-based structure that failed to reach consensus, and seeking to transform politics while refusing to become political. Ironic as it may seem, the impact of the movement that many view only in the rear-view mirror is becoming stronger and clearer with time.[4]

Even the corporate world joins the reflection extravaganza, demonstrating its concern about the leaderless strategies and reminding us that social media use alone will not result in a plan. Foreign policy strategists Eric Schmidt and Jared Cohen at Google remarked:

> Future revolutions will produce many celebrities, but this aspect of movement-making will retard leadership development necessary to finish the job. Technology can help find the people with leadership skills – thinkers, intellectuals and others – but it cannot create them. Popular uprisings can overthrow dictators, but they're successful afterward only if opposition forcers have a good plan and can execute it. Building a Facebook page does not constitute a plan; actual operational skills are what will carry a revolution to a successful conclusion.[5]

It seems that Silicon Valley is in need of some introspection itself as it has so far shown little interest in the democratization of 'operational skills'. Instead, most social media platforms deliberately create diffuse 'clouds' of impressions; private experiences and micro opinions are then made operational by machines. The tech elite has prioritized neither problem-solving nor effective communication tools, let alone online decision-making procedures. The idea of 'start-ups' has consciously been reduced to short-term business models. Why can't we start-up a non-profit? Ever heard of it? Imagine start-ups categorically rejecting venture capital, associated with higher education and culture? Sounds almost European. They would be tactically ignored and, of course, do not exist, particularly not in Europe, which is in an iron grip of neoliberal entrepreneurial thinking conjoined with austerity regimes.

Walled gardens like Facebook and Twitter make it hard to estimate the real size and impact of one's semi-private conversations (including the public 'clicktivism' *à la* Avaaz). Is 'direct action' becoming even more symbolic (and informational) than it already was? The hybrid of urban space and cyberspace, as dreamed up in the nineties, is a fact when looking at the Movement of the Squares (from Tahrir and Puerta del Sol to Taksim, Euromaidan and Hong Kong). Aside from a few internet gurus such as Clay Shirky and Jeff Jarvis – who were only able to read such 'Facebook revolutions' as giant input devices in the name of 'citizen journalism' supposedly executed in the name of US-American (market) values – there is little patience amongst op-ed writers for studying in detail what's at stake here (with the exception of, for instance, Paolo Gerbaudo,[6] Zeynep Tufekci[7] and Eric Kluitenberg).[8]

Should we speak of a theoretical deficit, or rather an overproduction of real-time reporting? Social grooming and an addictive 'presentation of the self' culture may be sociological facts but say surprisingly little about the organizational questions that I am asking here. Luckily, there's no longer a need to call for engagement. Discontent is thriving. The Age of Indifference is over. But how is today's solidarity being shaped? Is it only a matter of 'capturing' and 'channelling' political energies that are floating around us? No matter where you look, one gets the feeling that problems are piling up, yet urgency is only in its infancy and we have not even remotely started to explore the full potential of the internet in making organizational machines, discursive platforms and tools of collective desire.

Activism never restricted itself to the slow and invisible process of advocacy. It can be boring to define yourself as a citizen and criticize mainstream media coverage. We left the long twentieth century a while ago.[9] The struggle is no longer over engagement and the 'right' content. 'Movimentalism'[10] is not a preliminary form of 'collective awareness' either. In many forms of institutional politics, the role of 'civil society' is reduced to that of an input device. Thanks, we got your message, now shut up. This contradicts another neoliberal phrase, which says that citizens should not just complain and instead 'embody' solutions (and not merely suggest them). We only have a right to complain if we have alternatives on hand that demonstrably work. Current political bureaucracies can no longer deal with anger. Their numbness in turn infuriates the popular voice. Another result is repression for nothing, outbursts of an excessive show of force and out-of-the-blue violence by authorities, which no one seems to be able to explain. To contradict in public these days all too easily leads to arrests, injuries and sometimes worse: to shooting cops killing protesters.

Resistance grows out of a sudden existential crisis. There is a 2.0 of everything: racism, violence, unemployment, migration, poverty and pollution. In such circumstances, taking action is not a gesture of boredom or prosperity. Activists have fires to fight. Yet, urgency in itself does not easily translate into specific political forms. We need to 'invent' them, time and again. The creation of such 'new institutional forms' will not be done for us. 'Our institutions are beaming light that makes me think of the twinkling stars of which astronomers tell us they have died a long time ago', says Michel Serres, who observes that philosophers have failed to anticipate future forms of knowledge. So what are our contemporary forms? How about radical think tanks or 'thought collectives'? Can we think beyond the NGO

185

office culture and the start-up? Gangs and tribes are social units of the past, but what's replacing them? The swarm, mob, network?

As The Accelerate Manifesto writes, 'We need to build an intellectual infrastructure.'[11] Think sustainable networks that spread progressive knowledge, with strong ties between all countries and continents. Yes, there is the obligation to represent and build larger structures, but the avalanche of catastrophic occurrences only seems to grow. Initially impulsive, activism nowadays quickly mutates into a daily informational routine. The problem is not one of consciousness or commitment but one of the sustainable organizational form in which we express our discontent and then build on it, turning it into ways of life not hell-bent on exploitation and mass-scale destruction. This explains the shift in attention towards political parties such as the Five Star Movement, pirate parties from Sweden to Germany, Syriza in Greece, the United Left in Slovenia and Podemos in Spain, but also funky concepts such as the multitude and swarm, fresh critiques of horizontalism, the communism 2.0 of Jodi Dean and others, as well as the emergent net.political entities, from Wikileaks and Anonymous to Avaaz.

Most criticisms of social movements are known, justified and predictable. Yes, movements such as Occupy 'expend considerable energy on internal direct-democratic process and affective self-valorisation over strategic efficacy, and frequently propound a variant of neo-primitivist localism, as if to oppose the abstract violence of globalised capital with the flimsy and ephemeral "authenticity" of communal immediacy' (Accelerate Manifesto). This critique may be valid for US activism but doesn't seem to resonate with the situation in Southern Europe and the Middle East where collective therapy sessions are not such a priority. Activism in the North-West of Europe is in need of controversial debates and less consensus. An exclusivist lifestyle implicitly signals to others not belonging to the tribe to not bother trying to join. The problem with Occupy was not the obsession with its own decision-making rituals but its limited capacity to build coalitions. The issue became one of a performativity trap. At some point, the intensity of internal debate and collective affirmation needs to turn to the outside and engage that which it abhors. When activism promotes itself as a counterculture, the ability of its memes to travel outside of the issue-context becomes limited, and starts to run contrary to the 99% slogan. Cyberpolitics faces a similar problem: how can we get rid of its libertarian / liberal hipster image and politicize the unemployed masses of young people across the globe that will never get a share in the mega profits of 'their' Google and Facebook? When will we see the first user strike demanding an end to the free?

Activism is about saying: 'Enough is enough; we've got to stand up and do something.' Refusal is foundational. Just Say No. Cry out loud that you can no longer bear it. Tell the world that you no longer care. For the positivist managerial class, this is the hard part, as they would rather skip the schizo-part of today's society and deal only with reasonable and balanced people, united in their willingness to implement bottom-up alternatives – perfect humans for whom resistance is a rational choice, not connected with any bodily issues or existential misgivings. In the positivist view, revolution can be managed like any other event that requires logistics, delegation and related decision-making processes (including the social noise that comes with it). A fear is still amongst us that all emotions will, ultimately, lead to Stalinism or fascism. It is true that the despair of the rebel often ends up in a catastrophic, violent event, one that will be overdetermined by the agenda of others.

Autopoiesis of the General Assembly

Social movements that experienced the 'general assembly' model[12] claim that they are (re-) inventing democracy. The emphasis is on new modes of consensus-seeking for large constituencies that gather in real life. However, experiences with the 'general assembly' model have created a black box – namely, how the execution of collective decisions really works. What happens after consensus has been reached in a 'movement without organisation'? And, equally important, how do we look back at it after the event is over? Once the exhilarating and exhausting gathering can no longer take place because of evictions and the like, we easily get excited about the 'performativity' of the repeat chorus, the 'concerted actions of the body' (as described by Judith Butler)[13] and the social spectacle of the lively decision-making rituals of public assembly. Instead of criticizing resistance as entertainment and the simulated politics of staged media events, the proposed alternative route here is to counter-balance the centrality of the ritualized assembly with a multitude of organizational pillars that strengthen the underlying structure of a movement.

Marina Sitrin and Dario Azzellini remark that 'there is a growing movement of refusal – and simultaneously, in that refusal, a movement of creation'.[14] But what exactly is created here? It is the Event itself, a manifestation of the social that occurs inside a temporary autonomous zone that tears apart the monotone monads of the everyday. The Event itself is the aim, a pure act of self-disruption. For once we live in the present. Join the lonely heart's club band that jams deep into the night. The flight from banality cannot be staged alone. The liberation of the consumerist present can only be achieved in a collective act that borders on religious repentance. The raised issues and demands are often anything but radical – but the form will be.

Direct democracy without its own executive apparatus, no matter how small, can easily become a spectacle without consequences. The emphasis on horizontality starts to become a theatrical play. Anestis from Athens, recounting the situation at the large Syntagma Square assembly:

> We voted for many things, but everything we voted for didn't have a concrete end. We voted in favour of the refusal to pay metro or bus tickets, but the next day nobody went to the metro station or the bus station to talk to the people and prevent them from paying. We voted that we need a new constitution, yes ... ha-ha, we voted to refuse to pay the national debt. So what? We realised that there was too much talking and practically no action.[15]

The general assembly is not a power-free zone. As in all political processes, agenda setting is decisive, as is the power over the executive apparatus. 'The need to listen to each other', no doubt, is a value in itself – but only tells half of the story. The affective and trust-based politics of the assemblies creates a sense of sociality, which was lost for many years. Democracy, as practised by the social movements, is first and foremost an internal matter, aiming also against the rise of an implicit, invisible vanguard from spontaneously arising social movements. The emphasis here is on the democratization of social movements themselves, which in the past had to deal with 'disruptive individuals', macho personalities and 'the tyranny of the eccentric'.[16] The absent other here is the silent majority, the liberal mainstream. In many cases, there is no clear divide between different factions otherwise. This is the main reason why the general assembly is focused on reaching consensus – an exodus from the fuzzy cloud. The ritual is more about expressing the obvious than overcoming fundamental differences between rival factions, let alone implementing a programme and social–political infrastructure that survives after the ecstasy of the event.

The general assembly aims at streamlining the common language. The group that gathers is already homogeneous and all it needs to do is find out, through the exchange of arguments, what the consensus consists of. Needless to say, this is a lengthy process whose outcome cannot be known beforehand. Antagonistic politics (as described by Chantal Mouffe) are oddly out of place here.[17] The main problem with these procedures is not their reproduction of empty rituals and their new, inevitable forms of exclusion but the assumption that the general assembly represents society and is thus reinventing democracy at large. For a brief moment there is no lethargy anymore: we are overcoming the sectarian divides of the past and making a claim on a new majority position. This is the promise, from the inclusive 99% slogan to the 2014 Podemos populist rhetoric that no longer wants to be defensive and instead will reclaim the self-confidence necessary to win.[18] No more factions, no more minorities. The message is clear: we have finally managed to go beyond the fragments. For a moment, we see Derrida's 'democracy to come' appearing before our very own eyes. Not as a system, but as a democratic culture in action. Whether we are actually reinventing democracy through such brief collective experiences remains questionable. What happens when assemblies scale up – not only in size but in terms of what's at stake – and move beyond the crisis into a more permanent mode? This is a whole other matter altogether. And it is only then that representative democracy is really put to the test.

The silent, funny and somewhat nervous cult of hand signals flashing about during general assemblies looks odd to the anthropological outsider. The crowd gesturing seems to express a growing distrust in verbal expression and rhetoric. Hand signals are said to be an effective way of communication, fascinating to look at, to take part in, to fall in love with. We're not here to hear the same old arguments, what counts is the steady flow of the undisrupted (yet lengthy) procedure. After familiarizing oneself with the social body language, it is easy to observe that this NGO lingo, introduced by affinity groups, and guarded by trained facilitators, is no different from other decision-making processes. Despite the many hours it takes, this form of direct democracy is seen as remarkably efficient, ideal for the multitude pressed for time, knowing that the movement can – and will – disintegrate at any moment. We go under and disappear together, in agreement. To shake jazz hands, ask for clarification, demand a point of order, give a direct response and agree or disagree, all contributes 'to capture tendencies of opinion during debates involving large numbers of people'.[19] The 'temperature checks', brought in to avoid voting, aim at the collective experience of a visible consensus, overruling the looming possibility of emerging factions that fracture movements into fixed majority–minority stand-offs.[20]

Overcoming the nineties real–virtual dichotomy within the context of new political forms means rejecting both ongoing digital anxiety and offline romanticism as its cheap solution. 'Cutting the electronic leash' is corporate-speak for giving workers some time off – not a revolutionary strategy. But working on the ground, in the localities, facilities, with groups and reaching out is not done because of some nostalgic reason to reconnect with the all-too-human other. Theo from Thessaloniki puts it this way: 'Fighting against fascism means getting out into the neighbourhoods, getting to know your neighbours, getting organised with them, and building small struggles for our rights in the neighbourhoods. This is the first step to create real social relationships. And yes, this also means self-defence against the fascists.'[21] This is the task and challenge; internet participation is secondary to this.

Achtung! Feind hört mit! (Beware! The enemy is listening in!) Once the movement is under way, people will find out soon enough how to distinguish between networking as a secure P2P communication and the more diffuse ways in which the internet, and social media in particular, can be used to generate 'public conspiracy'. Internal strategy debates and future direct action plans are better not discussed online. The post-Snowden security issues have so far not been touched upon in the movement discourse, even though some are acutely aware of it and push for a crypto-approach when it comes to the electronic coordination of future actions. This urgent issue goes well beyond the moral question of whether movements and their active members should use Facebook and Twitter or, rather, alternative platforms. A political reality of the individualized Self pairs with the techno-social given of the network society. Centralist leftist party strategies are not the default. These days, the roles of spokesperson and 'leader' are problematic for a reason. This is not because of some late victory of historical anarchism or the relentless activism of a handful of anarchists in disguise. The centre-less network logic comes from media and has penetrated culture in a deep way, transforming power relations in movements. It will need a lot of (internal) violence to press movements back into a top-down model. This sociological reality is the main reason to pursue the concept further and design agendas of orgnets: the question of organization (what's to be done?) can no longer be distinguished from the network *a-priori*.

Social movements today face two key problems: a fundamental lack of time to let events unfold to their true potential, and of the self-organization skills to execute their own decisions. In the end, these two aspects are related. If movements were better organized, they would, in theory, have a better chance to withstand setbacks and be able to reappear. Because of the relative one-off organizational forms that are currently used, organized networks cannot resolve the issue of the Event as a compressed spectacle – for that we need a pharmacological mix of slow politics on the one hand, and the ability to accelerate our actions when the moment is right on the other. But orgnets can be part of long-term strategy to improve forms of self-organization. Movements need to think long-term and start to build their own infrastructure. Others will not do this for us.

In his 2013 book *Translating Anarchy: The Anarchism of Occupy Wall Street*, Mark Bray discusses the concept of a diversity of tactics, and this could very well also be applied to activist use of mainstream vs alternative (social) media. Bray discusses tactics in the context of ongoing debates around non-violence vs militant tactics, such as property destruction. The essay in the *Unlike Us Reader* by Tiziana Terranova and Joan Donovan on social media use by Occupy LA is a study of how this movement switched between different positions and cultures of use.[22] Despite wasting pages on identitarian navel gazing, *Translating Anarchy* provides us with a useful inside story of the inner workings of Occupy Wall Street (OWS) and its consensus-driven decision-making. However, *Translating Anarchy* is remarkably thin when it comes to critical media awareness, in particular if one takes into consideration that the identitarian anarchist Mark Bray was a member of the media group working for OWS during and after Zuccotti Park, talking to hundreds of journalists.

An equally useful insider's account is Linda Herrera's *Revolution in the Age of Social Media*, in which she provides us with a detailed account of the lead-up to the 25 January 2011 revolution in Egypt. She describes the history of the 'We Are All Khaled Said' Facebook page, which, at its height, in January 2011, had 390,000 members and 9 million hits a day. Without talking down its influence, Herrera dismisses the Facebook revolution meme that has since circulated in Western media: 'That movements use the media available to them as a way to reach out as far as possible is neither new nor surprising. To label the uprisings "digital" or "Facebook revolutions" is in the best case a misunderstanding and in the worst an attempt to down-play them.'[23] Having said that, she explains how the Facebook page did encourage the 25 January Revolution: 'The page did not cause

191

the revolution, and youth of the internet were not the only group active in it, but it is hard to imagine the revolt being put into motion without, firstly, the Tunisian revolution, and, secondly, the changing political culture, mentality, and networked behaviour of Egypt's wired youth.'[24] Herrera concludes: 'the generations coming of age with social media, virtual values, and virtual intelligence have a great capacity to unlock the mechanisms of ideology'. In the light of the pressing organization question of our time, this 'deconstructive' tendency might be necessary and liberating but how can it transcend the individual level and create new social forms not limited to the commercial agendas and template design of Facebook, both of which impact upon the mode of organization?

Organized Networks as Basic Units

> Organisation, which is, after all, only the practice of cooperation and solidarity, is a natural and necessary condition of social life.
>
> Errico Malatesta

If the nineteenth and twentieth centuries were preoccupied with the Social Question, and we have recently been struggling to make sense of the Media Question, the twenty-first century will be dominated by the Organization Question. What will replace the holy triangle of Party, Church and State and facilitate the aspirations of the chattering billions? Will we face a radical remake of the social movement itself? We may all have good ideas for how to arrange society in a different way, and be able to communicate these ideas, but how to get there? Will networks, corporations, groups or communities replace older social forms? As the Invisible Committee already remarked:

> Organisations are obstacles to organising ourselves. In truth, there is no gap between what we are, what we do, and what we are becoming. Organisations – political or labour, fascist or anarchist – always begin by separating, practically, these aspects of existence. It's then easy for them to present their idiotic formalism as the sole remedy to this separation. To organise is not to give structure to weakness. It is above all to form bonds.[25]

We can ask ourselves: what comes next, after the boredom is gone? David Foster Wallace accurately described the previous phase. In his essay on the 2000 McCain campaign, he asks why young voters are so uninterested in politics. He observes that it is 'next to impossible to get someone to think hard about why he's not interested in something. The boredom itself preempts inquiry: the fact of the feeling's enough'. This is also true about the observations of Jean Baudrillard concerning the inertia, the Silence of the Masses. But this state of affairs always comes to end at some point. Once the party has started, it is hard to stay on the outside. Wallace comments that politics is not cool: 'Cool, interesting, alive people do not seem to be the ones who are drawn to the political process.'[26] There is a 'deep disengagement that is often a defence against pain. Against sadness.' The demonstration that presents itself as a cool festival overcomes such a zero-degree mindset by creating Temporary Autonomous Zones that are inclusive, well beyond the multitudes of the past. This is based on a politics of affect that is purely bodily in nature and no longer fools around with 1930s visual language (as problematized by Walter Benjamin). If anything, the politics of aesthetics is audio-psychic in nature.

What's loss and desire in this digital networked age? The question may seem rhetorical, even utopian, but that's not how it is meant. Today's answer is all too often formulated in the language of offline romanticism. The way out is only being perceived as an exodus from technology as such, whereas technological proposals are often condemned as 'solutionism'. How can we design a radical agenda that avoids both extremes? As Chicago's Mayor Rahm Emanuel said: 'Never allow a crisis to go to waste. They are opportunities to do big things.' Let's seize that moment. Let's forget reformist agendas that emphasize individual solutions in which participation is reduced to an input device. In fighting censorship, surveillance and control by both states and monopolies (by dismantling actual infrastructure), there is a promise of a new culture of decentralization that is able to negotiate its rights on a federated level, with standards and protocols that benefit all.

Regained powers of negation alone cannot explain the sudden rise of hyper-large movements that seem to come out of nowhere. In a variation of what Corey Robin writes in *The Reactionary Mind* about contemporary conservatism, we could observe that in these post-Cold War times social movements do not primarily desire and demand but express a culture of loss. They mourn a lost future and show their collective desperation about the lack of public infrastructure and social facilities (education, healthcare, cheap housing), the disappearance of secure jobs and the prospect of a life without income security, dominated by debt. In a variation on Robin, we can say that protesters don't ask us to obey them but to feel sorry for them. They want to be seen as glorious losers, acting out their loss, celebrating their victim status. Outraged, they demand nothing but our sympathy.

The 1990s presumption of default harmony, with its 'unwilling-ness to embrace the murky world of power and violent conflict, of tragedy and rupture', is long gone.[27] The proposed concept of orga-nized networks can be considered a next stage in the worldwide quest for organizational forms that fit the age of digital media. It evolves from the workgroups that pop up spontaneously during events. Yet the difference here is an emphasis on the sustainability of self-organization. Whereas the event is short and ecstatic, and by its very nature local, the organized network can be local, while drawing in knowledge and experience from elsewhere to focus on the realiza-tion of ideas, projects and collaborations beyond the facilitation of the Event. Whereas the Event is geared towards immediate growth and visibility through all possible channels, small units focus on getting things done in the background. Executing decisions made during general assemblies, in online forums, or by the groups them-selves, is the prime aim.

Organizing is not mediating. If possible, groups conspire offline. When we organize towards the Event, we indeed communicate and try not to record our intentions. We arrange, debate, coordinate, make to-do lists and phone calls; we order necessary tools and equip-ment before we run outside to meet our political fate. Let's keep this in mind: informing your mates is not media work. In this age of social media, mobilization and public relations start to blend, much to the confusion of both activists and the institutional players, in media and society alike. Whereas for activists it is still possible to distinguish between internal channels and mainstream radio, newspapers and TV, this distinction can no longer be clearly made when we take the internet into account. Is tweeting, blogging, updating your status, posting to lists and responding to messages symbolic work at the level of representation or a material, social activity or both? The inherent impossibility of distinguishing between coordination, mobilization and publicity is one of the main drivers behind the current social media and activism debate.

We often overlook the mysterious tipping point where an issue, a small network, a local controversy, suddenly flips into a mass move-ment. Insiders might be able to reconstruct that particular moment, but can such one-offs be translated into strategic knowledge for all? Organized networks, however, cannot give an answer to this contem-porary mystery. In 2005, to deal with this and other central but neglected issues of organization in movements, my Australian media theorist friend Ned Rossiter developed the concept of 'orgnets'. The orgnet concept is a proposal, a possible answer to overcome the insular status of the subject-as-user in times of crisis for the traditional institutions such as political parties, unions and Western parliamentary constitutions. Social media tend to isolate their individualized users – in this case, those who want to do good and yet are only given individualized options for change. Orgnets are a possible answer to corporate strategies of internet giants that are out to exploit our weak ties (the 'friends of friends of friends') in order to increase their reach and their ever-growing data hunger.[28] How can we undermine the tendency to consume our own social life? Against the notion of sociality as an ever-expanding universe of possible clients and allies, orgnets emphasize the importance of strong ties with the aim of getting things done. Whereas corporate social networks promote eternal hyper-growth through sharing and updating, orgnets focus on the further development of (real-time) collaborative platforms.

Orgnets are a material condensation, in software and technical life, of what Tiqqun calls a 'commitment to commitment'. Activists know that the truth cannot be found in algorithms. Models are irrelevant and are only there to administrate the world. What concepts such as orgnets do is structure today's data flows. Comparable to the (potential) power of conceptual artworks, such proposals mingle in the titanic struggle over the planetary network architecture that defines our age. Code is necessary for operating systems; apps, databases and interfaces are highly dependent on abstract concepts. And this is where the role of science fiction writers, philosophers, literary critics and artists comes in. Software is not a given, an alien black box that receives us from outer space – even if we often experience it that way. It is written up by the geek next door.

The orgnet concept is clear and simple: instead of exploiting further the weak ties of the dominant social networking sites, orgnets emphasize intensive collaborations within a limited group of engaged users. The internet's potential should not be limited to corporate platforms that are out to resell our private data in exchange for free use. That option gives you silos ripe for NSA raids. Orgnets are neither avant-garde nor inward-looking cells. What's emphasized is the word 'organ'. With this, we do not mean a gesture of a return to nature or a regression into the (societal) body. Neither is it a reference to Aristotle's six-volume work called *Organon*, nor to the 'body without organs' notion (or Žižek's reversal of it, for that matter). The 'organ' of orgnets is a social-technical device through which projects are developed, relations built and interventions made. Here, we are speaking of the conjunction between software cultures and social desires. Crucial to this relationship is the question of algorithmic architectures, something largely overlooked by many activist movements who adopt – in what seems a carefree manner – commercially motivated and politically compromised social media platforms such as Facebook, Twitter and Google+.

For the fellow pragmatists amongst us, we can think of a next generation of work-group software that can run in parallel with publishing/campaign platforms and social media tools that help with mobilization. What's missing right now are small, task-driven decision-making applications that look more like chat environments and move away from the complex forum software that is usually developed only to be used on a large PC screen. Google dominates this field, with Google+ and the Writely software (sadly acquired and rebranded as Google Docs).

In contrast to David Graeber and others of the American Occupy movement, I am not obsessed with the 'democracy' question. I would prefer experimenting with decision-making software over consensus rituals and believe that movements should cultivate, and not be afraid of, controversies.[29] Whether movements split is not the prime concern right now. Let's remember that forking is how social-technical infrastructures are expanded and improved upon. The proposal is not to further experiment with the holistic community model, including its governance solutions. Orgnets are specific to our time in that they struggle with the way in which technology 'eats' itself into the dynamics of what is considered a group. Organized networks reverse social procedures in that these start off at the network level. The network is not a voluntary, bottom-up association of groups (as in the 1970s ideology) but manifests itself as the dominant everyday form of social life. How orgnets relate to each other, and to other organizational forms, is an interesting question, but one that cannot be properly addressed as long as the contours of the orgnets are only barely becoming visible. We have to get a better understanding of what's going on (and what's possible) at this basic level. Graeber writes: 'It's always better, if possible, to make decisions in smaller groups: working groups, affinity groups, collectives. Initiative should rise from below. One should not feel one needs authorisation from anyone, even the General Assembly (which is everyone), unless it would be in some way harmful to proceed without.'[30]

A justified critique should be applied to the presupposed 'vitalist impulse' of networks. What needs to be questioned is the assumption that social structures arise out of the blue. There is no emergence, no frictionless becoming, only trial and error, aimed at reaching the critical mass after which coalitions are built and separate actions snowball into a larger Event. What such Bergsonian metaphors seem to suggest is that what movements, in particular, must do is to free up the energy from inside: a liberation from inner desires in order to connect to the larger, moving swarm. What movements most of all do is surprise us (in particular the ones that are most involved). Instead of debunking the 'emergence' idea, it is perhaps better to frame historically certain political configurations in order to get a better understanding of what could work now, in comparison to the turbulent era forty years ago (the Golden Age of pop culture, social movements from feminism to squatting, armed struggle, decolonization and growing environmental/nuclear awareness). The big difference with the recent past is the poor state of the art of the 'rainbow coalition', the patchwork of minorities, as it was once called. Instead of 'affinity groups', we now have unstable networks with an informal core and weak ties amongst most of its members, in particular on its fringes.

In today's networks, we pass around status updates. If we take apart Twitter's question 'What's happening?', the event is taken as a given.[31] The corporate assumption is that, no matter how small, there is always an event in our lives that we can talk about. And it is especially this small talk that marketing experts are interested in. We do not find out about the origin of the happening, nor do we deconstruct the urge to press occurrences into the news category. Is a microblogging service that asks the strategic question 'What's to be done?' an option? How could its design look? What's important here is the implementation, on the software level, of a so-called 'open conspiracy'.

Instead of assuming the existence of a movement, there are cores, cells, small structures that work hard to pull issues off the ground, groups that often barely know each other and that operate in different locations and contexts. One thing is certain: there is nothing heroic about their work. We cannot predict where their efforts will lead. Ever since the 1970s, networking these initiatives has been seen as a vital first step to get a movement up and running. This grassroots approach, so closely tied to the notion of direct democracy within a local setting, has been confronted with additional models of 'summit hopping' (as practised by the Global Justice Movement). Their aim has been to confront global elites in their local habitat – at G-8, G-20 and EU, IMF and World Bank meetings – enabling spasmodic revolts in which networked coordination is limited to during the event itself (e.g. Paris 2005, the 2011 London riots, the Blockupy protests against the opening of the ECB headquarters in Frankfurt, March 2015).[32] The wave of protests in 2011–13 can be seen as a more hybrid model, as they contained elements of both of the above-mentioned forms of protest. Their action aimed at local/national impacts but these are easy to identify with across the globe. Current movements scale up very fast (in part because of the use of social media during the days of mobilization), yet, as street crowds, they disintegrate just as quickly.

Leaderless Events

It can be productive to contrast the current debate on organization with, for instance, the West-German 'Spontis', the horizontalists of their time that opposed the Marxist-Leninist, Trotskyist and Maoist groups and their top-down vanguard strategies, believing in the power of small, local groups that popped up unexpectedly, in a variety of contexts, each time using different names, without spokespersons. These days, it is the swarming masses that are spontaneous. They can no longer so easily be programmed by a consumerist-liberal consensus. However, the uprisings no longer seem to be 'initiated' by small groups of (anarchist) activists, either. Today's uprisings are much less predictable and often do not have a clearly defined ideological agenda. The 2013–14 Euromaidan protests in Kiev are a standout example here with their wide range of factions, from anarchists and civil society middle-class liberals to militant nationalists and fascists. At such moments, the snowballing network effect is overtaking the capacity to organize. Ironic strategies that 'blow up' conventional meaning through absurdist and playful interventions no longer spark these events. The media themselves offer enough contradictory material to create dialectical cascades for 1,001 events already. But that's not the point. There is overwhelming evidence. Big data, small data, it doesn't matter. Mass consciousness is there, the work has already been done, debates have been held and problems identified, time and again. What is lacking is the collective imagination on how to organize education, housing, communication, transport and work in a different, more sustainable way.

In the former West, the crowd is no longer a threat. At best it is a carnivalesque symbol, a signal for frictions in society (but which ones?). We are all products of The Century of the Self.[33] No matter how powerful the image of large gatherings of protesters may be, there is always an element of entertainment in it, produced for individual consumption. For many, rioting is a form of extreme sports, confronting the mix of police and the military, heavily supported by mobile units of the surveillance apparatus. Despite all the violence, the question posed here is how to create non-eventful forms of organization that work in the background and form possible bridges between events. Are 'crystals' still the cause of events?[34] If the answer is yes, let's create one, two, many of them, and stop waiting for the Zeitgeist to change.

A main issue is the question of leadership in internet culture. There is not much claim to fame here. The celebrity-centred SPO-model (Single Person Organization), as practised by Wikileaks' Julian Assange, has proven to be disastrous, comparable to a similarly closed 'cabal' circle, and the main reason for Wikipedia's stagnation. Less controversial are rotating moderation models, as in the case of some email lists (such as Empyre), and the 'karma' voting systems operated by users, as in the case of Slashdot. News aggregator Hacker News is using a similar system to weigh the ranking of postings on geeky forum websites. However, so far, no voting or moderation system has become popular in circles of artists and activists. Instead, most of us prefer to give our votes to Facebook and Twitter in the form of likes and retweets.

Another issue these days is the absence of political demands. In the current technological landscape, social media do not focus on transparent technologies of agenda-setting, discursive preparations of policies and decision-making procedures. David Graeber writes: 'We have little idea what sort of organisations, or for that matter, technologies, would emerge if free people were unfettered to use their imagination to actually solve collective problems rather than to make them worse.'[35] It is clear that this issue can't be limited to diversity quandaries and real existing differences of interest. Relevant for both social movements and organized networks is the (potential) influence of the Online Absent Other. It is both politically correct and a comfort for all to state that others who cannot be there in person will be able to steer and not merely witness events. Cameran Ashraf of Global Voices claims: 'Being so connected to something you are disconnected from is, I believe, deeply disturbing to your psyche. Sooner or later things make sense and your mind realises it's been seeing and reading one thing and living another. At that moment it just happens – you "go dark". Vanish.'[36]

Whistleblowing projects confront these questions of demand, execution and connection like any other. In September 2013, three months into the Edward Snowden / NSA scandal, Slavoj Žižek wrote in the *Guardian*: 'We need a new international network to organise the protection of whistleblowers and the dissemination of their message.'[37] Note that Žižek utilizes the two central concepts of the argument being developed here: a network that organizes. Once we have all agreed on this task, it is important to push the discussion further and zoom in on the organizational dimension of this timely effort.

These days, there are many Wikileaks clones. Only some of them, such as Balkan Leaks and Global Leaks, manage to survive. We still have the outstanding technical debate on how to build functioning anonymous submission gateways. I have made it clear that WikiLeaks itself is a negative role model because of the personality cult of its founder and editor-in-chief Julian Assange, whose track record of failed collaborations and falling-outs is impressive, not to mention the unreconstructed gender drama (not uncommon in hacker circles) that led to his never-ending self-imposed hiding in the London Ecuadorian embassy. Apart from this debate about governance, we need to look further into the question of what the network model, in this context, precisely entails. A step that WikiLeaks never dared to take is the one of national branches, based in either nation states or linguistic territories.

To run a virtual global advocacy network, as Žižek suggests, looks sexy because of its cost-effective, flexible nature, but the small scale of Single Person Organizations also makes it hard to lobby in various directions and create new coalitions. Existing networks of national digital civil rights organizations should play a role here, yet haven't so far. And it is important to discuss first why digital civil rights organizations like the US-based Electronic Frontier Foundation and European Digital Rights network, or the German Chaos Computer Club for that matter, have not yet created an appealing campaign that makes it possible for artists, intellectuals, writers, journalists, designers, hackers and other irregulars to coordinate efforts, despite their differences. The same can be said of Transparency International and journalist trade unions. The IT nature of the proponents seems to make it hard for existing bodies to take up the task of protecting and engaging this new form of activism. The June 2013 NSA revelations by whistleblower Edward Snowden have been an opportunity to create new alliances, this time more successfully coordinated by Glenn Greenwald, Laura Poitras, Jacob Appelbaum and others, who work together to analyse and publish documents through the Western mainstream press, from the *Guardian* to *Der Spiegel*.

As much as mainstream social media platforms come with an almost guaranteed capacity to scale as mass networking devices, they are not without problems, many of which are familiar: security of communication (infiltration, surveillance and a wilful disregard of privacy), logic or structure of communication (micro-chatting among friends coupled with broadcasting notices for the many subscribed to the cloud), and an economy of 'free labour' (user-generated data, or 'the social production of value'). Social media architectures have a tendency to incite passive–aggressive behaviour. Users monitor what others are doing from a safe distance while constantly fine-tuning their envy levels. All we're able to do easily is to update our profile and tell the world what we're doing. In this culture of 'sharing', all we can do is display our virtual empathy. Organized networks radically break with the updating and monitoring logic, and shift the attention away from watching and following diffuse networks to getting things done, together.

Autonomy, self-organization and collective property are all values that keep our untimely spaceships afloat and ensure that we can continue our hospitality for generations to come. Yet we all know the danger of boredom, repetition and routine when the management of alternative spaces becomes an aim in itself, and decay inevitably sets in. Redesigning contested spaces has not been the proper answer to the issues that we're confronted with. Hands-on renovations are often presented as the best possible way out of the daily malaise – but they are not. What we've faced over the past ten to fifteen years are changes in 'the social' itself. Do we still need collective spaces when people no longer come together that often? Once you walk away from the closures of identity politics and the whatever attitude of the nihilists, a whole range of new questions opens up, ready to be taken on. What is the future atelier when the artist primarily works on a computer? How can we join the debates and design efforts over the issue of alternative currencies? Why are libraries and coffee shops so popular at a time when no one is supposed to read anymore and bookstores are closing down one after the other? Building on Richard Sennett, Bernard Stiegler and Peter Sloterdijk, what are future crafts that are not retromantic? What are tomorrow's subversive professions? Can we go beyond the sustainability call[38] and fully blend the digital with the social into the urban tissue? Can we provide a radical alternative to Uber, Airbnb and the Starbucks-as-office model? How do we invent new forms of productivity that go beyond the McJobs mode of the service economy-in-ruins?

Instead of focusing on the downward spiral of the (self-)administrated world, it is time to leave behind the dwelling blues, break open the depressive state of mind that is associated with the visible remains of past subcultures and see how we can reconstitute the social. Show us your design. What should collaboration look like? What does it mean when we say distributed and federated? In order to get there, we need to take a radical and, for some, rather unpleasant step: the realization that the social of today is technical. Even though a political economy reading can come up with interesting results (precarity, declining middle class, globalization of poverty and work), from an organizational point of view it is crucial to include media forms and network architectures.

The question I pose here is how to create non-eventful forms of organization that get the job done in the background. If crowd crystals, Leninist kernels, Trotskyist cells and other avant-garde social formations are no longer the cause of events, we might have to move away from the cause–effect thinking altogether. The Spectacle, with its auto-generated intensity of affect goes against the Time of Organization. The complex and muddy coordination between different levels and interests cannot beat the real-time spread of memes. Organized networks grow in response to the universal solution of the algorithm. We organize against aggregation, multiplication and scale. We want seriality, not scale, and voluntarily step back from the viral model that inevitably culminates in the backlash of the sell-out and the Initial Public Offering (the Termidor of the dotcom age when companies were brought to the stock market months after their launch), with management buy-outs and first waves of lay-offs. Beware: how many fall-outs can you afford before you no longer have any more friends? Not many. More and more movements are doing away with leadership – and thriving.

If we look back at recent upheavals, we see bursts of 'social media' activity. From Tahir to Taksim, from Tel Aviv to Madrid, from Sofia to Sao Paolo and Black Lives Matter in the US, what they have in common is communication peaks, which fade away soon after the initial excitement, much in line with the festival economy that drives the Society of the Event. There is also this peculiar feedback loop in which the urgency of the event is tied to the 24-hour news cycle of mainstream media. Once the spectacle has been leached of newsworthy content, the coordination of political passion seems somehow to lose its way. Corporate social networking platforms such as Twitter and Facebook are considered useful to spread rumours, forward pictures and reports, and comment on established media (including the Web). But no matter how intense the street events may have been, they often do not go beyond creating 'short ties'. The temporary autonomous spaces they erect feel more like festivals, revolts without consequences.

There is growing discontent over the event-centred movements. The question of how to reach a critical mass is essential here. Instead of contrasting the Leninist party model with the anarcho-horizontalist celebration of the general assembly, the orgnet proposition is to integrate the general networked intellect into the organization debate. We've come a good 150 years since the Marx–Bakunin debates. It is time to integrate technology into the social tissue and no longer see computers and smart phones as alien tools. The organized networks model has a luxury problem, like most internet applications: it runs the risk of not being able to deal with the (tens of) thousands of users that will get involved. This is the state of exception in which the Event takes over, history takes over, and we experience the brief moments of the extra-technological. But these are the exception. What we need to focus on in the years to come is the time in-between, the long intervals when there is time to build sustainable networks, exchange ideas, set up working groups and realize the impossible, on the spot.

Today's uprisings no longer result from extensive organizational preparations in the background – nor do they produce new networks of 'strong ties'. What's left is a shared feeling: the birth of yet another generation. Even though small groups have often worked on the issues for many years, their efforts are usually focused on advocacy work, designing campaigns, doing traditional media work or organizing those who are immediately affected by the crisis on the ground – important work, but not precisely about preparing for the Big Riot.

Is longing for sustainable forms of organization wishing for too much, when the world seems to be in perpetual flux? Very little stability defines labour and life as we know it. Ideologies have been on the run for decades. So too are political networks amongst activists. At best we can speak of a blossoming of unexpected temporary coalitions. We can complain about social media causing loneliness but, without a thorough re-examination of social media architectures, such sociological observations can easily turn into forms of resentment. What presents itself as social media critique these days often leaves users with a feeling of guilt, with nowhere to go, except

203

to return to the same old 'friends' on Facebook or 'followers' on Twitter. There is more in this world than self-improvement and empowerment. Network architecture needs to move away from the user-centred approach towards task-related design, undertaken in a protected mode.

One of the first observations we need to make is that Anonymous is the missing element in Žižek's list of Assange, Manning and Snowden. Despite several setbacks, Anonymous remains an effective distributed effort to uncover secrets and publicize them, breaking with the neoliberal assumption of the individual as hero who operates out of a subjective impulse to crack the code in order to make sensitive material public. The big advance of anonymous networks is that they depart from the old-school logic of print and broadcasting media that needs to personalize their stories, thereby creating one celebrity after the other. Anonymous is many, not just Lulzsec.

Towards the end of her 2013 book *Agonistics*, Chantal Mouffe calls for social movements and political party factions 'to establish a synergy between different forms of intervention. The objective should be to jointly launch a counter-hegemonic offensive against neoliberalism. It is high time to stop romanticising spontaneism and horizontalism'. She calls on activists to 'accept becoming part of a progressive "collective will" engaged in a "war of position" to radicalise democratic institutions and establish a new hegemony'.[39] This may sound strategic, aiming at power, claiming hegemony, but it leaves the techniques of this democratization of movements – and networks – undiscussed. Before we rush into coalitions, the question of how movements themselves can become more resilient, able to bounce back and reappear, needs to be resolved.

Networks are not goals in themselves and should be made subordinate to organizational purposes. Internet and smart phone-based communication was once new and exciting. This caused some distraction, but distraction itself is becoming boring. The positive side of networks (in comparison to the group) remains their open architecture. What networks need to 'learn' is how to split off or fork once they start getting too big. Intelligent software can assist us to dissolve connections, close conversations and delete groups once their task is over. We should never be afraid to end the party in our constant search to move the social.

NOTES

INTRODUCTION: PREPARING FOR UNCOMMON DEPARTURES

1   Writing in 2015, it is twenty years since the inception of the nettime list, and twenty years since Richard Barbook and Andy Cameron wrote their infamous 'Californian ideology' essay. The Institute of Network Cultures published a twentieth-anniversary edition of the essay in November 2015: http://networkcultures. org/publications.
2   For social media statistics in the USA, see www.pewinternet. org/2015/08/19/mobile-messaging-and-social-media-2015.
3   Radical options are limited as no one has yet come up with concrete proposals to 'cut-up' the internet (not even in the artistic–subversive sense *à la* William Burroughs). The fear of 'Balkanization' runs deep. No one dreams of a weird parallel universe these days (not even Silk Road and other Dark Web initiatives materialize them). Interoperability is the unspoken a-priori of all communication systems. The only option left is to go crypto.
4   On 27 August 2015, 'Facebook hit an unprecedented benchmark: one billion users in a single day. ' "This was the first time we reached this milestone, and it's just the beginning of connecting the whole world", Mark Zuckerberg wrote.': http://money. cnn.com/2015/08/27/technology/facebook-one-billion-users-single-day/index.html.
5   Tarleton Gillespie, 'The politics of platforms', *New Media & Society*, 12 (2010), pp. 248–350. He writes: 'Platforms are typically flat, featureless and open to all. They are anticipatory, but not casual. The word itself suggests a progressive and egalitarian arrangement, promising to support those who stand upon it. The

term retains a populist ethos: a representative speaking plainly and forcefully to his constituents. In any of platform's senses, being raised, level and accessible are ideological features as much as physical ones.'

6 See Sascha Lobo in Spiegel Online on platform capitalism: www. spiegel.de/netzwelt/netzpolitik/sascha-lobo-sharing-economy-wie-bei-uber-ist-plattform-kapitalismus-a-989584.html; *Der Spiegel* Online, 3 September 2014; and Sebastian Olma, 'Never mind the sharing economy: here's platform capitalism', http:// networkcultures.org/mycreativity/2014/10/16/never-mind-the-sharing-economy-heres-platform-capitalism, 16 October 2014.

7 Michael Seemann, *Digital Tailspin*, Amsterdam, Institute of Network Cultures, 2015, pp. 39–42. In this strategic text, Seemann states that 'platforms provide the infrastructure that the next society will operate on. In the future, every politically active individual will have to learn to deal with them.' More on this, in German, in the on-stage dialogue between Michael Seemann and Sebastian Giessmann during Re:publica, Berlin, May 2015.

8 Hans Maarten van den Brink has argued in a similar fashion in the small Dutch-language anthology he put together, in which he framed the 'loss of independence' of classic media makers as a starting point for designing a new public media landscape. See: Hans Maarten van den Brink (ed.), *Onaf, over de zin van onafhankelijkheid in cultuur en media*, Amsterdam, Nieuw Amsterdam Uitgevers, 2013.

9 An obvious reference here would be the MIT Platform Studies book series http://platformstudies.com/started in 2009 by Nick Montfort and Ian Bogost: https://mitpress.mit.edu/index. php?q=books/series/platform-studies. Another would be Anne Helmond's Ph.D. at the University of Amsterdam (published online in August 2015) titled *The Web as Platform: Data Flows in Social Media*: www.annehelmond.nl/2015/08/28/dissertation-the-web-as-platform-data-flows-in-the-social-web/#respond.

10 Zeynep Tufekci, 'What happens to #Ferguson affects Ferguson', medium.com, 14 August 2014.

11 See *Forbes*, 26 August 2014.

12 See also 'When clicks reign, the audience is king', by Ravi Somaiya, *NYT*, 16 August 2015: 'There have been complaints from various corners of the media world that online news has deteriorated, and that it is now focused on the viral at

the expense of the substantive': http://mobile.nytimes.com/2015/08/17/business/where-clicks-reign-audience-is-king.html?referrer=&_r=0.

13 www.sociallyquantum.com/2015/05/facebook-is-going-to-suppress-click.html.

14 Taboola founder, www.bbc.com/news/business-29322578, 30 September 2014.

15 Corey Robin, *The Reactionary Mind*, New York, Oxford University Press, 2011, pp. 98–9. It is important here to de- and re-politicize the conservative as a figure operating in, and tied to, a wider techno-cultural context.

16 Berlin is widely considered a (global) centre for computer hackers, geeks and digital civil rights activists, combined with a modest start-up culture and still-thriving contemporary scene, primarily because of its affordable housing, cheap food and good public infrastructure. The resulting critical mass makes it easy to operate NGOs and campaigns out of Berlin (such as, for instance, TacticalTech and irights.info).

17 In her report of the 2015 Transmediale festival in Berlin, the Norwegian-Australian academic Jill Walker writes: 'Too much of the program so far has been one-sided criticism of datafication and social media that is so simplistic that it makes things worse. Chanting a list of all the things we track is cool. But once that's done, is it really helpful to basically just do that again and again?' (http://jilltxt.net/?p=4221). The Berlin strategy is obviously a better answer to such an interpassive view that defends innocent Big Data research and talks down criticism to appear as subjective complaint. The Berlin digital rights scene deals with this by building coalitions to put genuine internet controversies on longer-term political agendas, based on a strong ecology between diverse initiatives, rooted in different sections of society, from The Chaos Computer Club, Transmediale, *Berliner Gazette* to Netzpolitik and their re:publica gatherings.

18 No matter how important historical studies – such as those by Fred Turner at Stanford – or the history of net cultures circle around Michael Stevenson and the WebCultures mailinglist (webcultures.org) may be, these tend towards explanations from and for the past, unfortunately – not the present. Ruptures since the late 1990s, when business and finance moved in, have been simply too big, combined with a 'conservative revolution' that already started back in the 1970s, for the internet's historical-present to be robustly articulated.

19 Robin, *The Reactionary Mind*, pp. 171–3.
20 Robin, *The Reactionary Mind*, p. 193.
21 Peter Thiel, *From Zero to One: Notes on Startups, or How to Build the Future*, London, Virgin Books, 2014, p. 20.
22 Frank Pasquale, *The Black Box Society: The Secret Algorithms That Control Money and Society*, Cambridge, Mass., Harvard University Press, 2015, p. 141.
23 Julian Assange, *When Google Met Wikileaks*, New York / London, O/R Books, 2014. If Thiel plays the role of the right-wing libertarian, an ideal *agent provocateur*, Eric Schmidt is the reasonable *Realpolitiker*, not unlike the European Labor politician.
24 Petra Löffler, *Verteilte Aufmerksamkeit, Eine Mediengeschichte der Zerstreuung*, Zurich, diaphanes, 2014. See also my interview with her, which focuses on the link between her historical material and the present debate: *The Aesthetics of Dispersed Attention, an Interview with German Media Theorist Petra Loeffler*, published on the nettime list, 24 September 2013, and in NECSUS #4, November 2013, www.necsus-ejms.org/the-aesthetics-of-dispersed-attention-an-interview-with-german-media-theorist-petra-loffler. Also see her lecture at Unlike Us #3, Amsterdam, March 2013. There is more on this in chapter 2.
25 Bernard Stiegler reads these tensions also as a symptom of the abandonment of new generations by the so-called 'analogous natives' that are still in control of most of our institutions.: 'The pharmacology of the mass media has as its main goal the replacement of the intergenerational transmission of prescriptions. Such prescriptions, in which the entry into civility always consists, are replaced by the control of behaviour, constantly transformed by marketing – and via its main carriers, the productions of the programme industries' (*States of Shock*, Cambridge, Polity, 2015, p. 219).
26 David Weinberger, *Too Big to Know*, New York, Basic Books, 2012.
27 More on Morozov in my review of *Save Everything, Click Here*, published in *Open Democracy*, 23 April 2013: www.opendemocracy.net/geert-lovink/eugene-morozov-attacks-internet-consensus-single-handed. I disagree with Morozov's attack on what he calls 'McLuhanesque medium-centrism' – in this case, internet-centrism. In my view, we need a lot more critical scholars that take the internet very seriously, and start

to get an understanding of its functioning from the inside, as a technology, a *Kulturtechnik*, an industry and infrastructure of political economy, and not merely read its populist surface in the cultural studies style. Techno-determinism is an essential stage in such a learning curve, whilst a broader understanding of neoliberal society (and its history) remains another vital pillar. Also, in Morozov's universe, artists, activists and coders are absent, or only appearing as idiots.

28 Evgeny Morozov, 'Socialize the data centres!', *New Left Review* 91 (Jan./Feb. 2015), pp. 45–66.

29 According to Stephen Fidler, reporting for the *Wall Street Journal* from Brussels, Europe won't go for old-style regulation, nor will it choose the Chinese model (building an Alibaba to replace Amazon, a Baidu instead of Google). Instead, it will go for an 'insiders' model. According to Mr Oettinger of the EC, 'European industrial champions would build digital platforms that will dominate the future' (22 May 2015). This means not just barring US companies, but also frustrating European start-ups, and, it goes without saying, civil society initiatives.

30 Franco Berardi, *The Uprising: On Poetry and Finance*, Los Angeles, Semiotext(e), 2012, p. 15, referring to a letter from Bill Gates to John Seabrook.

31 Written in dialogue with the introduction to Bernard Stiegler, *States of Shock, Stupidity and Knowledge in the 21st Century*, Cambridge, Polity, 2015, p. 3.

32 One way towards this would be a critical rereading of classic texts and their legacies, as done, for instance, by Stiegler in his 2012 *States of Shock*. He particularly looks at the 'postmodern' period in the work of Lyotard, in order to finally think together parallel currents in philosophy with shifts in the knowledge industry, from the perspective of a political economy of the digital. One of his verdicts reads: 'The flabbiness of philosophy's political and economic propositions seems, after the fact, to amount to a terrible blindness to what was beginning to transpire with the conservative revolution and the first steps towards financialization' (p. 100). Another approach would be along the lines of Andrew Culp's *Anarchist Without Content* blog that proposes a radical shift from the Joyous Deleuze to the Dark Deleuze: 'What good is joy in this world of compulsive positivity? It is time to move from the chapel to the crypt. There is sufficient to establish a counter-canon.' The Dark Deleuze glossary contains concepts such as Destroy Worlds, Asymmetry,

Interruption, Unfolding, Cataclysmic and The Powers of the False: https://anarchistwithoutcontent.wordpress.com.

33 For a definition of a collective awareness platform, see http://caps-conference.eu and http://ec.europa.eu/digital-agenda/ en/collective-awareness-platforms-sustainability-and-social-innovation.

34 An example could be the art project of Ine Poppe and Sam Nemeth who ran into refugees arriving from Syria during their holiday on the Greek island of Lesbos in May 2015. They became friends with one of them, Ideas, and decided to follow his journey on WhatsApp. Their blog: http://ideasodyssey. blogspot.nl. A report: http://mashable.com/2015/07/03/syrians-europe-whatsapp-refugees.

35 Gabriella Coleman, *Hacker, Hoaxer, Whistleblower, Spy: The Many Faces of Anonymous*, London / New York, Verso, 2014.

36 See https://freebarrettbrown.org: 'Barrett Brown is an imprisoned US journalist. He was described as an unofficial spokesperson for Anonymous before he renounced his ties to the collective in 2011. In 2012, the FBI raided his house, and later that year Barrett was indicted in 12 federal charges relating to the 2011 Stratfor hack. The most controversial charge, linking to the hacked data, was dropped, but in 2015 Brown was still sentenced to 63 months in prison.'

37 Coleman, *Hacker, Hoaxer*, p. 43.

38 Smari McCarthy, 'Engineering our way out of fascism', a keynote lecture at the free software conference FSCONS 2013 (http:// smarimccarthy.is/2014/05/28/engineering-our-way), written in the aftermath of the Snowden revelations. McCarthy's goal here is 'decentralizing everything, encrypting everything, and hardening all of the endpoints', and, further, providing these services to the next 5 billion people; 'Bottom line: if you're developing software and you aren't developing that software for the benefit of all humanity, you are helping the fascists.'

39 See the special section in the *Nation*, 27 May 2015, with contributions by Janelle Orsi, Frank Pasquale, Nathaniel Schneider, Pia Mancini and Trebor Scholz. The authors discuss ways in which tech platforms must be opened up to the commons: 'We have a choice: keep using platforms that widen the wealth gap, or build tech platforms as commons' (Janelle Orsi). Shared ownership and control are critical. Trebor Scholz proposes to start building platform co-op apps: 'To make good digital labor a reality, it is essential for like-minded people to organize, form

kernels of self-organization, and fight for basic democratic rights for cloud workers.'

40 David Berry and Alex Galloway, 'A network is a network is a network: reflections on the computational and the society of control', *Theory, Culture & Society* (2015).

1 WHAT IS THE SOCIAL IN SOCIAL MEDIA?

1 https://en.wikipedia.org/wiki/Sociocybernetics.
2 Quoted from the manuscript chapter of Chris Chesher, 'How computer networks became social', in: Chris Chesher, Kate Crawford and Anne Dunn, *Internet Transformations: Language, Technology, Media and Power* (publication – with Palgrave Macmillan, 2015 – cancelled).
3 It is rarely acknowledged, for example, that as early as 1953 two computers in different locations were able to 'talk' to each other via modems.
4 Nietzsche, 'I go into solitude so as not to drink out of everybody's cistern. When I am among the many I live as the many do, and I do not think I really think. After a time it always seems as if they want to banish my self from myself and rob me of my soul', in *Daybreak: Thoughts on the Prejudices of Morality*, ed. Maudemarie Clark and Brian Leiter, trans. R. J. Hollingdale, Cambridge, Cambridge University Press, 1997 p. 491.
5 Jean Baudrillard, 'The masses: implosion of the social in the media', trans. Marie Maclean, *New Literary History*, 16.3, 'On Writing Histories of Literature' (Spring, 1985), pp. 577–89: www.jstor.org/stable/468841.
6 All quotes by Michael Hardt and Antonio Negri are from *Declaration*, New York, Argo-Navis, 2012, pp. 18–21.
7 Hardt and Negri, *Declaration*, p. 35 (both quotes).
8 See the exchange 'The $100bn Facebook question: will capitalism survive "value abundance"?' on the nettime list, early March 2012. Brian Holmes writes there, in different postings: 'What I have found very limiting in the discourse around so-called web 2.0 is the use of Marx's notion of exploitation in the strict sense, where your labor power is alienated into the production of a commodity and you get an exchange value in return'; 'For years I have been dismayed by a very common refusal to think. The dismaying part is that it's based on the work of European history's greatest political philosopher, Karl

211

Marx. It consists in the assertion that social media exploits you, that play is labor, and that Facebook is the new Ford Motor Co.'; 'The "apparatus of capture", introduced by Deleuze and Guattari and developed into a veritable political economy by the Italian Autonomists and the Multitudes group in Paris, does something very much like that, though without using the concept of exploitation'; 'Social media do not exploit you the way a boss does. It emphatically _does_ sell statistics about the ways you and your friends and correspondents make use of your human faculties and desires, to nasty corporations that do attempt to capture your attention, condition your behaviour and separate you from your money. In that sense, it does try to control you and you do create value for it. Yet that is not all that happens. Because you too do something with it, something of your own. The dismaying thing in the theories of playbour, etc, is that they refuse to recognise that all of us, in addition to being exploited and controlled, are overflowing sources of potentially autonomous productive energy. The refusal to think about this – a refusal which mostly circulates on the left, unfortunately – leaves that autonomous potential unexplored and partially unrealised.'

9   Eva Illouz, *Cold Intimacies: The Making of Emotional Capitalism*, Cambridge, Polity, 2007.
10 Private email correspondence, 5 March 2012.
11 Albert   Benschop,   *Virtual*   Communities:www.sociosite.org/ network.php.
12 See Robert Pfaller, *Ästhetik der Interpassivität*, Hamburg, Plilo Fine Arts, 2008 (in German), and Gijs van Oenen, *Nu even niet! Over de interpassieve samenleving*, Amsterdam, van Gennep, 2011 (in Dutch).
13 See Avital Ronell, *The Telephone Book*, Lincoln, University of Nebraska Press, 1989, starting with p.2: 'You're saying yes, almost automatically, suddenly, sometimes irreversibly. Your picking it up means the call has come through. It means more: you're its beneficiary, rising to meet its demand, to pay a debt. You don't know who's calling or what you are going to be called upon to do, and still, you are lending your ear, giving something up, receiving an order.' The historical case here is Heidegger's acceptance of a telephone call he received in 1933 from the SA Storm Trooper Bureau (p. 6). Heidegger traces his relationship to National Socialism to this call. Ronell's project is to prove that Heidegger walks into a trap: 'I want to trace this trap to

one day, one event. I am going to take the same call several times, and then try to move beyond it' (p. 16).

14 Baudrillard, 'The masses': www.jstor.org/stable/468841.

15 See www.theatlantic.com/technology/archive/2012/12/bruce-sterling-on-why-it-stopped-making-sense-to-talk-about-the-internet-in-2012/266674. Sterling wrote: 'In 2012 it made less and less sense to talk about "the Internet", "the PC business", "telephones", "Silicon Valley", or "the media", and much more sense to just study Google, Apple, Facebook, Amazon and Microsoft. These big five American vertically organised silos are re-making the world in their image. If you're Nokia or HP or a Japanese electronics manufacturer, they stole all your oxygen. There will be a whole lot happening among these five vast entities in 2013. They never compete head-to-head, but they're all fascinated by "disruption".'

16 'The majority of traffic on the internet this year was from bots, according to Incapsula's Bot Traffic Report 2014. This year saw 56 percent of all website traffic coming from bots, with 29% of those bots being considered "bad", and 27% being "good"': www.scmagazine.com/bot-traffic-overall-decreased-from-2013-incapsula-report-says/article/390564.

17 For the English translation of this essay, 'In the shadow of the silent majorities ... or, the end of the social', trans. Paul Foss, Paul Patton and John Johnston, see, for instance: http://autonomous university.org/sites/default/files/Baudrillard_Shadow-of-the-Silent-Majorities.pdf.

18 Catch-phrase of Professor Professor, a Bavarian character who speaks English with a heavy German accent in the BBC animation series *The Secret Show* from 2007.

19 www.nytimes.com/2012/02/25/us/25iht-currents25.html?_r=1.

20 Read more at http://successcreeations.com/438/definition-of-social-media/#ixzz1nJmIQl1c.

21 Andrew Keen, *Digital Vertigo*, New York, St Martin's Press, 2012, p. 13.

2 AFTER THE SOCIAL MEDIA HYPE: DEALING WITH INFORMATION OVERLOAD

1 This chapter continues the research in the first chapter of my *Networks Without a Cause: A Critique of Social Media* (Cambridge, Polity, 2011), entitled 'Psychopathology of information overload'.

2   Dambisa Moyo, *How the West was Lost*, London, Penguin Books, 2011.

3   Peter Sloterdijk: 'What the internet is all about: organon of the world spirit, basic technology to provide global democracy, the new Crystal Palace, a universal bazar. At the same time it is a digital railway station district, at best a virtual Hyde Park where every aroused citizen can blast their complaints from a crate' (my translation), in: *Zeilen und Tage: Notizen 2008–2011*, Berlin, Suhrkamp Verlag, 2012, p. 325.

4   See the series of articles in the German weekly *Die Zeit* on truth and propaganda in the internet age, July 2015: www.zeit.de/2015/26/journalismus-medienkritik-luegenpresse-vertrauen-ukraine-krise.

5   James Gleick, 'Librarians of the Twitterverse', *New York Review of Books*, 16 January 2013: www.nybooks.com/blogs/nyrblog/2013/jan/16/librarians-twitterverse.

6   Re-reading Christopher Lasch, *The Culture of Narcissism: American Life in an Age of Diminishing Expectations*, New York, Warner, 1979, is essential here. The subtitle of his classic text could be easily updated and re-framed for the present. In particular his question, 'Have we fallen in love with ourselves?', has been answered. 'Having displaced religion as the organising framework of American culture, the therapeutic outlook threatens to displace politics', he writes (p. 42). We can all agree that this process is completed, resulting in a 'democratic deficit', and that diminished expectations have led to new forms of protest and discontent.

7   Geert Lovink, 'The aesthetics of dispersed attention: an interview with German media theorist Petra Löffler' in NECSUS (Autumn 2013): www.necsus-ejms.org/the-aesthetics-of-dispersed-attention-an-interview-with-german-media-theorist-petra-loffler.

8   The river is a favourite metaphor of RSS inventor and blogger Dave Winer who has turned this idea into an entire social media philosophy. See www.scripting.com.

9   Clay A. Johnson, *The Information Diet: A Case for Conscious Consumption*, Sebastopol, Calif., O'Reilly, 2012.

10   Peter Sloterdijk, *Du musst dein Leben ändern*, Frankfurt am Main, Suhrkamp, 2009, translated into English as *You Must Change Your Life*, Cambridge, Polity, 2014.

11   See his interview with Salon.com: www.salon.com/2012/12/29/slavoj_Žižek _i_am_not_the_worlds_hippest_philosopher.

12 Howard Rheingold, *Net Smart: How to Thrive Online*, Cambridge, Mass., MIT Press, 2012.
13 Tom Chatfield, *How to Thrive in the Digital Age*, London, PanMacmillan, 2012.
14 See, for instance, the ambivalent report of Paul Miller on his year offline from the internet: https://www.theverge.com/2013/5/1/4279674/im-still-here-back-online-after-a-year-without-the-internet. His summary: 'you don't need to go on a yearlong internet fast to realise your sister has feelings'. A collective effort is, for example, The National Day of Unplugging (http://nationaldayofunplugging.com/about-us), organized by Reboot, which aims 'to rekindle connections and re-imagine Jewish lives full of meaning, creativity, and joy'.

3 A WORLD BEYOND FACEBOOK: THE ALTERNATIVE OF UNLIKE US

1 Dark visions from Europe arise.: 'We witness the rise of a new absolute power. Google transfers its radical politics from cyberspace to reality. It will earn its money by knowing, manipulating, controlling the reality and cutting it into the tiniest pieces' (FAZ, 30 April 2014, written by Shoshana Zuboff).
2 See Terry Eden: 'Literally everyone I know is doing amazing stuff! Sure, there's the odd moan about a crappy commute, or a missed Christmas present. But everyone is so unnervingly upbeat all the time. I wonder what this does for our mental health? When all you see is the relentless cheeriness of all your friends, suddenly finding yourself miserable can be deeply distressing. Your friends are always flying off somewhere exotic, and buying new cars, and having exciting careers. You just sit in your underwear wondering if visiting Vimeo rather than YouTube counts as a life changing experience ... It's no longer a case of "keeping up with the Joneses" – you now have to keep up with everyone you've ever met, no matter what the cost': http://shkspr.mobi/blog/2012/12/why-facebook-makes-me-feel-like-a-loser.
3 On Facebook, Dick El Demasiado wrote the following entry: 'I just discovered that the so-called re-vamped Myspace has erased all of everybody's dialogues and interaction. Without a single warning, just because of change of marketing, they just have erased the little humanity that was in their service. This means a whole generation has lost their love notes, fan dialogues, intercultural exchange and first approaches. If Anne Frank would

have had Myspace we wouldn't know about her feelings anymore' (28 July 2013, via Josephine Bosma).

4   See the Ph.D. thesis of Taina Bucher, 'Programmed sociality: a software studies perspective on social networking sites', Faculty of Humanities, University of Oslo, 2012, http://tainabucher. com. In this, she develops a sophisticated theory of social media as black boxes, going back to the original meaning of the concept, coming from cybernetics.

5   In her Ph.D. study on trolls, 'This is why we can't have nice things', Whitney Phillips is expressing the same fear: 'It became painfully apparent that I was no longer writing a study of emergent subcultural phenomena. I was instead chronicling a subcultural lifestyle ... I spent many a sleepless night worried that my dissertation would be outdated before I finished writing it' (p. 45). Her study has now been published as *This Is Why We Can't Have Nice Things: Mapping the Relationship between Online Trolling and Mainstream Culture*, Cambridge, Mass., MIT Press, 2015.

6   http://www.jstor.org/stable/468841Jean   Baudrillard,   'The masses: implosion of the social in the media', trans. Marie Maclean, *New Literary History*, 16.3, 'On Writing Histories of Literature' (Spring 1985), p. 577: www.jstor.org/stable/468841.

7   See Hannah Arendt's chapter on the Social Question in *On Revolution*, New York, The Viking Press, 1963, p. 6: 'Marx's transformation of the social question into a political force is contained in the term "exploitation", that is, in the notion that poverty is the result of exploitation through a "ruling class" which is in the possession of the means of violence.' See https:// archive.org/stream/OnRevolution/ArendtOn-revolution_djvu. txt.

8   www.nybooks.com/articles/archives/2010/nov/25/generation-why.

9   Cory Doctorow, 'Lockdown, the coming war on general-purpose computing', http://boingboing.net/2012/01/10/lockdown.html.

10   For more information on the Unlike Us network, the related email list, upcoming events, including the blog and (academic) publications, see: http://networkcultures.org/wpmu/unlikeus.

11   http://europe-v-facebook.org/EN/en.html. For more on its class action, see https://www.fbclaim.com/ui/page/faqs?lang=en.

12   See, for instance, the conference in Berlin on 1 August 2013, with talks given by Christian Grothoff, Carlo von lynX, Jacob Appelbaum and Richard Stallman: https://gnunet.org/

internetistschuld. Its slogan was 'You broke the Internet. We'll make ourselves a GNU one.'

13 Christian Fuchs, *Social Media – a Critical Introduction*, London, Sage, 2014.

14 Vito Campanelli, *Web Aesthetics*, Rotterdam, INC/NAi Publishers, 2010.

15 Examples of artistic projects in this context vary from Crystal Pillars by Constant Dullaart, FriendFracker by Lozano-Hemmer and Reed (http://lozano-hemmer.com/friendfracker. php), Incautious Porn (http://incautious.org), Owen Mundy's www.commodify.us, Julien Deswaef's bot on Facebook (http:// loveMachine.cc), the whatever button (www.shifteast.com/the-whatever-button-likes-it-all), and Wages for Facebook by Laurel Ptak (wagesforfacebook.com).

16 As discussed in, for instance, Paolo Gerbaudo, *Tweets and the Street: Social Media and Contemporary Activism*, London, Pluto Press, 2012.

17 April Glaser and Libby Reinish, 'How to block the NSA from your Friends List', *Slate* (17 June 2013): www.slate.com/blogs/ future_tense/2013/06/17/identi_ca_diaspora_and_friendica _are_more_secure_alternatives_to_facebook.html.

18 A good introduction to the alternative social media initiatives is the work of Robert Gehl, a Salt Lake City scholar and active member of Unlike Us. See his book *Reverse Engineering Social Media: Software, Culture, and Political Economy in New Media Capitalism*, Philedelphia, Temple Press University, 2014, and his website www.robertwgehl.org.

19 https://ello.co, quoted on 24 September 2014 when the service was launched.

20 Michael Dieter commented on the Unlike Us list: 'There's something really appealing about how they're inverting certain expectations of mainstream UX, critically commenting on it and using their apparent poverty of features to an advantage. In this respect, they actually represent a consensual design experiment against the worst excesses of "dark patterns" and "growth hacking" in social media (http://modelviewculture.com/pieces/ the-fantasy-and-abuse-of-the-manipulable-user). Things like foregrounding the profile delete button and a general policy of following the users and buttons are cool.'

21 Christian Fuchs, Unlike Us mailinglist, 26 September 2014.

22 www.dailydot.com/technology/diaspora-ello-facebook-battle-of-social.

23 Comment of Aral Balkan: https://aralbalkan.com/notes/ello-goodbye.
24 http://venturebeat.com/2013/06/05/with-12m-in-funding-ne3twork-aims-to-build-a-web-experience-based-on-your-interests.
25 http://schedule.sxsw.com/2013/events/event_IAP407. Dave Winer: 'What comes next is an easy way for the generation of people who grew up on Facebook to create their own social networks, accessible only by the people they want to share it with': http://threads2.scripting.com/2013/march/whatComesAfterFacebook.
26 An example would be the Dutch corporate research report entitled 'The dark side of social media', produced by Sogeti Nederland: vint.sogeti.com/wp-content/uploads/2013/04/VINT-The-Dark-Side-of-Social-Media-Alarm-Bells-Analysis-and-the-Way-Out.pdf.
27 Firechat review: http://breizh-entropy.org/~nameless/random/posts/firechat_and_nearby_communication.
28 The You Broke the Internet campaign offers 'theory and practice of a complete encrypted and obfuscated new internet stack, enabling us to unfold a carefree digital living': http://youbroketheinternet.org.
29 Information provided by Hellekin on the Unlike Us mailing list, 17 February 2014.
30 Carlo on the Unlike Us list, 24 June 2015: 'What it takes is legislation that forbids companies from accessing any conversations between people.' See also www.youbroketheinternet.org/#legislation.

4 HERMES ON THE HUDSON: MEDIA THEORY AFTER SNOWDEN

1 A phrase, still used in the early nineties, by the Australian cyber-feminist collective VNS-Matrix.
2 Zeynep Tufekci, 'Is the Internet good or bad? Yes. It's time to rethink our nightmares about surveillance': www.medium.com, 17 February 2014.
3 Alexander Galloway, Eugene Thacker and McKenzie Wark, *Excommunication: Three Inquiries in Media and Mediation*, Chicago, University of Chicago Press, 2014. Note: an earlier version of this chapter on the trio's work appeared in e-flux journal #54 (April 2014): www.e-flux.com/journal/hermes-on-the-hudson-notes-on-media-theory-after-snowden.

4   Siegfried Zielinski, ... *After the Media: News from the Slow-fading Twentieth Century*, Minneapolis, Univocal Publishing, 2013.

5   Galloway, Thacker and Wark, *Excommunication*, p. 29.

6   Galloway, Thacker and Wark, *Excommunication*, p. 153.

7   Leo Strauss, *Persecution and the Art of Writing*, Chicago, University of Chicago Press, 1988, p. 25.

8   See the web archive of the Nettime mailing list for a more detailed account of the 'post-digital' debate, March 2014: http://nettime.org/Lists-Archives/nettime-l-1403/threads.html.

9   Galloway, Thacker and Wark, *Excommunication*, p. 21.

10   Galloway, Thacker and Wark, *Excommunication*, p. 10.

11   Niklas Luhmann, *Social Systems*, Stanford, Stanford University Press, 1995, Preface to the German Edition, p. xlv.

12   The mono-disciplinary social science approach that North-American sociologists established in 1999, with the founding of the Association of Internet Researchers, has so far not been challenged or changed. AoIR is run as a North-American academic professional association, with its resulting cultural specificities, such that the emphasis is on social science peer-review journals, conferences in hotels, early bird discounts and board elections, thereby limiting itself to the internet researchers who chose to have a career in Anglo-Saxon universities with their particular career paths and related lingo ('early career' scholars, tenure track etc.). This not only leaves out programmers, philosophers, designers and artists, but also does not recognize the reality that most internet 'researchers' in fact work inside corporations and civil society organizations, and not in academia.

13   http://bit.ly/NwwoIm.

14   http://monoskop.org/The_Media_Are_With_Us.

15   Tufekci, 'Is the Internet good or bad?'.

16   Jonathan Crary, *24/7: Late Capitalism and the Ends of Sleep*, New York, Verso, 2013.

5 INTERNET REVENUE MODELS – A PERSONAL ACCOUNT

1   Isaiah Berlin, 'Two concepts of liberty', in: *The Proper Study of Mankind*, New York, Farrar, Straus and Giroux, 1998, p. 192.

2   'Popper, Soros and pseudo-masochism', posted on 2 May 2012: http://andreworlowski.com/2012/05/02/popper-soros-and-pseudo-masochism.

3   See, for instance, the Free4What campaign from November 1999, developed during the Temporary Media Lab project, hosted by the Kiasma Museum in Helsinki: http://project.waag.org/free.

4   A recent example is Peter Osnos, 'The enduring myth of the "free" internet', *The Atlantic* (February 2013), http://m.theatlantic.com/technology/archive/2013/02/the-enduring-myth-of-the-free-internet/273515/. See also Nathaniel Tkacz, 'From open source to open government: a critique of open politics', *Ephemera*, 12.4 (2012), and his book *Wikipedia and the Politics of Openness*, Chicago/London, University of Chicago Press, 2015.

5   A first draft of this chapter appeared in the Paris-based *CMD Magazine*'s special issue on 'Money' (Summer 2015), edited by Shulea Chang.

6   See 'Free! Why $0.00 is the future of business', www.wired.com/techbiz/it/magazine/16-03/ff_free?currentPage=all. See also Anderson's book, which came out not long after this Wired cover story: Chris Anderson, *Free: How Today's Smartest Businesses Profit by Giving Something for Nothing*, New York, Hyperion, 2009. Robert Levine's critical book *Free Ride: How Digital Parasites are Destroying the Culture Business, and How the Culture Business Can Fight Back* was published soon after by Anchor Books, New York, in 2011. However, Levine doesn't mention that the old copyright system didn't work for artists, and only seems to be concerned with the business interests of the traditional culture industries such as print, TV, film and record labels.

7   Nathaniel Tkacz investigates this question in *Wikipedia and the Politics of Openness*. According to him, Popper only defines openness in a negative way – namely, as not fascism and not communism. It is only in the past decades (after 1989?) that the *force of the open* has been put into action. Whereas Tkacz deals with openness, I am more interested here in 'the free'.

8   I am a proud content producer. Unlike Rick Falkvinge, I do not think that the word 'content' is an evil invention of the copyright lobby. On 30 August 2015, Rick wrote on the Torrent Freak site that 'the word "content" means that there must also be a "container", and that container is the copyright industry'. From the perspective of independent publishing, this is simply not the case. Our own channels also need content (https://torrentfreak.com/when-youre-calling-culture-content-y-150830). However, I

agree with Falkvinge that language matters. In my understanding, I would distinguish content from (meta)data and code, and
from the context and the wider ecology in which any creative
expression is situated.

9   Jochai Benkler, *The Wealth of Networks*, New Haven, Yale
University Press, 2006, p. 37.

10 Ole Bjerg, *Making Money: The Philosophy of Crisis Capitalism*,
London, Verso, 2014.

11 See the classic text by Arthur Kroker and Michael Weinstein,
Data Trash: Theory of the Virtual Class, New York, St Martins
Press, 1994, which suffered, like so many studies of its time,
from a speculative overestimation of a 'politics of the body'
related to 'virtual reality' and a relative neglect of the network
capacities of the internet and mobile phones, because the internet didn't fit into French theory's categories of the time (and still
doesn't).

12 See https://en.wikipedia.org/wiki/Kurt_Baschwitz: 'Baschwitz
contributed to the founding of a "seminarium" for mass psychology, public opinion and propaganda at the University of
Amsterdam. In 1972 it was renamed the Baschwitz Institute
for collective behaviour studies, before merging with the public
opinion section within the department for communication
studies in 1985.'

13 See her reassessment fifteen years later, posted on the INC
website: http://networkcultures.org/blog/2015/01/29/paulina-
borsook-cyberselfish-15-years-after-part-1.

14 See http://bad.eserver.org/faq/what_is_bad_subjects.html/en.

15 For the archive of the project, see www.medialounge.net/lounge/
workspace/index.html.

16 More on this on the iDC list, the email forum of the Institute of
Distributed Creativity, led by the New School scholar Trebor
Scholz: http://blog.gmane.org/gmane.culture.media.idc/month=
20100201.

17 See, for instance, https://news.yahoo.com/huffington-posts-
unpaid-bloggers-taking-arianna-court-20110412-081829-782.
html.

18 The archive of the radio show is available online, hosted by
archive.org, thanks to Margreet Riphagen who led the digitization of the 120 one-hour radio programmes produced between
1987 and 2000 (however, the interview with Chaum is not yet
digitized). Relevant from the same period is an essay by the
German media theorist Bernhard Vief called 'Digital Geld' in:

Florian Rötzer (Hg.), *Digitaler Schein: Ästhetik der elektronischen Medien*, Frankfurt am Main, Suhrkamp Verlag, 1991. As with most German media theorists, Vief connects money to the known theory universe of the time, such as McLuhan and Baudrillard. By 1991, the digital networks at the London stock exchange had already been in place for many years. The effect of the so-called 'Big-Bang' in terms of market deregulation in the 1980s is unthinkable, with the simultaneous introduction of PCs, terminals and electronic networks. Vief struggles with the question of whether digital money is hardware or software, and with the virtual appearance of it all.

19 It is important in this context to point to the early writings of the Greek ex-minister of finance, Yanis Varoufakis, on Bitcoin. Many reports in 2015 made a direct connection between the Greek debt crisis and cyber-currencies as a possible alternative to the Euro.

6 THE MONEYLAB AGENDA: AFTER FREE CULTURE

1 Large parts of this chapter were initially written together with Nathaniel Tkacz, with whom I worked on the founding of the MoneyLab project in 2012–13. I have turned our shared positions into a single voice (from 'we' to 'I') only to be consistent with the book form. Credit and thanks also go to Patricia de Vries who started at INC in 2013 and became the MoneyLab producer of the first conference in March 2014, MoneyLab #2 in December 2015, and the MoneyLab reader that came out in April 2015 (Geert Lovink, Nathaniel Tkacz, Patricia de Vries, *MoneyLab Reader: An Intervention in Digital Economy*, Amsterdam, Institute of Network Cultures, 2015).

2 David Graeber, *Debt: The First 5,000 Years*, Brooklyn, Melville House Publishing, 2011.

3 See Scott Patterson, *Dark Pools*, New York, Random House, 2012, p. 315.

4 Rudolf Hilferding, *Finance Capital: A Study in the Latest Phase of Capitalist Development*, London, Routledge, 2005. Online text available at https://www.marxists.org/archive/hilferding/1910/finkap/index.htm. Thanks to Ruud Vlek for introducing me to this classic, back in 1981.

5 For more on this argument, see Franco Berardi and Geert Lovink, 'A call to the Army of Love and to the Army of Software',

www.nettime.org/Lists-Archives/nettime-l-1110/msg00017. html. How to regulate high-frequency trading? By slowing it down? An overall ban? How does humankind 'forget' lethal weapons – in this case, algorithms?

6   In English translation: Joseph Vogl, *The Specter of Capital*, Stanford, Stanford University Press, 2014. See also https:// en.wikipedia.org/wiki/Joseph_Vogl.

7   See, for instance, Andrew Goffey's entry on the algorithm in Matthew Fuller (ed.), *Software Studies: A Lexicon*, Cambridge, Mass., MIT Press, 2006. On the pop science end of the scale, see Christopher Steiner, *Automate This: How Algorithms Came to Rule the World*, New York, Portfolio/Penguin, 2012, and Frank Pasquale's *Black Box Society*.

8   Peter North, *Alternative Currency Movements as a Challenge to Globalisation?* Burlington, Ashgate, 2006, p. 3.

9   More on this can be found in the interview with Eduard de Jong, a former DigiCash employee, by Nathaniel Tkacz and Pablo Velasco in Lovink, Tkacz and de Vries, *MoneyLab Reader*, pp. 258–67.

10   In Popper's *Digital Gold*, we find a detailed account of Bitcoin's early dependency on Silk Road.

11   Jean-François Blanchette, *Burdens of Proof: Cryptographic Culture and Evidence Law in the Age of Electronic Documents*, Cambridge, Mass., MIT Press, 2012.

12   See http://networkcultures.org/wpmu/mycreativity, and Geert Lovink and Ned Rossiter (eds.), *MyCreativity Reader: A Critique of Creative Industries*, Amsterdam: Institute of Network Cultures, 2007, available at http://networkcultures.org/wpmu/ portal/publication/mycreativity-reader-geert-lovink-ned-rossiter.

13   See the three articles in the crowdfunding section of the Lovink, Tkacz and de Vries, *MoneyLab Reader*, for first outcomes in this area.

14   See Ethan Mollick, 'The dynamics of crowdfunding: determinants of success and failure', *Social Science Research Network* (25 March 2013): http://papers.ssrn.com/sol3/papers. cfm?abstract_id=2088298.

15   Inge Ejbye Sørensen, 'Crowdsourcing and outsourcing: the impact of online funding and distribution on the documentary film industry in the UK', *Media, Culture & Society*, 34.6 (2012), pp. 726–43.

16   Ian Bogost, 'Kickstarter, crowdfunding platform or reality show?', *Fast Company* (18 July 2012): www.fastcompany.

com/1843007/kickstarter-crowdfunding-platform-or-reality-show.

17   See Brett Scott, *The Heretic's Guide to Global Finance: Hacking the Future of Money*, London, Pluto Press, 2014, and his blog: http://suitpossum.blogspot.ca.

18   www.investopedia.com/articles/financialcareers/08/quants-quantitative-analyst.asp.

19   Philip Mirowski, *Never Let a Serious Crisis Go to Waste*, London / New York, Verso, 2013, p. 333.

20   Mirowski, *Never Let a Serious Crisis Go to Waste*, p. 356.

21   Costas Lapavitsas, *Profiling Without Producing: How Finance Exploits Us All*, London / New York, Verso, 2013, p. 138. Max Keiser happens to be an early supporter of Bitcoin and has launched his own crypto-currency, the MaxCoin.

22   See www.zerohedge.com and http://rt.com/shows/keiser-report.

23   See, for instance, www.mobilemoneysummit.com, where Visa Inc. is one of the sponsors.

24   See https://temporaryculture.wordpress.com/san-precario2.

7 FOR BITCOIN TO LIVE, BITCOIN MUST DIE

1   This essay was written together with Patrice Riemens in 2014–15 and slightly rewritten for this publication.

2   www.theguardian.com/world/2014/jul/08/kyrgyzstan-bitcoin-experiment-migrant-savings.

3   Ippolita, *In the Facebook Aquarium*, Amsterdam, Institute of Network Cultures, 2015.

4   I'm reminded of a running joke here from the glorious era of French intellectualism that conjures Nizan and Sartre in their student days at the Ecole Normale Supérieure, vying with each other in deconstructing the difference between 'the notion of concept' and 'the concept of notion'. 'Trust' and 'value' make good candidates for such a game.

5   Geek suprematism, run by an 'algocracy' (http://philosophicald-isquisitions.blogspot.nl/2014/01/rule-by-algorithm-big-data-and-threat.html).

6   As Nathaniel Popper writes in *Digital Gold* (London, Penguin Books, 2015), five years after its invention, Bitcoin 'was still used almost entirely for speculation, gambling and drugs dealing'. On the same page, Popper mentions the 'built-in incentives discouraging people from using it' and describes the hoarding as

deflation: 'What were all these locked-up virtual coins worth if no one was doing anything with them?' (pp. 219–20). The Ponzi scheme is noticed too but Popper is too much caught up in the excitement of being amongst pioneers that he shies away from directly criticizing the Bitcoin architects for all these fundamental problems.

7 https://en.wikipedia.org/wiki/Ethereum.

8 Popper, *Digital Gold*, p. 336.

9 Yanis Varoufakis, 'Bitcoin and the dangerous fantasy of a-political money' (blogpost), http://yanisvaroufakis.eu/2013/04/22/bitcoin-and-the-dangerous-fantasy-of-apolitical-money. See also his later rejoinder on the many comments: http://yanisvaroufakis.eu/2014/02/15/bitcoin-a-flawed-currency-blueprint-with-a-potentially-useful-application-for-the-eurozone.

10 See Saskia Sassen's opening speech at MoneyLab #1 conference, Amsterdam, March 2014 (http://vimeo.com/90207380). See also http://networkcultures.org/wp-content/uploads/2014/05/MoneyLab_Conference_Report_2014.pdf, and her introduction to Geert Lovink, Nathaniel Tkacz, Patricia de Vries, *MoneyLab Reader: An Intervention in Digital Economy*, published by the Institute of Network Cultures, Amsterdam, 2015.

11 One should always remember that 'money' (coins, notes) are legal tender, but bank deposits are not, and that their protection is moot – and, above a certain sum, non-existent.

12 See Caroline Nevejan, 'Presence and the design of trust', Ph.D. dissertation University of Amsterdam, 2007: http://nevejan.org/presence.

8 NETCORE IN UGANDA: THE I-NETWORK COMMUNITY

1 The reference used here would be the report of the trend forcasting group k-hole.net from October 2013 called *Youth Mode: A Report on Freedom* (http://khole.net/dl?v=4). The Urban Dictionary defines normcore as 'a subculture based on conscious, artificial adoption of things that are in widespread use, proven to be acceptable, or otherwise inoffensive. Ultra-conformists' (www.urbandictionary.com/define.php?term=normcore).

2 Think of the dialectics between networking and notworking as described in Geert Lovink, 'The Principle of Notworking',

Hogeschool van Amsterdam, 2005: http://networkcultures.org/blog/publication/the-principle-of-notworking-geert-lovink.

3   In the list discussions, advertisement promises are often compared to the somewhat different reality on the ground – for instance in the case of the greatest carrier in the country, MTN, or the performance of new players. Take Cavin Mugarura, defending Vodafone: 'Vodafone is here to make a buck and they are providing a service which is better than the available competition, they are not Red Cross or National Water which is providing contaminated water to its citizens hence the typhoid outbreaks' (18 March 2015).

4   Margaret Sevume, email interview, 4 April 2015.

5   Margaret Sevume, i-network, 2 December 2014.

6   Margaret Sevume, i-network, 20 March 2015.

7   Discussion on the i-network list, 1 April 2015.

8   Green Mugerwa, i-network, 24 November 2014.

9   'Mwesigwa, you said: "Point is maturity, responsibility, experience and professionalism has nothing to do with age." I say: Sometimes it does' (James Mwesigwa).

10   www.i-network.or.ug/index.php?option=com_content&view=article&id=462:i-networks-decade-of-ict-knowledge-sharing&catid=161:q2-newsletter-2010&Itemid=185.

11   *Daily Monitor*, 19 November 2011.

12   'The SEACOM submarine fibre optic network system was launched on 23 July 2009. The cable network serves to directly connect South Africa and Eastern Africa with Europe and Southern Asia, covering a distance of over 17,000 km worth of fibre optic technology' (www.seacom.mu).

13   Joshua Twinamasiko, i-network, 15 May 2010.

14   The group consisted of Ali Balunywa, Guido van Diepen, Wouter Dijkstra, Kai Henriquez and Ben White.

15   In 2015, about 25 per cent of the population is connected to the internet in Uganda, equaling 8.5 million people out of a population of 35 million. Since 2012, an average of 1 million new users have been added to the internet each year. In 2012, the total number of users was 5.7 million, in 2013 it was 6.8 million, and in 2014 users numbered 7.3 million (figures from the Ugandan Communications Commission).

16   Living in a Christian orthodox village, north of Amersfoort, in early 1975 I became a member of the local 'Wereldwinkel' group, a lively shop that sold 'third World' products and leftist political literature, with subjects ranging from anti-colonial

struggles, to feminism, to anti-militarism – a defining experience in terms of my political socialization that also shaped my interests in literature and philosophy.

17 For a summary of these networks, see Geert Lovink, 'ICT after development: the Incommunicado agenda', in: Geert Lovink, *Zero Comments*, New York, Routledge, 2007, pp. 161–84. In the same book there is a similarly focused chapter to this one, about the first five years of the Delhi new media centre Sarai.

18 See Geert Lovink and Soenke Zehle, *Incommunicado Reader*, Amsterdam, Institute of Network Cultures, 2006. I have summarized the debates of the Incommunicado network in *Zero Comments*. The <incom> mailinglist ceased to exist around mid-2010. No attempts were made to organize a second meeting after the first Incommunicado conference in June 2005 in De Balie in Amsterdam.

19 According to Wikipedia, the first BRIC summit, held in Yekaterinburg on 16 June 2009, was attended by the leaders of Brazil, Russia, India and China.

20 See his blog 'ICTs for development', https://ict4dblog.wordpress.com, and his Centre for Development Informatics at the University of Manchester: www.cdi.manchester.ac.uk.

21 A version of the interview transcription can be found at http://chimurengachronic.co.za/the-internet-is-afropolitan.

22 Quotes are from the interview transcription: http://chimurenga-chronic.co.za/the-internet-is-afropolitan.

23 www.fastcodesign.com/1665425/jan-chipchase-lays-out-3-deep-trends-affecting-tech-today.

24 Nishant Shah and Fieke Jansen (eds.), *Digital AlterNatives with a Cause?* Bangalore / The Hague, CIS/HIVOS, 2011.

25 See http://pctechmag.com/2015/04/ugandans-get-onto-mobofree.

26 www.businessdailyafrica.com/Corporate-News/M-Pesa-customers-get-access-to-seven-African-countries/-/539550/2694034/-/ur4epu/-/index.html. The regional expansion of M-Pesa prompted David Mushabe to respond: 'Not heard of Ugandan enterprise expanding in that sense. Is it that we lack technical capacity or business leadership? In terms of money transfer in the region, banks can now pack their bags' (24 April 2015). According to Geria Richard, 'the culture of informality is the reason mobile money and indeed mobile telephony is succeeding in Africa. In Europe the culture of formality explains the growth of banks and the little interest in mobile money.'

27 See, for a summary of his Ph.D., Henry Warwick, *Radical Tactics of the Offline Library*, Amsterdam, Institute of Network Cultures, 2014.
28 David Okwii, i-network, 19 February 2015.
29 Quoted from the press release of the Aurecon report *Data for a 21st Century Africa*: www.modernghana.com/news/595009/1/data-for-a-21st-century-africa.html.
30 www.kccc.interconnection.org/aboutus.htm.

9 JONATHAN FRANZEN AS SYMPTOM: INTERNET RESENTMENT

1 Maddie Crum, 'Jonathan Franzen slams Jennifer Weiner, again', *The Huffington Post*, 13 February 2015: www.huffingtonpost.com/2015/02/13/franzen-weiner_n_6680962.html.
2 Jonathan Franzen, ' "I Just Called to Say I Love You": cell phones, sentimentality, and the decline of public space', *MIT Technology Review*, 19 August 2008: www.technologyreview.com/article/410623/i-just-called-to-say-i-love-you.
3 His publisher had already embellished *The Corrections* 800,000 second print run with Oprah's Book Club seal when he pontificated: 'I see this as my book, my creation, and I didn't want that logo of corporate ownership on it.' Farrar, Straus and Giroux's own logo, part of the Holtzbrinck conglomerate and much bigger than Oprah's business, was not at the forefront of his mind.
4 Quoted in www.telegraph.co.uk/culture/hay-festival/9047981/Jonathan-Franzen-e-books-are-damaging-society.html, written by Anita Singh, 29 January 2012.
5 Jonathan Franzen, *The Kraus Project*, New York, Farrar, Straus and Giroux, 2013, p. 301.
6 It is widely known that Franzen prefers Windows machines to Macs. 'The PC "sobers" what you're doing; it allows you to see it unadorned', he has said, echoing the distinction that Umberto Eco made in 1994 between the protestant MS-DOS and the Catholic Mac. See: Franzen, *The Kraus Project*, pp. 9–10.
7 Franzen, *The Kraus Project*, p. 142.
8 The fact that this email list on the 'cultural politics of the net' survived and remains a very interesting space for critical reflection is in itself remarkable. However, the ironical 'sustainable

growth' curve of its subscriber base also tells us something about the constant threat of (self-)marginalization and stagnation that plagues such initiatives: from 2,000 in September 2001, to 3,250 in July 2004, 4,000 in December 2006, and 4,500 in September 2015.

9 Sherry Turkle, *Alone Together: Why We Expect More from Technology and Less from Each Other*, New York, Basic Books, 2011.

10 Jonathan Franzen, *Farther Away: Essays*, New York, Farrar, Straus and Giroux, 2012, pp. 6–7.

11 In the VPRO documentary 'The world according to Wikipedia', from 2008, Tim O'Reilly said about Keen that 'his whole pitch, I think he was just pure and simple looking for an angle, to create some controversy to sell a book, I don't think there's any substance whatever to his rants' (quoted from http://en.wikipedia.org/wiki/Andrew_Keen).

12 Franzen, *Farther Away*, p. 8.

13 Franzen, *Farther Away*, p. 52.

14 Maria Bustillos, 'Jonathan Franzen, come join us', *The New Yorker*, 18 September 2013: www.newyorker.com/books/page-turner/jonathan-franzen-come-join-us.

15 Mic Wright in the *Telegraph*, 16 September 2013: http://blogs.telegraph.co.uk/technology/micwright/100010517/jonathan-franzen-sounds-off-pompously-about-the-internet-prepare-for-a-really-really-bad-book.

16 Franzen, *Farther Away*, p. 144.

17 See my contribution to the e-flux journal publication, Julieta Aranda, Brian Kuan Wood and Anton Vidokle (eds.), *The Internet Does Not Exist*, Berlin, Sternberg Press, 2015. According to the editors, the internet does not exist because you can't see it, 'it has no shape, no face'. Writing in 2015, the editors admit 'we are still trying to climb onboard, to get inside, to be part of the network. But we will never get inside something that isn't there. ... Just try to get in, you can't' (p. 5). Is this a conceptual problem? Or because of some socio-economic status? A lack of technical literacy? We can only guess.

18 The one time there's talk of protest, it is set in far-away Lithuania: 'The usual crowd of anarchists openly carried banners and placards and privately, in the pockets of their cargo pants, carried powerful bar magnets with which they hoped to erase much data from the center's new Global

Desktops. Their banners said REFUSE IT and COMPUTERS ARE THE OPPOSITE OF REVOLUTION' (Franzen, *The Corrections*, p. 397).

19 Leon Wieseltier, 'Among the disrupted', *The New York Times*, 7 January 2015. Wieseltier writes that 'the processing of information is not the highest aim to which the human spirit can aspire, and neither is competitiveness in a global economy. The character of our society cannot be determined by engineers.' With Michel Serres he asks: 'How can we master our own mastery?'

20 Jonathan Franzen, *The Corrections*, London, Fourth Estate, 2001, p. 181.

21 As Stephen Marche puts it: 'The characters' lives are aimed, with single-minded purpose, toward the achievement of comfortable and socially acceptable financial security, which is threatening always to collapse or is in the process of collapsing. If Raymond Carver was the master of the death of the American dream, Franzen is the chronicler of its ghostly persistence – the combination of economic growth with deepening insecurity' ('Literature for the second Gilded Age', *Los Angeles Review of Books*, 16 June 2014).

22 Douglas Coupland on his isolated holidays in Chili: 'I take a Stephen King novel and a historical biography that will not contain mentions of televisions or mobile phones. It is like temporal tourism; it feels like California in 1910. I do three weeks and then I want to go back' (interview in the *Guardian* by Tim Adams, 19 October 2014).

23 Franzen, *The Corrections*, p. 51.

24 Note that 'Zorn' can be translated as both 'rage' or 'anger' as there are no separate words for these affects in German. For an overview of the structure of anger in this book, see the review: berlinbooks.org/brb/2010/12/rage-and-time.

25 See the event at Erasmus University and Worm in Rotterdam, May 2014, which stated that 'we have often been told that, throughout modern history, resentment has been the basic affective pathology of ideologies of protest on the left and the right. From Romanticism to Jacobinism, from Marxism to National-Socialism, and from feminism to post-colonialism, in each case "explosions" of envious but impotent anger would explain why utopian struggle unavoidably leads to violent dystopia.' The organizers asked: 'Does neoliberalism not cultivate resentment as a strategy of control, a tactic fostering of sad passions such

as envy, hope, nostalgia, indignation and anxiety in people who, in the name of an exhaustive self-preservation that leaves all utopian critique in its wake, will renounce their own power and give in to secrecy and cowardice, turning their guilt inward and their hatred outward?': www.worm.org/home/view/event/11668.

26 Peter Sloterdijk, *Rage and Time: A Psychopolitical Investigation*, New York, Columbia University Press, 2010, p. 283.

27 Franzen, *The Corrections*, p. 117.

28 University of California, Santa Barbara, killer Elliot Rodge: 'You deserve it, just for the crime of living a better life than me. All you popular kids. You've never accepted me, and now you'll all pay for it.'

29 Jeffrey Bernstein's review of the English translation *Rage and Time*, in: *Continental Philosophy Review*, 44.2 (2011), pp. 253–7.

30 You have to love Wikipedia: 'The term shitstorm has come into inflationary use by German-speaking media since 2010 to describe any clamour of outrage on the internet, especially by posting and writing in social media. It was voted *Anglicism of the year 2011* by a jury in Germany. It was voted *Word of the Year* in Switzerland 2012. The opposite of a shitstorm is a candystorm.'

31 Franzen became renowned for his animosity towards Oprah Winfrey, a media saga that continues to this day with Jennifer Weiner, who invented the term 'Franzenfreude' to signal women novelists' resentful relationship to his celebrity: 'Schadenfreude is taking pleasure in the pain of others. Franzenfreude is taking pain in the multiple and copious reviews being showered on Jonathan Franzen.' (Of course, the more accurate term would be 'Schadenfranzen', or even 'Franzenangst', as this Tumblr points out: http://oughtabeagermanwordforthat.tumblr.com/post/1081433318/the-trouble-with-franzenfreude). In what way is there a technical component to this amplification of patriarchal affect online? Does the current meme architecture of social media promote such moods? Gamergate and the subsequent exodus of IT women from Silicon Valley seem to validate this thesis.

32 Michelle Goldberg, 'In defense of Jonathan Franzen', *The Daily Beast*, 26 September 2013: www.thedailybeast.com/articles/2013/09/26/jonathan-franzen-is-right-twitter-is-horrible.html.

33 Franzen interview with *Scratch* magazine by Manjula Martin (Q4 2013): http://scratchmag.net/article/52749949c873d951eb 2ec90e/the_scratch_interview_with_jonathan_franzen.
34 Jonathan Franzen, 'What's wrong with the world', *The Guardian*, 13 September 2013 (no longer available online).
35 Franzen, 'What's wrong with the world', p. 128.
36 Franzen, 'What's wrong with the world', p. 13.
37 Franzen, 'What's wrong with the world', p. 116.
38 Franzen, 'What's wrong with the world', p. 127.
39 Franzen, 'What's wrong with the world', p. 11.
40 Franzen, *The Kraus Project*, p. 11.
41 For Franzen, there can be no multi-tasking: 'Kraus's resistance to music while working is a point of identification with me. I'm always amazed when writers report listening to Beethoven or Arcade Fire while at work. How do they pay attention to two things at once?' (*The Kraus Project*, p. 67).
42 Franzen, *The Kraus Project*, p. 33.
43 Franzen, *The Kraus Project*, p. 12.
44 Franzen, *The Kraus Project*, p. 12.
45 Franzen, *The Kraus Project*, p. 140.
46 Franzen, *The Kraus Project*, p. 140. Here there are clear connections to Evgeny Morozov, *To Save Everything, Click Here: Technology, Solutionism and the Urge to Fix Problems that Don't Exist*, London, Allen Lane, 2013.
47 Franzen, *The Kraus Project*, p. 141.
48 Franzen, 'What's wrong with the world'.
49 Franzen, 'What's wrong with the world', p. 146.
50 Unlike me, also endlessly deciphering newspapers in search of alternative ideas, intellectual and political debates, but in my case *Die Tageszeitung* from Berlin. At the time, I showed zero interest in the other side and looked down on the conservative financial papers as alien, historical relics of the disastrous, outgoing twentieth century.
51 Franzen, *The Kraus Project*, p. 274.
52 Franzen, *The Kraus Project*, p. 273.
53 Joe Fasler, 'Jonathan Franzen on the 19th-century writer behind his internet skepticism', *The Atlantic*, 1 October 2013: www.theatlantic.com/entertainment/archive/2013/10/jonathan-franzen-on-the-19th-century-writer-behind-his-internet-skepticism/280168.
54 Fasler, 'Jonathan Franzen on the 19th-century writer behind his internet skepticism'.

10 URBANIZING AS A VERB: THE MAP IS NOT THE TECH

1   This chapter is an updated version of an original draft, written in March 2012. Thanks go to Tom Apperley and Linda Wallace for valuable comments and edits, and Rob van Kranenburg and Marc Tuters for their extensive input and inspirational work on the politics and aesthetics of RFID / Internet of Things and locative media, respectively. For more on radio-frequency identification (RFID)see https://en.wikipedia.org/wiki/Radio-frequency_identification.

2   See the seventh 2005 issue of the online *Fibreculture Journal* (http://seven.fibreculturejournal.org), dedicated to distributed aesthetics. I have given my own summary and interpretation of this collaborative investigation in the chapter 'Theses on distributed aesthetics' in: Geert Lovink, *Zero Comments: Blogging and Critical Internet Culture*, New York, Routledge, 2007.

3   An example of how not to approach the topic would be to lament the SmartCap, a gadget which reads our level of fatigue while driving around town for our boss: www.smartcap.com.au.

4   The term 'urbanising technologies' originates from Saskia Sassen. You can find her definition here: https://lsecities.net/media/objects/articles/urbanising-technology/en-gb/. Her thesis is that our technologies have not yet been sufficiently 'urbanized'. She stresses the limits of intelligent systems and calls for 'the need to design a system that puts all that technology truly at the service of the inhabitants, and not the other way around: the inhabitants as incidental users'.

5   For instance, see the German anthologies *Stadt am Netz, Ansichten von Telepolis*, ed. Stefan Iglhaut, Armin Medosch, Florian Rötzer, Mannheim, Bollmann, 1996; and *Virtual Cities, Die Neuerfindung der Stadt im Zeitalter der globalen Vernetzung*, ed. Christa Maar and Florian Rötzer, Basel, Birkhäuser, 1997. In both cases, it remains unclear what is being discussed: the use of computer networks in optimizing centralized urban planning, or bottom-up IT usage by citizens to network neighbourhoods and strengthen democratic participation through self-organization? Both? In a way, twenty years later, this confusion still exists.

6   According to Usman Haque, the corporate smart-city rhetoric is all about efficiency, optimization, predictability, convenience and security: 'You'll be able to get to work on time; there'll be a seamless shopping experience, safety through cameras, et cetera. Well, all these things make a city bearable, but they don't make

a city valuable.' Quoted from www.theguardian.com/cities/ 2014/dec/17/truth-smart-city-destroy-democracy-urban-thinkers-buzzphrase.

7   See Norbert Elias' two-volume study *The Civilizing Process*, Oxford, Blackwell, English translation, 1969 and 1982 (original in German, 1939).

8   'Publicness' is taken from the title of Jeff Jarvis' 2011 book, and is a term this Google evangelist uses to defend the internet's culture of sharing data inside the massively distributed new platforms, while defending violations of privacy by corporations like Facebook and Google. I am using the term here to point at the collective potential to create (and design) new manifestations of what could be called 'the public sphere'. According to Jarvis, publicness needs its advocates, just like privacy. The problem here is how to develop common ownership after the neoliberal state has withdrawn from the commons' protection and regulation, to favour fiscal-legal oversight only.

9   Richard Dawkins, *The Selfish Gene*, Oxford, Oxford University Press, 1996, and Geert Lovink, 'The Memesis Network Discussion', in: Ars Electronica Festival 1996, *Memesis, The Future of Evolution*, Vienna / New York, Spinger, 1996, pp. 28–39. An update of the meme story can be found in Limor Shifman, *Memes in Digital Culture*, Cambridge, Mass., MIT Press, 2013.

10 One example I like is Elisabeth Noelle-Neumann's 'Spiral of Silence' media theory, developed in her 1984 book *The Spiral of Silence: A Theory of Public Opinion – Our Social Skin*), recently revisited by Christie Barakat at the *SocialTimes*. According to the theory, 'people tend to remain silent when they feel that their views are in the minority. The model is based on three premises: 1) people have a "quasi-statistical organ", which allows them to know the prevailing public opinion, even without access to polls; 2) people have a fear of isolation and know what behaviour will increase their likelihood of being socially isolated; and 3) people are reticent to express their minority views, primarily due to fear of being isolated. The closer a person believes that his or her opinion is similar to the prevailing public opinion, the more they are willing to disclose that opinion publicly. As the perceived distance between public opinion and a person's personal opinion grows, the more unlikely the person is to express their opinion.' See Christie Barakat, 'Why quora won't scale',

SocialTimes, 13 September 2012: http://socialtimes.com/why-quora-wont-scale_b104711.

11 See http://en.wikipedia.org/wiki/Occupy_movement. From the same group comes the book *Meme Wars* (New York, Seven Stories Press, 2012), authored by Adbusters founder Kalle Lasn. Another example would be 'rethink' – Rethink Everything.

12 One of the first critical publications to explore maps and networks is Peter Hall and Janet Abrahams, *ELSE/WHERE: MAPPING – New Cartographies of Networks and Territories*, Minnesota, School of Design, 2006: http://elsewheremapping.com.

13 See, for instance, www.visualcomplexity.com/vc, http://infosthetics.com, http://flowingdata.com, and Junk Charts (http://junkcharts.typepad.com) by Kaiser Fung, 'the web's first data visualisation critic'.

14 http://bureaudetudes.org.

15 https://wiki.ushahidi.com.

16 http://blog.tropo.com/2011/12/09/tropo-ushahidi-awesome.

17 See www.othermarkets.org/index.php?tdid=10.

18 As a starting point, see, for instance, the Wikipedia entries http://en.wikipedia.org/wiki/Aadhaar, and http://en.wikipedia.org/wiki/Unique_Identification_Authority_of_India#Book_on_AADHAAR. See also http://aadhararticles.blogspot.com and, for an update, www.moneylife.in/article/new-government-is-going-back-to-aadhaar/38576.html.

19 See www.gizmag.com/go/3685. Wikipedia defines it as such: 'Wireless dating, Widating or Bluedating is a form of dating which makes use of mobile phone and Bluetooth technologies. Subscribers to the service enter details about themselves and about their ideal partner, as they would for other on-line dating services. When their mobile phone comes in the vicinity of that of another subscriber (a radius of about 10 meters) the phones exchange details of the two people. If there is a match, then both users are alerted and can seek each other out and directly chat using Bluetooth. Settings can include an option which restricts alerts to subscribers who have a friend in common' (http://en.wikipedia.org/wiki/Bluedating).

20 See www.theatlantic.com/technology/archive/2014/10/firechat-the-hong-kong-protest-tool-aims-to-connect-the-next-billion/381113.

21 Quoted from https://en.wikipedia.org/wiki/Phatic_expression.

22 '(Im)mobility, exploring the limits of hypermobility', *Open Magazine*, 21 (2011), Rotterdam, NAi Publishers / SKOR.

23 https://en.wikipedia.org/wiki/Accelerationism.

24 See, for instance, his article: http://networkedpublics.org/locative_media/beyond_locative_media. On 28 October 2015, Marc Tuters defended his Ph.D. research at the University of Amsterdam, entitled *Kosmoikos: The Search for Location in a Networked Age*.

25 http://networkcultures.org/wpmu/portal/publications/network-notebooks/the-internet-of-things.

26 Alexander R. Galloway, *Protocol*, Cambridge, Mass., MIT Press, 2004.

27 See, for instance, www.cryptophone.de.

28 See http://diydrones.com.

29 See, for instance, the Herma initiative: http://herma.duekin.com.

30 The discussion in this chapter is purposively speculative and does not include close readings of the smart city rhetoric and its specific research agendas. For that, see, for instance, the Social Cities of Tomorrow conference in Amsterdam, 14–16 February 2012, organized by The Mobile City initiative www.socialcities-oftomorrow.nl/ and www.themobilecity.nl), and the work by Martijn de Waal, who is playing a key role in this research context.

31 Simon Reynolds, *Retromania*, London, Faber and Faber, 2012.

32 http://theoccupiedtimes.org/?p=11969.

33 Eric Kluitenberg, *Legacies of Tactical Media, The Tactics of Occupation: From Tompkins Square to Tahrir*, Amsterdam, Institute of Network Cultures, 2011.

11 EXPANDED UPDATES: FRAGMENTS OF NET CRITICISM

1 https://en.wikipedia.org/wiki/Hyperlink.

2 www.becker-posner-blog.com/archives/2009/06/the_future_of_n.html.

3 www.techcrunch.com/2009/06/28/how-to-save-the-newspapers-vol-xii-outlaw-linking/

4 See https://c3.nasa.gov/dashlink/privacy/#disclaimer.

5 See Carolin Gerlitz and Anne Helmond, 'The like economy: social buttons and the data-intensive web', *New Media & Society* 15.8 (2013), p. 1348, and Daily Dot on the rise of fake likes: www.dailydot.com/technology/facebook-fake-likes.

6 On 7 July 2015, the B2C website reports: 'Link profiling may become a thing of the past, replaced by a centralized, Google directed, proto-artificially intelligent algorithm that taps into the company's vast (and growing) Knowledge Vault to rank websites based primarily on relevance and factual information instead of the number and quality of incoming links' (www.business2community.com/seo/forget-link-building-time-embrace-google-knowledge-vault). The writer Chris Holton calls it 'from linking to thinking', but doubts whether this is such a good step in the first place.

7 Thanks to Henry Warwick for copy-editing this fragment and for his never-ending streams of ideas. A first draft of this text appeared initially in Peter Piller, *Archive Materials*, Cologne, Verlag der Buchhandlung Walther König, 2014, pp. 87–91 (separate edition in German).

8 Wolfgang Ernst, 'The immediateness of the retrieval of immense volumes of data through online databases contends with an increasingly maximum usability period, which contemporary culture knowingly accepts', in Claudia Giannetti (ed.), *AnArchive(s)*, Oldenburg, Edith-Russ-Haus für Medienkunst, 2014, p. 176.

9 A deliberate provocation from my side, in friendly dialogue with German media theorist Siegfried Zielinski, in Giannetti, *AnArchive(s)*, p. 17.

10 As explained well in the BBC documentary *Google and the World Brain* from 2013.

11 Henry Warwick, *Radical Tactics of the Offline Library*, Amsterdam, Institute of Network Cultures, 2014, p. 49.

12 Robert Hughes, *Culture of Complaint*, New York, Warner Books, p. 4.

13 Reference to Günther Anders, *Die Antiquiertheit des Menschen* (Munich, C. H. Beck, 1956) – in English, 'The Obsolescence of Humankind' (never translated).

14 Corey Robin, *The Reactionary Mind*, New York, Oxford University Press, 2011, p. 98.

15 It remains to be seen whether Google sets the trend or will remain the exception with their foreign policy efforts, as documented in publications by Eric Schmidt and Jared Cohen, *The New Digital Age: Reshaping the Future of People, Nations and Business*, London, John Murray, 2013.

16 Arthur Kroker and Michael Weinstein, *Data Trash: The Theory of the Virtual Class*, Montreal, New World Perspectives, 1994.

17   Quoted in T. B. Bottomore, *Elites and Society*, Harmondsworth, Penguin Books, 1966, p. 9.

12 OCCUPY AND THE POLITICS OF ORGANIZED NETWORKS

1   This chapter is part of an ongoing collaboration with Ned Rossiter. I consider him the co-author of this piece as our concepts and materials cannot really be distinguished, even though much of this particular essay was written especially for this occasion. The argument can be read as an update of the concluding chapter of the third book in this series, *Zero Comments* (2007), and of the essay 'Organising networks in culture and politics' in the fourth volume *Networks Without a Cause: A Critique of Social Media*, Cambridge, Polity, 2011.

2   Writing about the 'unnatural relative calm of the spring of 2012', Slavoj Žižek observes: 'what makes the situation so ominous is the all-pervasive sense of blockage: there is no clear way out and the ruling elite is clearly losing its ability to rule' (*The Year of Dreaming Dangerously*, London,Verso, 2012, p. 197.

3   See http://daviddegraw.org/manhattan-project-for-the-evolution-of-society, 20 May 2013.

4   Michael Levitin, 'The Triumph of Occupy Wall Street', *The Atlantic*, 10 June 2015.

5   Eric Schmidt and Jared Cohen, *The New Digital Age: Reshaping the Future of the People, Nations and Business*, London, John Murray, 2013, p. 129. To get a better understanding of the corporate agenda of these two authors, Julian Assange's introduction 'Beyond good and "Don't be evil"' in his book *When Google Met Wikileaks*, New York / London, O/R Books, 2014, is highly recommended.

6   Activist-scholar and author of *Tweets and the Streets: Social Media and Contemporary Activism*, London, Pluto Press, 2012. The key phrase in his book is: 'It is communication that organises, rather than organisation that communicates' (p. 139). Focusing on organized networks, however, is not to emphasize 'liquid organizing' or 'choreographic leadership'. The problem with liquid is that, once it has vaporized, it is unlikely to return again, as moistness, in the same spot. Rather, we should strengthen social ties in order to overcome the problem of temporality. In Gerbaudo's view, organization remains a problem of overview and coordination. Instead of going 'beyond

the fragments', the proposition here is to strengthen the fragments.

7 See for instance her blog post, 'Is there a social-media fueled protest style?', 1 June 2013: http://technosociology.org/?p= 1255.

8 Eric Kluitenberg, *Legacies of Tactical Media*, Amsterdam, Institute of Network Cultures, 2011. See also 'Affect space, witnessing the Movements of the Squares', an essay he wrote as part of his Ph.D. research at the University of Amsterdam (March 2015): www.academia.edu/12867911/Affect_Space __Witnessing_the_Movement_s_of_the_Squares.

9 *Leaving the 20th Century* is the title of the first anthology in English of Situationist texts, put together by Chris Gray, published by FreeFall in 1974. The title comes from a 1964 text where it says: 'It is high time to put an end to the dead time that has dominated this century and to finish the Christian era with the same stroke. The road to excess leads to the palace of wisdom. Ours is the best effort so far towards leaving the 20th century.' The organized network concept can be read as a contribution to the debate around what comes next after the avant-garde. In this sense, we have not yet left behind the post-Situationist period. What's significant here is the inability of events to inter-connect and create chain reactions, despite all the available – and utilized – global communication tools.

10 Reference to the somewhat obsessive (Italian) way of talking about 'the movement' as a living entity with its own will that is (not) doing this or that, not thinking, not acting, falling into lethargy, and yet desiring, discussing, moving on, overcoming, creating and hitting back.

11 '#Accelerate Manifesto' by Alex Williams and Nick Srnicek. See criticallegalthinking.com/2013/05/14/accelerate-manifesto-for-an-accelerationist-politics, 14 May 2013.

12 See https://en.wikipedia.org/wiki/General_assembly_(Occupy _movement).

13 From the contribution by Judith Butler, *Notes Toward a Performative Theory of Assembly*, Cambridge, Mass., Harvard University Press, 2015.

14 Marina Sitrin and Dario Azzellini, *They Can't Represent Us! Reinventing Democracy from Greece to Occupy*, London / New York, Verso, p. 5.

15 Sitrin and Azzellini, *They Can't Represent Us!*, p. 96.

16 Sitrin and Azzellini, *They Can't Represent Us!*, pp. 64–5. The main threat, it reads here, is 'that discussions are ... dominated by individuals'.

17 I am with the late Tony Judt here. In his 2010 political testament *Ill Fares the Land* (New York, The Penguin Press, 2010), he wrote: 'The disposition to disagree, to reject and to dissent – however irritating it may be when taken to extremes – is the very lifeblood of an open society. We need people who make a virtue of opposing mainstream opinion. A democracy of permanent consensus will not remain a democracy.' (p. 180). Needless to say, Judt was an analogue native and doesn't mention the internet or media even once, so trolls do not really fit into this scheme. Nonetheless, we need to foster visible and organized factions. Leninists hate this as factions threaten the organic unity as articulated and synthesized by the Party. Leninism itself breeds sectarianism, conspiracies and ultimately expulsions. Unfortunately, these issues are not history. Luckily, in theory there has never been consensus, and always the anxiety of who or what to belong to (https://lareviewofbooks. org/essay/rock-your-world-or-theory-class-needs-an-reality-upgrade).

18 See 'Luke Stobart, understanding Podemos', parts 1–3 (November/December 2014): http://left-flank.org/2014/11/05/ explaining-podemos-1-15-m-counter-politics.

19 Sitrin and Azzellini, *They Can't Represent Us!*, p. 65.

20 These observations are, in part, based on my own involvement in the Rethink UvA group that was formed during the occupation of the main administration building, Maagdenhuis, at the University of Amsterdam in March/April 2015. See www. rethinkuva.org. A real source of inspiration for this chapter is Sitrin and Azzellini's up-to-date comparison between recent social movements in Greece, Spain and the US and earlier ones in Argentina and Venezuela. Positive reflections such as these sometimes border on the religious, yet leave enough room for critical self-reflection – this was invaluable original research that cries out for further theorization.

21 Sitrin and Azzellini, *They Can't Represent Us!*, p. 86.

22 Tiziana Terranova and Joan Donovan, 'Occupy Social Networks: The Paradoxes of Using Corporate Social Media in Networked Movements', in: Geert Lovink and Miriam Rasch (eds.), *Unlike Us Reader: Social Media Monopolies and their*

Alternatives, Amsterdam, Institute of Network Cultures, 2013, pp. 296–311.

23 Linda Herrera, *Revolution in the Age of Social Media: The Egyptian Popular Insurrection and the Internet*, London / New York, Verso, 2014, p. 7.

24 Herrera, *Revolution in the Age of Social Media*, p. 5.

25 The Invisible Committee, *The Coming Insurrection*, Los Angeles, Semiotext(e), 2009, p. 15.

26 David Foster Wallace, 'Up Simba', in: *Consider the Lobster*, New York, Back Bay Books, 2005, pp. 186–7.

27 Variations of a fragment (including the quote) in Corey Robin, *The Reactionary Mind*, New York, Oxford University Press, 2013, pp. 172–3.

28 The orgnet proposal can also be read as a response to the 'Carl Sagan Deleuzians', as Alexander Galloway calls them: 'Remember Carl Sagan and his awestruck odes to the "billions and billions of stars"?' – in 'Conversation between David M. Berry and Alexander R. Galloway', *Theory, Culture & Society* (June 2015).

29 Experiments in recent years have been rather small and short-lived but nonetheless interesting. Think of the employment of the Loomio software during Occupy and inside the Spanish Podemos party, and the Liquid Feedback experiment of the German Pirate Party. More on this can be found in the valuable research that Anja Adler in Essen and Berlin is doing on this topic, and in the New World Academy Reader #3: *Leaderless Politics*, Utrecht, BAK, 2013.

30 David Graeber, *The Democracy Project: A History, a Crisis, a Movement*, New York, Spiegel & Grau, 2013, p. 78.

31 According to Mashable Twitter's change of slogan in November 2009, from 'What are you doing?' to 'What's happening?'. The shift 'acknowledges that Twitter has grown far beyond the more personal status updates it was originally envisioned to convey, and has morphed into a sort of always-on, source-agnostic information network'.

32 See http://blockupy.org/en. Here it reads: 'Blockupy is part of a European wide network of various social movement activists, altermondialists, migrants, jobless, precarious and industry workers, party members and unionists and many more. Together we want to connect our struggles and powers beyond nation-state lines and create a common European movement, united in diversity, which can break the rule of austerity and will start to

build democracy and solidarity from below. As a transnational movement we oppose explicitly each and every attempt for racist, nationalist or anti-Semitic divisions as well as conspiracy theories to interpret the world.'

33 In his 2002 *Century of the Self* documentary series, Adam Curtis brilliantly explains the shifting position of the individual as a member of the crowd, from a grey, anonymous member of a potentially always dangerous mob that can arise and attack, to an isolated, inward-looking consumer who is no longer concerned about the condition of others in his or her proximity. This cultural shift corresponds with the disappearance of the cultural pessimism of the mass psychology discipline, which was replaced by the scientific positivism of (social) media marketing techniques: https://en.wikipedia.org/wiki/The_Century_of_the _Self.

34 Reference to the crowd crystal theory of Elias Canetti in *Crowds and Power*, London, Penguin, 1981, pp. 85–7: 'Crowd crystals are the small, rigid groups of men, strictly delimited and of great constancy, which serve to precipitate crowds. ... Their unity is more important than their size.' Canetti remarks that the crowd crystal is constant, it never changes its size.

35 See Graeber, *The Democracy Project*, and the review by Kelefa Sanneh in the *New Yorker*: www.newyorker.com/magazine/2013/ 05/13/paint-bombs.

36 http://advocacy.globalvoicesonline.org/2013/04/17/the-psychological-strains-of-digital-activism.

37 Slavoj Žižek, 'Edward Snowden, Chelsea Manning and Julian Assange: our new heroes', *The Guardian*, 3 September 2013: www.theguardian.com/commentisfree/2013/sep/03/snowden-manning-assange-new-heroes#start-of-comments.

38 See www.sustainism.com.

39 Chantal Mouffe, *Agonistics: Thinking the World Politically*, London / New York, Verso Books, 2013, p. 127.

SELECT BIBLIOGRAPHY

RELEVANT MAILINGLISTS, BLOGS, WEBSITES

Air-l, list of the Association of Internet Researchers, www.aior.org.
Coin Desk, news site on cybercurrencies, www.coindesk.com.
Hacker News, collaborative IT news filtering, http://news.ycombinator.com.
I Cite, blog of Jodi Dean, http://jdeanicite.typepad.com.
IDC, mailinglist of the Institute for Distributed Creativity, http://mailman. thing.net/cgi-bin/mailman/listinfo/idc.
Nettime-l, International mailinglist for net criticism, www.nettime.org.
Nettime-nl, Dutch list for Internet culture and criticism, www.nettime.org.
Netzpolitik, German news blog on digital civil rights, https://netzpolitik.org.
Pando Daily, investigate journalism from inside Silicon Valley, http://pando. com.
Public Seminar, blog of the New School staff (NYC), www.publicseminar. org.
Rough Type, blog of ICT critic Nicholas Carr, http://www.roughtype.com/ index.php.
Scripting News, Dave Winer on RSS and other blogging technologies, http:// scripting.com.
The Daily Dot, 'original reporting about internet life', www.dailydot.com.
Vice, global/American news site, https://www.vice.com/en_us.
Zero Hedge, 'On a long enough timeline the survival rate for everyone drops to zero', www.zerohedge.com.

BOOKS

Apprich, Clemens, Slater, S. B. and Schultz, O. J. (eds.), *Provocative Alloys: A Post-Media Anthology*, Lüneburg, Post-Media Lab & Mute Books, 2013.

243

Arendt, Hannah, *On Revolution*, New York, The Viking Press.

Assange, Julian, *When Google Met Wikileaks*, New York / London, O/R Books, 2014.

Assange, Julian, et al. *Cypherpunks: Freedom and the Future of the Internet*, New York / London, O/R Books, 2012.

Bazzichelli, Tatiana and Cox, Geoff (eds.), *Disrupting Business: Art and Activism in Times of Financial Crisis*, Databrowser 05, Brooklyn, Autonomedia, 2013.

Benkler, Jochai, *The Wealth of Networks*, New Haven, Yale University Press, 2006.

Berardi, Franco, *The Uprising: On Poetry and Finance*, Los Angeles, Semiotext(e), 2012.

Berardi, Franco and Sarti, Alessandro, *RUN Morphogenesis*, Kassel, Documenta, 2012.

Bilton, Nick, *Hatching Twitter: A True Story of Money, Power, Friendship and Betrayal*, New York, Portfolio/Penguin, 2013.

Bishop, Claire, *Artificial Hells: Participatory Art and the Politics of Spectatorship*, London / New York, Verso Books, 2012.

Bray, Mark, *Translating Anarchy: The Anarchism of Occupy Wall Street*, Winchester, Zero Books, 2013.

Brink, Hans Maarten van den (ed.), *Onaf, over de zin van onafhankelijkheid in cultuur en media*, Amsterdam, Nieuw Amsterdam Uitgevers, 2013.

Broeckmann, Andreas and knowbotic research, *Opaque Presence: Manual of Latent Invisibilities*, Zurich, Diaphanes, 2010.

Carr, Nicholas, *The Glass Cage: Automation and Us*, New York, W. W. Norton & Company, 2014.

Carr, Nicholas, *The Shallows: What the Internet is Doing to Our Brains*, New York, W.W. Norton & Company, 2014.

Caygill, Howard, *On Resistance: A Philosophy of Defiance*, London, Bloomsbury, 2013.

Chatfield, Tom, *How to Thrive in the Digital Age*, London, Macmillan, 2012.

Coleman, Gabriella, *Hacker, Hoaxer, Whistleblower, Spy: The Many Faces of Anonymous*, London / New York, Verso, 2014.

Cramer, Florian, *Anti-Media: Ephemera on Speculative Arts*, Rotterdam, NAi Uitgevers, 2013.

Crary, Jonathan, *24/7: Late Capitalism and the Ends of Sleep*, London / New York, Verso Books, 2013.

Dardot, Pierre and Laval, Christian, *The New Way of the World: On Neoliberal Society*, London / New York, Verso Books, 2013.

Deibert, Ronald J., *Black Code: Inside the Battle for Cyberspace*, Toronto, McLelland & Stewart, 2013.

Doctorow, Cory, *Information Doesn't Want to Be Free: Laws for the Internet Age*, San Francisco, McSweeney's, 2014.

Easterling, Keller, *Extrastatecraft: The Power of Infrastructure Space*, London / New York, Verso Books, 2014.

e-flux journal, *The Internet Does Not Exist*, Berlin, Sternberg Press, 2015.

Eggers, Dave, *The Circle: A Novel*, London, Penguin Books, 2013.

Fanon, Franz, *Black Skin, White Masks*, New York, Grove Press, 2008 [1952].

Franzen, Jonathan, *The Corrections*, London, Fourth Estate, 2001.

Franzen, Jonathan, *The Discomfort Zone: A Personal History*, New York, Farrar, Straus and Giroux, 2006.

Franzen, Jonathan, *Farther Away: Essays*, New York, Farrar, Straus and Giroux, 2012.

Franzen, Jonathan, *Freedom*, London, Fourth Estate, 2010.

Franzen, Jonathan, *How to be Alone: Essays*, New York, Farrar, Straus and Giroux, 2002.

Franzen, Jonathan, *The Kraus Project*, New York, Farrar, Straus and Giroux, 2013.

Franzen, Jonathan, *The Twenty-Seventh City*, New York, Farrar, Straus and Giroux, 1988.

Fuchs, Christian, *Social Media – A Critical Introduction*, London, Sage, 2014.

Galloway, Alexander, *Protocol*, Cambridge, Mass., MIT Press, 2004.

Galloway, Alexander, Thacker, Eugene and Wark, McKenzie, *Excommunication: Three Inquiries in Media and Mediation*, Chicago, University of Chicago Press, 2014.

Gerbaudo, Paolo, *Tweets and the Street: Social Media and Contemporary Activism*, London, Pluto Press, 2012.

Giannetti, Claudia (ed.), *AnArchive(s)*, Oldenburg, Edith-Russ-Haus für Medienkunst, 2014.

Graeber, David, *Debt: The First 5,000 Years*, Brooklyn, Melville House, 2011.

Graeber, David, *The Democracy Project: A History, a Crisis, a Movement*, New York, Spiegel & Grau, 2013.

Graeber, David, *The Utopia of Rules: On Technology, Stupidity, and the Secret Joy of Bureaucracy*, London, Melville House Publishing, 2015.

Han, Byung-Chul, *Im Schwarm: Ansichten des Digitalen*, Berlin, Matthes & Seitz, 2013.

Hardt, Michael and Negri, Antonio, *Declaration*, New York, Argo-Navis, 2012.

Heidenreich, Ralph and Heidenreich, Stefan, *Mehr Geld*, Berlin, Merve Verlag, 2008.

Herrera, Linda, *Revolution in the Age of Social Media: The Egyptian Popular Insurrection and the Internet*, London / New York, Verso Books, 2014.

Hughes, Robert, *Culture of Complaint*, New York, Oxford University Press, 1994.

Johnson, Clay A., *The Information Diet: A Case for Conscious Consumption*, Sebastopol, Calif., O'Reilly, 2012.

Judt, Tony, *Ill Fares the Land*, New York, The Penguin Press, 2010.

Kapuscinski, Ryszard, *The Shadow of the Sun: My African Life*, London, Penguin Books, 2001.

Keen, Andrew, *Digital Vertigo: How Today's Social Revolution Is Dividing, Diminishing, and Disorienting Us*, New York, St Martin's Press, 2012.

Lanier, Jaron, *Who Owns the Future?* London, Penguin Books, 2013.

Lapavitsas, Costas, *Profiting Without Producing: How Finance Exploits Us All*, London / New York, Verso Books, 2013.

Leister, Oliver and Röhle, Theo (eds.), *Generation Facebook: Über das Leben im Social Net*, Bielefeld, transcript Verlag, 2011.

Levine, Robert, *Free Ride: How Digital Parasites Are Destroying the Culture Business, and How the Culture Business Can Fight Back*, New York, Anchor Books, 2011.

Löffler, Petra, *Verteilte Aufmerksamkeit: Eine Mediengeschichte der Zerstreuung*, Zurich, diaphanes, 2014.

Lovink, Geert, *Networks Without a Cause: A Critique of Social Media*, Cambridge, Polity, 2011.

Lovink, Geert, *Zero Comments: Blogging and Critical Internet Culture*, New York, Routledge, 2007.

Lovink, Geert and Rasch, Miriam, *Unlike Us Reader: Social Media Monopolies and their Alternatives*, Amsterdam, Institute of Network Cultures, 2013.

Lovink, Geert, Tkacz, Nathaniel and de Vries, Patricia, *MoneyLab Reader: An Intervention in Digital Economy*, Amsterdam, Institute of Network Cultures, 2015.

Lowenstein, Roger, *The End of Wall Street*, New York, Penguin Books, 2011.

Luhmann, Niklas, *Social Systems*, Stanford, Stanford University Press, 1995 [1984].

Lukacs, Georg, *History and Class Consciousness*, London, Merlin Press, 1971.

Mason, Matt, *The Pirate's Dilemma: How Hackers, Punk Capitalists and Graffiti Millionaires Are Remixing Our Culture and Changing the World*, London, Penguin Books, 2008.

Mejias, Ulises Ali, *Off the Network: Disrupting the Digital World*, Minneapolis, University of Minnesota, 2013.

Mirowski, Philip, *Never Let a Serious Crisis Go to Waste*, London / New York, Verso Books, 2013.

Moretti, Franco, *Graphs, Maps, Trees, Abstract Models for Literary History*, New York / London, Verso Books, 2005.

Morozov, Evgeny, *The Net Delusion: How Not to Liberate the World*, London, Penguin Books, 2011.

Morozov, Evgeny, *To Save Everything, Click Here: Technology, Solutionism and the Urge to Fix Problems that Don't Exist*, London, Allen Lane, 2013.

Mouffe, Chantal, *Agonistics: Thinking the World Politically*, London / New York, Verso Books, 2013.

New World Academy Reader #3, Leaderless Politics, Utrecht, BAK, 2013.

Nietzsche, Friedrich, *Zur Genealogie der Moral*, Leipzig, Reclam, 1988 (1887).

Oenen, Gijs van, *Nu even niet! Over de interpassieve samenleving*, Amsterdam, Uitgeverij van Gennep, 2011.

Olsthoorn, Peter, *De Macht van Facebook, Onweerstaanbaar!* Leeuwarden, Uitgeverij Elikser, 2012.

Orwell, George, *All Art is Propaganda: Critical Essays*, Boston, Mariner Books, 2009.

Pasquale, Frank, *The Black Box Society: The Secret Algorithms That Control Money and Society*, Cambridge, Mass., Harvard University Press, 2015.

Patterson, Scott, *Dark Pools: The Rise of A.I. Trading Machines and the Looming Threat to Wall Street*, New York, Random House, 2012.

Patterson, Scott, *The Quants: How a New Breed of Math Whizzes Conquered Wall Street and Nearly Destroyed It*, New York, Random House, 2010.

Phillips, Whitney, *This Is Why We Can't Have Nice* Things, Cambridge, Mass., MIT Press, 2015.

Popper, Nathaniel, *Digital Gold: The Untold Story of Bitcoin*, New York, Allen Lane, 2015.

Reynolds, Simon, *Retromania*, London, Faber and Faber, 2012.

Rheingold, Howard, *Net Smart: How To Thrive Online*, Cambridge, Mass., MIT Press, 2012.

Robin, Corey, *The Reactionary Mind*, New York, Oxford University Press, 2013.

Rushkoff, Douglas, *Program or be Programmed: Ten Commands for a Digital Age*, New York, O/R Books, 2010.

Sassen, Saskia, *Expulsions: Brutality and Complexity in the Global Economy*, Cambridge / London, Harvard University Press, 2014.

Schmidt, Eric and Cohen, Jared, *The New Digital Age: Reshaping the Future of People, Nations and Business*, London, John Murray, 2013.

Scott, Brett, *The Heretic's Guide to Global Finance, Hacking the Future of Money*, London, Pluto Press, 2014.

Serres, Michel, *De wereld onder de duim: Lofzang op de internetgeneratie*, Amsterdam, Boom, 2014.

Sitrin, Marina and Azzellini, Dario, *They Can't Represent Us! Reinventing Democracy from Greece to Occupy*, London / New York, Verso Books, 2014.

Sloterdijk, Peter, *Du musst dein Leben ändern*, Frankfurt am Main, Suhrkamp Verlag, 2009.

Sloterdijk, Peter, *Rage and Time: A Psychopolitical Investigation*, New York, Columbia University Press, 2010 [2006].

Sloterdijk, Peter, *Zeilen und Tage: Notizen 2008–2011*, Berlin, Suhrkamp Verlag, 2012.

Stalder, Felix, *Digital Solidarity*, Lüneburg, Mute/PML Books, 2013.

Steyerl, Hito, *The Wretched of the Screen*, Berlin, Sternberg Press, 2012.

Stiegler, Bernard, *For a New Critique of Political Economy*, Cambridge, Polity, 2010.

Stiegler, Bernard, *Taking Care of Youth and the Generations*, Stanford, Stanford University Press, 2010.

Stiegler, Bernard, *Uncontrollable Societies of Disaffected Individuals*, Cambridge, Polity, 2013.

Stiegler, Bernard, *What Makes Life Worth Living*, Cambridge, Polity, 2013.

Strauss, Leo, *Persecution and the Art of Writing*, Chicago, University of Chicago Press, 1988.

Sweezy, Paul M., *The Theory of Capitalist Development*, New York and London, Modern Reader Paperbacks, 1970 [1942].

Taleb, Nassim Nicholas, *The Black Swan: The Impact of the Highly Improbable*, London, Penguin Books, 2010.

Taylor, Astra, *The People's Platform: Taking Back Power and Culture in the Digital Age*, New York, Metropolitan Books, 2014.

Thiel, Peter, *From Zero to One: Notes on Startups, or How to Build the Future*, London, Virgin Books, 2014.

Tiqqun, *How Is It To Be Done?* London, Bandit Press, 2010.

Tiqqun, *Introduction to Civil War*, Los Angeles, Semiotext(e), 2010.

Tkacz, Nathaniel, *Wikipedia and the Politics of Openness*, Chicago/London, University of Chicago Press, 2015.

Turkle, Sherry, *Alone Together: Why We Expect More from Technology and Less from Each Other*, New York, Basic Books, 2012.

Vogl, Joseph, *Das Gespenst des Kapitals*, Zürich, diaphanes, 2010.

Wittkower, D. E. (ed.), *Facebook and Philosophy*, Chicago, Carus Publishing, 2010.

Zielinski, Siegfried, ... *After the Media: News from the Slow-fading Twentieth Century*, Minneapolis, Univocal Publishing, 2013.

Žižek, Slavoj, *The Year of Dreaming Dangerously*, London / New York, Verso, 2012.